The Death Penalty Today

The Death Penalty Today

Edited by Robert M. Bohm

CRC Press
Taylor & Francis Group
Boca Raton London New York

CRC Press is an imprint of the
Taylor & Francis Group, an **informa** business

CRC Press
Taylor & Francis Group
6000 Broken Sound Parkway NW, Suite 300
Boca Raton, FL 33487-2742

First issued in hardback 2017

ISBN-13: 978-1-4200-7011-8 (pbk)
ISBN-13: 978-1-1384-6348-6 (hbk)

Visit the Taylor & Francis Web site at
http://www.taylorandfrancis.com

and the CRC Press Web site
http://www.crcpress.com

Library of Congress Cataloging-in-Publication Data

The death penalty today / [editor] Robert Bohm.
p. cm.
Includes bibliographical references and index.
ISBN 978-1-4200-7011-8 (alk. paper)
1. Capital punishment--United States. 2. Capital punishment--Moral and ethical aspects--United States. I. Bohm, Robert M. II. Title.

KF9227.C2D43 2008
345.73'0773--dc22 2007042040

Contents

2

DEATH PENALTY OPINION, MEDIA ACCESS TO EXECUTIONS, CONSENSUAL EXECUTIONS, AND THE RELATIONSHIP BETWEEN LYNCHING AND THE DEATH PENALTY

Introduction

In the late eighteenth century, Dr. Benjamin Rush (1747–1813), a Philadelphia physician and signer of the Declaration of Independence, was among the most vocal opponents of the death penalty in the United States (Bedau, 1982, p. 13). Rush questioned the biblical support for capital punishment and the belief that it was a general deterrent to crime. He did not believe that the example of executions dissuades people from carrying out crimes they have contemplated committing. To the contrary, he thought that capital punishment might increase crime (Filler, 1967, p. 106; Gorecki, 1983, p. 85).

More than two centuries later, religious justifications and deterrence are no longer key issues in the death penalty debate. At the beginning of the twenty-first century, the death penalty is still as controversial as it was in the late eighteenth century, but different issues now drive the debate. The ten chapters in this book examine some of those new issues. In the first part of this book, the focus is on miscarriages of justice, including the current lethal injection controversy, and innocence. The second part of the book addresses death penalty opinion, media access to executions, consensual executions, and the relationship between lynching and the death penalty. Following is a brief description of each of the chapters.

In Chapter 1, "Errors in Capital Cases and What Can Be Done about Them," Robert M. Bohm describes the types of errors that occur in capital cases and provides an inventory of possible remedies. He argues that errors in capital cases happen with regularity and frequency, and the special procedural safeguards provided in capital cases do not significantly reduce them. According to Bohm, implementing the remedies described in his study could significantly reduce errors but that strategy would create a dilemma for death penalty opponents because to significantly reduce errors in capital cases might increase the legitimacy of a process that abolitionists are trying to undermine. He notes that although the public is becoming increasingly aware of problems with administering capital punishment, it may not make any difference because policy makers are unlikely to do much about them. If policy makers addressed the problems, they would have to admit the likelihood that many other criminal cases that do not receive nearly the scrutiny of capital cases also must be infected with errors.

In response to recent revelations about continuing problems with administering the death penalty, such as those described in Chapter 1, several states have created investigative bodies charged with the task of reviewing their death penalty systems. James R. Acker, in Chapter 2, "Scrutinizing the Death Penalty: State Death Penalty Study Commissions and Their Recommendations," examines thirteen death penalty study commissions and their work. Acker describes the origins, participants, and charges of the commissions, summarizes their essential findings and recommendations, and provides observations about the studies' potential to help shape future death penalty laws and practices.

In Chapter 3, "Themes of Wrongful Executions in the Post-*Furman* Era," Talia Roitberg Harmon identifies common themes among eighteen factually innocent capital defendants who were executed in the post-*Furman* era. She examines the evidence that suggests the defendants were factually innocent, the potential causes of the wrongful convictions, and the factors that led to the executions despite significant doubt about the defendants' guilt. She also provides a summary of the geography, the timeframe, and the races of the executed innocents and their victims. These datasets are then compared to the population of post-*Furman* executions more generally to identify any significant differences between the two populations.

Cathleen Burnett, in Chapter 4, "Making It Work: Compensation for the Wrongfully Convicted," describes how society deals with the reintegration problems of death row inmates who have been exonerated and released from prison. She notes that the exonerated frequently leave prison with just a bus ticket and a suit of clothes because the legal system is not set up to take responsibility for their predicament. Ironically, had they been paroled from prison, observes Burnett, they would have been assigned a parole officer who at least could help them find a job and shelter. Burnett points out the inadequacies of the three options currently available to the exonerated, and then relates the obstacles she has encountered in trying to implement an administrative solution to the problem in Missouri.

In Chapter 5, "A Painless Cocktail? The Lethal Injection Controversy," Gavin Lee describes the interesting but troublesome development of lethal injection as a method of execution. Lethal injection is now the execution method employed by all death penalty jurisdictions but one, Nebraska, which still provides for electrocution but rarely executes (only three post-*Furman* executions). Almost 85 percent of the nearly 1100 post-*Furman* executions (as of August 10, 2007) have been carried out by lethal injection. Lee reveals the flaws with lethal injection, which has been chosen as superior to hanging, firing squad, electrocution, and lethal gas because it supposedly amounts to "no more than putting a condemned individual to sleep," causing a "painless death."

Findings from a survey of death penalty experts are presented by Matthew B. Robinson in Chapter 6, "Assessing Scholarly Opinion of Capital Punishment: The Experts Speak." Robinson randomly selected authors of death penalty books and articles published since 2001. The experts responded to questions about whether the death penalty achieves its goals of retribution, incapacitation, and deterrence; whether death penalty practice is plagued by problems such as race, class, and gender bias; and whether the death penalty is used against the innocent, and other problems.

In Chapter 7, "Police Managers' Attitudes toward Capital Punishment," Gennaro F. Vito, Geetha Suresh, and William F. Walsh present the results of their survey of mid-level police managers. Vito and his colleagues compare police managers' level of death penalty support with the level of death support expressed by prosecutors, legislators, public defenders, prison inmates, and criminologists. They also compare the death penalty attitudes of their police managers with the death penalty attitudes of both rank-and-file police officers and police chiefs.

In Chapter 8, "The United States Can't Televise an Execution Because It Will Make Condemned Men Feel Bad about the Death Penalty: Issues Raised by the Suit to Make McVeigh's Execution Public," Paul Leighton addresses the provocative question: why is a photographer at an execution of a criminal or, in McVeigh's case, why is it a crime to make a videotape of a mass murderer's execution? The answer to that question not only involves the First Amendment but also the related larger issues of whether an open democratic society should use the coercion of the criminal law to prevent photographic recordings of executions and to what degree and in what ways government should be held accountable to its citizens.

The nearly one in eight persons executed post-*Furman* who did not pursue all available avenues of appeal is the subject of Chapter 9, "'Let's Do It!': An Analysis of Consensual Executions," by Margaret Vandiver, David J. Giacopassi, and K. B. Turner. Vandiver and her colleagues provide a statistical overview of prisoners who dropped their appeals, contrasting them to those who have been executed only after all appeals were exhausted. Drawing on Durkheim's theory of suicide, they explore whether his categories of suicide are applicable to the phenomenon of consensual executions. Finally, they investigate individual cases to discover the various motives condemned prisoners have for dropping their appeals and to create a tentative typology of those motives.

In Chapter 10, "Some Hypotheses about Capital Punishment and Lynching," Hugo Adam Bedau begins to construct a theory about the relationship between capital punishment and lynching. He proposes and comments on 31 hypotheses. His underlying motive appears to be the development of another argument against capital punishment. As he explains, "If the death penalty shares many important features with lynching, and decent people have always known that lynching is a terrible criminal act, then for that reason we ought to oppose and abolish the death penalty."

As noted previously, the death penalty in the United States remains a hotly debated and controversial issue. However, in much of the rest of the world the death penalty is no longer a salient issue. On the occasions when the subject of capital punishment is raised, most of the countries that have abolished it simply express disdain for the countries that have retained it.

The United States is becoming increasingly isolated and reviled on the subject of the death penalty. At the beginning of the twentieth century, only three countries—Costa Rico, San Marino, and Venezuela—had abolished the death penalty for all crimes (Amnesty International, 2007). By 1977, only 16 countries had abolished the death penalty for all crimes, but, as of August 2007, 90 countries had abolished the death penalty for all crimes; another 11 countries had abolished it for all but exceptional crimes; and 29 countries had abolished it in practice (i.e., they retain the death penalty but have not carried out an execution for at least ten years and are believed to have a policy or established practice of not using the death penalty) (Amnesty International, 2007). More than 50 countries have abolished the death penalty since 1990 (Amnesty International, 2007). Since 1985, only four abolitionist countries have reintroduced the death penalty. Two of those countries, Nepal and the Philippines, have since abolished it again; and the two others, Gambia and Papua New Guinea, have not executed anyone since reintroducing the penalty (Amnesty International, 2007). So, as of August 8, 2007, about two thirds of the countries in the world, 130 of them, have abolished the death penalty in law or practice, including all of the United States' major allies except Japan (Amnesty International, 2007). Only 67 countries and territories have retained the death penalty (Amnesty International, 2007). Still, among the countries that have retained the death penalty only a few of them actually execute anyone in a given year. In 2006, for example, 91 percent of all known executions occurred in only five countries: China, Iran, Pakistan, Iraq, Sudan, and the United States (Amnesty International, 2007).

Even in the United States, 14 jurisdictions (13 states and the District of Columbia) do not have the death penalty (Death Penalty Information Center, 2007). Moreover, of the 39 jurisdictions (37 states, the U.S. government, and the U.S. military) that do have a death penalty, only five of those jurisdictions (Texas, Virginia, Oklahoma, Missouri, and Florida) account for about two thirds of all post-*Furman* executions (as of September 6, 2007). Texas, alone, executed nearly 37 percent of the total (Death Penalty Information Center, 2007). In short, the death penalty is actually used with some regularity in only a few of the world's countries and a few of the states within the United States.

The material presented in the chapters of this book clearly shows that more than thirty years after the Supreme Court reinstated the death penalty, it is still plagued by egregious problems. One wonders when death penalty states in the United States will join the fourteen jurisdictions in the United States and two thirds of the world's countries and realize that the goals of criminal justice can be achieved without resorting to the death penalty?

References

Amnesty International. (2007). The death penalty at http://web.amnesty.org/pages/deathpenalty-index-eng (accessed September 7, 2007).

Bedau, Hugo Adam. (Ed.) (1982). *The Death Penalty in America*, 3d ed. New York: Oxford University Press.

Death Penalty Information Center. (2007). Executions at www.deathpenaltyinfo.org/article.php?scid=8&did=186 (accessed September 7, 2007).

Filler, Louis. (1967). Movements to abolish the death penalty in the United States, in T. Sellin (Ed.) *Capital Punishment*. pp. 104–122, New York: Harper & Row.

Gorecki, Jan. (1983). *Capital Punishment: Criminal Law and Social Evolution*. New York: Columbia University Press.

Editor

Robert M. Bohm is a professor of criminal justice and legal studies at the University of Central Florida in Orlando and a fellow of the Academy of Criminal Justice Sciences. He has published numerous journal articles, book chapters, and books in the areas of criminal justice and criminology, including *Deathquest III: An Introduction to the Theory and Practice of Capital Punishment in the United States* (3rd ed., LexisNexis/Anderson, 2007), *The Death Penalty in America: Current Research* (Anderson, 1991), and *America's Experiment with Capital Punishment: Reflections on the Past, Present, and Future of the Ultimate Sanction* (2nd ed.), with James R. Acker and Charles S. Lanier (Carolina Academic Press, 2003). He served as president of the Academy of Criminal Justice Sciences in 1992–1993.

Contributors

James R. Acker
Professor
School of Criminal Justice
University at Albany
Albany, New York

Hugo Adam Bedau
Tufts University
Medford, Massachusetts
and
Board of the Capital Punishment Research Initiative
Albany, New York

Robert M. Bohm
Professor
Criminal Justice and Legal Studies
University of Central Florida
Orlando, Florida

Cathleen Burnett
Associate Professor
University of Missouri
Kansas City, Missouri

David J. Giacopassi
Professor
Department of Criminology and Criminal Justice
The University of Memphis
Memphis, Tennessee

Talia Roitberg Harmon
Associate Professor
Department of Criminal Justice
Niagara University
Lewiston, New York

Gavin Lee
Department of Criminology, Law & Society
University of California, Irvine
Irvine, California

Paul Leighton
Associate Professor
Department of Sociology, Anthropology & Criminology
Eastern Michigan University
Ypsilanti, Michigan

Matthew B. Robinson
Associate Professor
Criminal Justice and Criminology
Appalachian State University
Boone, North Carolina

Geetha Suresh
Assistant Professor
Department of Justice Administration
University of Louisville
Louisville, Kentucky

K. B. Turner
Associate Professor
Department of Criminology and Criminal Justice
The University of Memphis
Memphis, Tennessee

Margaret Vandiver
Professor
Department of Criminology and Criminal Justice
The University of Memphis
Memphis, Tennessee

Gennaro F. Vito
Professor
Department of Justice Administration
University of Louisville
Louisville, Kentucky

William F. Walsh
Director
The Southern Police Institute
Louisville, Kentucky
and
Professor
Department of Justice Administration
College of Arts and Sciences
University of Louisville
Louisville, Kentucky

1

Miscarriages of Justice and Innocence

Errors in Capital Cases and What Can Be Done about Them

1

ROBERT M. BOHM

Contents

Introduction

When assessing the administration of capital punishment in the United States, it is helpful to distinguish between how the death penalty might be administered ideally, and the way it is administered in practice. To support the death penalty is to support actual practice and not some unobtainable ideal. It is noteworthy, in this regard, that much of the Supreme Court's workload during the last three decades has been devoted to refining capital punishment procedures: to making the process work "right." The record of that effort clearly shows that the death penalty in the United States remains very much a work in progress.

Among the problems with capital punishment is the ever-present possibility of executing an innocent person. Whether an innocent person has actually been executed during the modern era of capital punishment is debatable.[1] What is not controversial is the troublesome frequency with which errors are made in capital cases. For example, a study of the fully reviewed state death sentences imposed between 1973 and 1995 found that two-thirds were reversed at one of the appeal stages because of serious or prejudicial errors (Liebman et al., 2000). In 82 percent of the reversals by state post-conviction courts the defendant deserved a sentence other than death when the errors were cured on retrial, and in 7 percent of the reversals the defendant was found to be innocent of the capital crime. From 1973 through June 2007, 124 people in 25 states had been released from death rows because of evidence of their innocence (Death Penalty Information Center, 2007).

The number of death penalty appeal reversals has been decreasing dramatically in recent years, not because of greater fairness in the system or fewer constitutional errors, but rather because death row inmates are simply less likely to prevail. Nearly all constitutional errors today are subject to harm analysis and "proving that an error was harmful is difficult or impossible" (Dow, 2005, pp. xxii–xxiii and 44). Still, the percentage of death penalty cases overturned by the appellate courts since the reestablishment of capital punishment has far exceeded the percentage of appellate reversals of all other noncapital felony cases, which, in most states, probably does not exceed one percent (White, 1987, p. 10). The purpose of this chapter is to describe the types of errors that occur in capital cases and to provide an inventory of possible remedies.

Two General Types of Errors

Most errors in capital cases are probably never discovered, but of those that are, there are two general types: "harmless" errors and "serious" or "prejudicial" errors (see Coyne & Entzeroth, 2001, p. 540; Liebman et al., 2000). A serious or prejudicial error is one that can be shown by the defendant to have likely affected the outcome of the trial or to be the type of error that generally results in reversals. In addition—and this is important—the error has to be properly preserved. A harmless error is one, which by proof beyond a reasonable doubt, did not contribute to the verdict. Appellate courts will reverse convictions and sentences only for serious or prejudicial errors that have been properly preserved.

Prior to the mid-1960s, there was no harmless error and nearly any mistake, especially a violation of a defendant's constitutional rights, was considered serious or prejudicial even if it did not affect the outcome of the trial. In cases tainted by such error, appellate courts almost always reversed convictions. Critics complained that the practice allowed clearly guilty defendants to escape justice because of minor errors, "legal technicalities" that probably did not adversely affect the trial's outcome. In 1967, the Supreme Court created the harmless error rule in *Chapman v. California*. The rule provided that violations of a defendant's rights do not require remedy (reversal of conviction or sentence) unless the error or errors are serious or prejudicial.

At each appeal stage, what constitutes serious or prejudicial error becomes more restrictive mostly due to the requirement that error be properly preserved. For example, most state direct appeals courts will not grant relief based on error, even if the error affected the outcome of the trial, if three conditions are not met: (1) a timely objection was not made at the trial, (2) a motion for a new trial based on the objection is not made in a timely fashion after the trial ends, and (3) the objection is not properly asserted in a timely appeal (Liebman et al., 2000). Defendants may suffer even though the failure to properly preserve the error is entirely their defense attorneys' fault. Several capital defendants have been executed despite obvious prejudicial errors because of their lawyers' failure to properly preserve their objections (when objections were made in the first place). Even in the case of a claim of innocence based on new evidence, 33 death penalty states require that such a claim be made within six months of the final appeal. Virginia, which has the shortest deadline in the United States, requires the claim to be made within twenty-one days following conviction. Only seven states allow the motion at any time. Consequently, most prisoners who claim innocence based on new evidence can get state relief only by applying to the governor for executive clemency (Scheck et al., 2001, pp. 282 and 340).

Why Errors Occur in Capital Cases

As law professor Samuel Gross surmises, "The basic cause for the comparatively large number of errors in capital cases is a natural and laudable human impulse: We want murderers to be caught and punished" (1996, pp. 499–500). Many of the errors that contribute to wrongful convictions in capital cases occur long before the case goes to trial. Some of the sources of those errors are discussed in the following sections.

Shoddy Investigation and Misconduct by the Police

Many errors in capital cases are a product of shoddy investigation by the police, who sometimes identify the wrong person as the criminal. According to Gross, "This is the critical stage, where most errors occur" (1998, p. 133). When a capital crime is committed, there is usually great pressure on the police to solve it. When the police are unable to do so within a reasonable amount of time, they sometimes cut corners and jump to conclusions. They (or others who aid them) may even go so far as to lose, destroy, or manufacture evidence against a suspect. For example, in 1993, the West Virginia Supreme Court of Appeals ruled as invalid hundreds of blood tests that West Virginia prosecutors had used over a ten-year period to link defendants to crime scenes (see *The Charlotte [NC] Observer*, 1993, p. 8A). The state police serologist in every case had lied about, made up, or manipulated evidence to win convictions. There was also evidence that the serologist's supervisors may have ignored or concealed complaints of his misconduct. At least 134 prisoners may have been entitled to new trials because of the falsified testimony that put them in prison.

More recently, an FBI investigation found that an Oklahoma City police crime laboratory chemist had misidentified or misinterpreted evidence or testified improperly in court in several cases. The investigation was prompted by DNA evidence that disproved her testimony against Jeffrey Pierce who was released from prison in May 2001, after serving 15 years on a rape conviction. A second state investigation focused on 23 capital trials in which her testimony helped gain convictions. Ten of those defendants have already been executed. Most controversial is the case of Malcolm Rent Johnson who was executed for rape and murder on January 6, 2000. At Johnson's trial, she testified that six samples of semen taken from the victim's bedroom were consistent with Johnson's blood type. However, when the evidence was re-examined after Johnson's execution, there was no semen present. This same police chemist, who was involved in about 3000 cases from 1980 to 1993, had been criticized for years. (In 1994 she stopped doing laboratory work after she was promoted to a supervisory position.)

In another case, two appellate courts ruled that this police chemist gave false testimony about semen evidence in the 1992 rape and murder trial of Alfred Brian Mitchell. In August 2001, Mitchell's rape conviction was overturned because of her false testimony (his murder conviction was upheld). State officials and the FBI scrutinized her work in about 1200 cases, including the cases of three death row inmates. She was fired from her job in September 2001 after a hearing by an administrative panel into her alleged misconduct. (See Accusations, 2001; Hastings, 2001; Yardley, 2001a,b; for more examples, see Scheck et al., 2001, Chapter 5.) Note that in both these examples the errors were discovered (posthumously in Malcolm Johnson's case); how many such errors go undetected cannot be known.

Eyewitness Misidentification and Perjury by Prosecution Witnesses

Decades of research show that eyewitnesses are just not very good at identifying criminal offenders especially when the eyewitnesses are under stress or are attempting to identify offenders of a different race. Oftentimes the witnesses who are most certain of their identification are the least likely to be correct (Scheck et al., 2001, p. 58). Although eyewitness misidentification is probably less common in capital cases than it is in noncapital cases,[2] it still was the second most important factor, accounting for 16 percent of the errors in the capital cases discovered in a study by Professors Bedau and Radelet (1987).

In noncapital cases, the crime victim is often able to identify the offender; in capital cases, that is not possible. Consequently, in capital cases, the police frequently must rely on evidence from other people, such as accomplices, jailhouse snitches, other disreputable characters, and even the defendant himself or herself. Some offenders implicate innocent people to divert suspicion from themselves. Other people, who may or may not have had a role in the crime, perjure themselves for money or for other favors from criminal justice officials, such as the dropping of charges in another unrelated case. It should come as no surprise, then, that perjury by prosecution witnesses is the foremost cause of wrongful convictions in capital cases. Bedau and Radelet (1987) identified witness perjury as a factor in 35 percent of the wrongful convictions that they discovered (also see Harmon, 2001). Furthermore, recent exploratory research shows that when allegations of witness perjury are raised on appeal, innocent capital defendants are 27 times more likely to be exonerated and released from death row than are innocent defendants who did not raise perjury issues on appeal and are eventually executed (Harmon and Lofquist, 2005).

False Confessions

The third most common cause of errors in capital cases is false confessions, which accounted for 14 percent of the errors in the cases discovered by Bedau and Radelet (1987). Police officers in the United States have powerful techniques for extracting confessions:

> They confuse and disorient the suspect, they lie about physical evidence, about witnesses, about statements by other suspects; they pretend that they already have their case sealed and are only giving the suspect a chance to explain his side of the story; they pretend to understand, to sympathize, to excuse; they play on the suspect's fears, his biases, his loyalty to family and friends, his religion; they exhaust the suspect and wear him down; in some cases, they use violence, even torture. (Gross, 1996, p. 485; also see Scheck et al., 2001, p. 116)

By using such coercive and manipulative methods, the police are often successful in getting guilty defendants to confess. Sometimes, however, they get innocent people to confess, too.

Guilty Pleas by Innocent Defendants

Another source of error in capital cases is guilty pleas by innocent defendants. Because of their fear of being executed, some innocent people charged with capital crimes plead guilty to lesser, noncapital offenses. Professor Radelet and his colleagues list 16 cases of innocent people in the twentieth century who pled guilty to noncapital murder to avoid the possibility of execution (Radelet et al., 1992).

Prosecutor Misconduct

Prosecutor misconduct is a principal cause of wrongful convictions in capital cases. For example, in a recent study of the 88 cases under post-*Furman* statutes (through December 31, 2000) in which people were completely exonerated of crimes for which they were sentenced to die, 30 instances of prosecutor misconduct were discovered in 27 (31%) of the cases (Miller-Potter, 2002; also see Harmon, 2001; Liebman et al., 2000; Scheck et al., 2001). Fourteen instances of prosecutor misconduct involved withholding exculpatory evidence, 12 instances involved the subordination of perjury, and 4 instances involved the use of improper evidence (Miller-Potter, 2002).

Prosecutors know that legal procedure prohibits them from withholding exculpatory evidence. A prosecutor's concealment or misrepresentation of evidence (typically referred to as a "Brady violation," see *Brady v. Maryland*, 1963) is grounds for an appellate court's reversal of a conviction or sentence. In the study of the 88 exonerations cited above, withholding exculpatory evidence accounted for more than half of all instances of prosecutor misconduct and was a factor in about 16 percent of the 88 cases (Miller-Potter, 2002; also see Liebman et al., 2000).

Because suborning perjury is a criminal offense, it is hard to believe that many prosecutors know in advance that their witnesses are lying under oath. Yet, how can prosecutors ignore or not suspect the obvious motives of jailhouse snitches and the questionable incriminating evidence they provide (see Scheck et al., 2001, Chapter 6)? It is also hard to believe that most prosecutors are not privy to inmate informer argot about their deceptive practices: "'Don't go to the pen-send a friend.' Or: 'If you can't do the time, just drop a dime.' [Or:] 'Trouble? You better call 1-800-HETOLDME'" (Scheck et al., 2001, pp. 165–167). Perjury by prosecution witnesses occurred in 13.6 percent of the cases in the aforementioned study of the 88 people sentenced to die who were exonerated. It accounted for nearly 45 percent of all cases of prosecutor misconduct (Miller-Potter, 2002). And, as noted previously, Bedau and Radelet (1987) identified witness perjury as a factor in 35 percent of the wrongful convictions that they discovered (also see Harmon, 2001). In their study, it was the foremost cause of wrongful convictions in capital cases.

Sometimes prosecutors fail to dismiss capital charges against ostensibly innocent defendants. Prosecutors may be reluctant to dismiss charges even when the case is a weak one, especially when there is public clamor for a conviction. Much of this has to do with ego. A sign seen in the Dallas County, Texas, prosecutor's office reads: "Convicting the guilty is easy. It's the innocent that keep us working late" (Lehner, 1996). The problem is that not only are some weak cases tried, but, as the quotation suggests, in some cases innocent defendants are convicted. In 20 of the 88 cases (22.7%) in which people sentenced to die were exonerated, lack of evidence was the primary reason for release (Miller-Potter, 2002).

DNA analysis has proven to be an important tool in the successful investigation, prosecution, and exoneration of criminal defendants, including defendants facing the death penalty. In ten (11.4%) of the 88 cases in the study cited above, DNA evidence was responsible for exoneration (Miller-Potter, 2002). Yet, despite relatively easy access to the technology, many local prosecutors refuse to release crime evidence for DNA analysis unless litigation is threatened or filed. They point out that they have no legal obligation to cooperate because once a trial has ended, a convicted defendant has no absolute right to prove his or her innocence. They argue that the offender's interest in proving his or her innocence is outweighed by the state's interest in the finality of judgment (Scheck et al., 2001, pp. xxi–xxii). Although refusing to release crime evidence for DNA analysis when possible innocence is at stake may not be prosecutor misconduct in a legal or technical sense, the belief that finality of sentence is more important than the preservation of innocent life is certainly debatable.

It is hoped that most prosecutors follow the rules. Some do not. What happens to those prosecutors who get caught engaging in misconduct in capital cases? The answer is not much. In a study of 381 murder convictions since 1963 that were reversed because of police or prosecutor misconduct, not one of the prosecutors who broke the law was convicted or disbarred for his or her misconduct. Most of the time, they were not even disciplined (Scheck et al., 2001, p. 226). Current laws also protect prosecutors from civil suits even when they knowingly allowed perjured testimony or deliberately concealed evidence of innocence (Scheck et al., 2001, p. 233).

Judicial Misconduct or Error

In capital trials, judges are responsible for allowing the jury a fair chance to reach a verdict on the evidence presented. Judges must ensure that their behavior does not improperly affect the outcome of the case. Before juries retire to deliberate and reach a verdict, judges instruct them on the relevant law. This involves interpreting legal precedents and applying them to the unique circumstances of the case.

In her examination of Missouri clemency petitions, Professor Burnett (2002, p. 103) found the following allegations of judicial misconduct or error: (1) "not permitting the defense to present evidence of an alternative theory of the case;" (2) "not permitting the defense to present certain mitigating evidence;" (3) "denying the right of defense experts to offer evidence;" (4) "failing to order a psychiatric examination prior to trial;" (5) "prejudging the case;" (6) "incorrectly finding fact;" (7) "refusing to give certain jury instructions;" (8) "failing to admonish the prosecutor for an improper closing argument;" (9) "allowing a highly prejudicial photograph during the penalty phase;" (10) "failing to permit withdrawal of a guilty plea;" and (11) "not having jurisdiction."

Bad Defense Lawyers

Law professor Gross (1996, pp. 492–493) claims that despite some of the problems just cited, the capital trial "plays a comparatively minor role in the production of errors in capital cases." Gross says the reason is that capital defendants usually have superior (as compared to other felony defendants) defense counsel: "Capital defendants . . . may be better represented than other criminal defendants. The attorneys who are appointed to represent them may be more experienced and skillful, and their defenders may have more resources at their disposal" (Gross, 1996, p. 496). The evidence, however, suggests that Gross may be wrong on this point.

Professor Bedau (1982, pp. 189–190) relates that "Experienced criminal trial attorneys . . . say that 'No really capable defense lawyer should ever lose a capital case.'" Research shows that "A lawyer's skill is the most important factor determining whether a defendant is sentenced to death or to life in prison" (Dow, 2005, p. 7). Most capital defendants, though, are not represented by capable defense attorneys, but by those who are inexperienced, overworked, understaffed, less resourceful, less independent, and who frequently lose capital cases (Bedau, 1982, p. 190; Bowers, 1984, p. 339).

A Texas study by the governor's judicial council found that three-quarters of murderers with court-appointed attorneys were sentenced to death, whereas only about a third of those represented by private lawyers were so sentenced (Andersen, 1983, p. 39; also see Harmon, 2001). Another study that compared innocent capital defendants who were eventually exonerated and released from death row and innocent capital defendants who were later executed discovered that defendants with private lawyers at trial were nine times more likely to be exonerated and released from death row than defendants with court-appointed attorneys (Harmon & Lofquist, 2005).

A 1990 *National Law Journal* study showed that criminal defendants in six states of the South—Alabama, Florida, Georgia, Louisiana, Mississippi, and Texas—often wound up on death row after being represented by inexperienced, unskilled, or unprepared court-appointed lawyers (Coyle et al., 1990; also see Burnett, 2002, pp. 66–68; Mello & Perkins, 2003, p. 369). The study found that many poor defendants sentenced to death (and nearly all capital defendants are poor) had lawyers who had never handled a capital trial before, lacked training in life-or-death cases, made little effort to present evidence in support of a life sentence, or had been reprimanded, disciplined, or subsequently disbarred. More recently, an investigation published in the *Chicago Tribune* on June 11, 2000, found that in Texas, "Attorneys in 40 capital cases 'presented no evidence whatsoever or only one witness during the trial's sentencing phase' [and that in] forty-three cases, the accused were represented by attorneys who were punished for professional misbehavior" (cited in Scheck et al., 2001, p. 336; also see Liebman et al., 2000). In 2002, the U.S. Supreme Court upheld the death sentence of Gary Cone from Tennessee, even though his attorney presented no mitigating evidence and did not argue for his client's life. It was reported that the attorney was mentally ill and later committed suicide. Nevertheless, the Court ruled 8–1 that the attorney's inaction did not amount to a complete absence of representation, and that the state court did not act unreasonably when it held that the attorney might have been making a tactical decision in not presenting evidence (*Bell v. Cone*, 2002). Even an attorney who sleeps through much of the trial is not necessarily considered ineffective (Bright, 2003, pp. 136–137; Mello & Perkins, 2003, pp. 371–372).

The *National Law Journal* study discovered a general failure of the states to provide effective assistance of counsel to capital defendants. Not much has changed since the study was first published. At the beginning of the 21st century, only half of the then-38 states with death penalty statutes had adopted minimum guidelines or standards or created an agency to promulgate standards for the appointment of counsel at either the trial or appellate level or both in capital cases (see, e.g., *In re Amendment to Florida Rules of Criminal Procedure*—Rule 3.112 Minimum Standards for Attorneys in Capital Cases, adopted July 1, 2000; also see Acker & Lanier, 1999).

In addition, and contrary to what Gross reports, defense counsel in capital cases (including those in states with minimum standards) rarely has the resources necessary to mount an effective defense. In the 1990s, for example, attorneys in Alabama were being paid only $20 an hour for out-of-court time in capital cases, with a limit of $2000 per case; Mississippi was limiting payment to $1000 a case (Bright, 1997, p. 11). As late as 2004, Florida had a $3500 cap on the payment for defense services in capital cases, meaning that state-funded lawyers in Florida capital cases would be paid an estimated $3.00 an hour (Acker & Lanier, 1999, pp. 448–449; Williams, 2005). A paralegal working on a federal bankruptcy case is paid more per hour than a defense attorney in a capital case in Alabama, Georgia, Mississippi, and Virginia (Bright, 2004, p. 168). It is not unusual for attorneys in capital cases to be compensated at less than minimum wage, and states are increasingly appointing attorneys in capital cases who submit the lowest bids (Bright, 1997b, pp. 816–821). Some jurisdictions have attempted to provide more adequate resources in capital cases, but in none could the provision of those resources be considered generous. Most provide woefully inadequate resources.

Even if the necessary financial resources were provided, that would not compensate entirely for deficient intellectual resources. Defense attorneys, however, are not entirely to blame for this problem. Capital jurisprudence is a highly specialized area of the criminal law, and most attorneys have not received instruction in it.[3] Nevertheless, many judges will appoint any lawyer licensed to practice law to represent a capital defendant, even if the lawyer's practice is limited mostly to real estate or divorce law (Bright, 2004, p. 169). Consequently, even when they are conscientious, they may make numerous mistakes. In sum, whether it is the result of a lack of training, experience, or heart, most capital defendants receive what appears to be ineffective legal representation.

Jury Problems

Research shows that jurors commonly misapprehend judges' capital-sentencing instructions, especially those pertaining to mitigating circumstances (Acker & Lanier, 2003, p. 113; Blankenship et al., 1997; Bowers et al., 2003, pp. 436–439; Frank & Applegate, 1998; Haney, 2003, pp. 474–477; Haney et al., 1994; Sandys & McClelland, 2003, pp. 402–406). Particularly troublesome is evidence from the Capital Jury Project indicating that nearly 75 percent of jurors, "Acknowledge that sentencing instructions did not guide their decision-making on punishment but served instead as an after-the-fact façade for a decision made prior to hearing the instructions" (Bowers, 1995; Bowers & Steiner, 1999; Bowers et al., 2003, pp. 425–428). Many jurors inappropriately made their sentencing decisions before the sentencing phase of the trial began, and oftentimes those decisions were pro-death (Bowers et al., 2003; Bowers and Foglia, 2003).

Data from the Capital Jury Project reveals that jurors frequently have mistaken views about the alternatives to a death sentence and, consequently, vote for death even though they would vote for life if they were assured that the defendant would never be released from prison or would not be released for a long time. Many of them do not believe that LWOP (life imprisonment without opportunity of parole) actually means that a defendant will be imprisoned for the rest of his or her life. In non-LWOP jurisdictions jurors want to know the minimum amount of time an inmate must serve before he or she is eligible for parole, and the average amount of time served before similar capital offenders have been released. Judges in many jurisdictions are legally barred from answering those questions. Many capital jurors believe murderers will be back on the streets far too soon, typically, in about 15 years (Bowers & Steiner, 1999). Ironically, in noncapital cases, the Supreme Court requires that jurors fully understand all available sentencing options (Bowers & Steiner, 1999, pp. 633–634, 715–716, and 717, n. 324).

Many jurors also underestimate their sentencing responsibilities, seeming to believe that they are only to follow a prescribed formula in determining a sentence in capital cases. For them, it is "the law" or "legal instructions" that ultimately determines whether a capital defendant lives or dies. For some jurors, "the law" or "legal instructions" "authorizes" them to impose the death penalty and, at the same time, relieves them of any personal responsibility in making the decision (Haney, 2005; Sundby, 2005; Bowers & Foglia, 2003). Other jurors assume that the sentence they impose is only preliminary and nonbinding because it will be reviewed and corrected, if necessary, by an appellate court (Acker & Lanier, 2003; Bowers et al., 2003, pp. 445–449; Hoffmann, 1995). In *Caldwell v. Mississippi* (1985), the Supreme Court opined that for jurors to believe that "The responsibility for any ultimate determination of death will rest with others" is an "intolerable danger."

Finally, jurors are unlikely to find defendants innocent of their crimes after the police and prosecutors failed to do so. Jurors have less information and experience than the police and prosecutors. Consequently, jurors are probably less to blame for errors in capital cases than are the police and prosecutors. (See Gross, 1998, pp. 145–146.)

The Illusive Hope of Clemency

Clemency generally provides the final opportunity to consider whether a death sentence should be imposed (see Acker & Lanier, 2000; Kobil, 2003).

All 50 states, the federal government, and the military have provisions for granting clemency. They allow the governor of a state or the president of the United States, when federal or military law is violated, to exercise leniency or mercy.

Chief Justice Rehnquist considers executive clemency the "fail safe" of the criminal justice system (cited in *Herrera v. Collins*, 1993, p. 415). It is the last, best chance of rectifying errors in capital cases. Unfortunately for those who would rely on clemency to correct errors made earlier in the process, recent experience contradicts the promise. Few death sentences have been commuted under post-*Furman* statutes because of increased media attention devoted to capital clemency deliberations and the realization by governors that a decision to commute a death sentence is likely to lead to political suicide. This is a change from the past. Prior to 1970, governors in death penalty states, "Routinely commuted up to a third of the death sentences that they reviewed," but since then commutations of death sentences have become rare events (Acker & Lanier 2000, pp. 212–213, Table 1 for the pre-1970s' figure; Baldus & Woodworth 2003, p. 506; also see Deiter, 1996, p. 26). Former Governor Ryan of Illinois is a notable exception (Davey & Mills, 2003).

An Inventory of Possible Remedies

The only sure way to put a stop to the numerous errors made in capital cases is to abolish the death penalty. However, short of total abolition are remedies that could substantially reduce the incidence of errors. The following sections describe some of those remedies.[4]

Good Attorneys Can Make a Difference

The most successful capital punishment defense attorney in American history was undoubtedly Clarence Darrow, who, in more than 100 capital trials, never had a client sentenced to death (cited in Acker & Lanier, 1999, p. 430). Most capital defendants do not have attorneys as talented as Darrow. Perhaps The Innocence Protection Act of 2004 and the ABA's 2003 capital defense guidelines will help change that. In addition, some death penalty states have created minimum standards for defense attorneys in capital cases. These developments are at least a start. It would also help if fees for court-appointed defense attorneys were raised to levels high enough to attract competent lawyers. A handful of states have attempted to address the legal representation problem in capital cases by creating centralized state funded agencies (capital defender offices or CDOs) comprised of defense attorneys who specialize in capital cases. Attorneys in these agencies defend indigent clients charged with capital crimes as well as advise and assist other appointed counsel in capital cases (Acker & Lanier, 1999, p. 437). Some of these agencies appear to be particularly effective in not only reducing the number of people sentenced to death but also the amount of capital litigation generally. Both situations likely reduce the number of errors.

Punish the Misconduct of Defense Attorneys

Most acts of misconduct by defense attorneys in capital cases should result in the attorney being disciplined by the state bar association. Where applicable, such disciplined attorneys should be removed from the roster of attorneys eligible to handle death penalty cases. For egregious cases of misconduct, defense attorneys should be disbarred.

Improve Police Investigations, Interrogations, and the Handling of Evidence

Police should keep an open and objective mind during investigations. They should investigate crimes rather than trying to build a case against a likely suspect. Once a suspect has been identified, the police should continue to pursue all reasonable leads, whether they point towards or away from the suspect. Police should be trained to avoid "tunnel vision" or "confirmatory bias" where the belief that a particular suspect has committed a crime often prevents an objective evaluation of whether there might be others who are actually guilty.

To reduce the number of false confessions, defense counsel should be provided to indigent suspects during police interrogation in potential death penalty cases. When there is doubt about whether the suspect is indigent, defense counsel should be provided. Police should also make a reasonable attempt to determine if a suspect is mentally retarded. If the suspect is deemed mentally retarded, the police should not ask leading questions (mentally retarded suspects are inclined to agree with the police version of events) and suggest that they believe the suspect is guilty.

In potential death penalty cases, the entire police custodial interrogation should be videotaped to help validate the interrogation and confessions. Where videotaping is not feasible during an interrogation, audiotaping should be substituted. Any nonrecorded statement by a homicide suspect, for example, in a patrol car on the way to the police station, should be repeated to the suspect on tape, and the suspect's comments recorded. Interviews with significant witnesses in homicide cases should also be electronically recorded.

To make sure that the police provide all the evidence in their possession to the prosecution: (1) all relevant evidence, including exculpatory evidence and its location, should be listed on schedules by the police, (2) specific police officers or employees should be assigned record-keeping responsibility, and

(3) prosecutors should be given certified written copies of the schedules by the police.

Improve Eyewitness Identification Techniques and Procedures

Experts agree that the accuracy of eyewitness identifications could be greatly improved if the following policy reforms were adopted in all jurisdictions. First, videotapes should be made of all line-ups, photo spreads, and other identification processes so that later any biases, suggestions, or hints that infected the process could be exposed and evaluated. Second, eyewitnesses should be given explicit instructions that the suspected perpetrator might not be in the line-up or photo spread, and therefore making an identification may not be possible. Third, independent examiners should conduct all line-ups and photo spreads. Fourth, to avoid dropping hints, examiners should not know who the suspect is. Fifth, eyewitnesses should be told that they should not assume that the examiner of the line-up or photo spread knows which person is the suspect in the case. Sixth, when the examiner does not know who the suspect is, a sequential procedure should be used. With a sequential procedure the eyewitness views only one line-up member or photo at a time, making a judgment ("Yes, it is" or "No, it isn't" the perpetrator) about each person before looking at another line-up member or photo. Seventh, nonsuspect line-up "fillers" should look like the witnesses' descriptions of the suspect and not the person who has been identified as the potential suspect. Eighth, witnesses should be required to rate the certainty of their identifications at the time they make them. This would provide fact finders important information weeks or months after the identifications were made. Ninth, police and prosecutors should be trained not to provide corroborating details to eyewitnesses. Such prompts tend to increase the certainty of identifications but to decrease their reliability. In addition, trial judges should inform jurors that eyewitness testimony should be judged in light of the other evidence in the case. Finally, convictions for murder based on the testimony of a single eyewitness or accomplice, without any other corroboration, should never be death eligible.

Improve the Work and Credibility of Crime Lab Technicians

To promote greater credibility in the work of crime lab technicians, such labs and their budgets should be independent and not under the supervision of a police department or prosecutor's office as is now typically the case. Crime labs should also be accredited by professional organizations and subjected to regulatory oversight and external blind proficiency testing (in which samples are sent in as ordinary evidence to corroborate the validity of results). Prosecutors who introduce scientific evidence should be required to provide all underlying documentation that was used in writing the report as well as the name of the technician or technicians who performed the work. Fundamental questions should be asked about the reliability of the evidence: Have the scientific tests been replicated? What is the error rate of the procedure? Did any controls fail? Have the methods been published in peer-reviewed journals? Agent-technicians who make mistakes should be disciplined. The reports should indicate what, if any, exculpatory inferences can be derived from the evidence. Every public defender's office should have at least one attorney with scientific evidence expertise.

Require DNA Testing

DNA testing should be required in cases in which DNA evidence is available and there is a reasonable probability that the defendant could be exonerated based on it. The testing should be conducted in a timely manner, within 7 to 14 days of the crime, if possible, to ensure that innocent suspects are not incarcerated too long and to improve the chances of catching the guilty. In May 2000, only two states—Illinois and New York—gave inmates the right to use the latest DNA testing (Alter and Miller, 2000). As of September 2006, 40 states gave inmates that right (Ferrero, 2006). The federal government and the states should provide adequate funding for the creation of a comprehensive DNA database. It is hoped that The Innocence Protection Act of 2004 is a step in that direction.

Set Rigorous Standards for Jailhouse Snitches or Informants

Before allowing a jailhouse snitch or informant to testify a committee of prosecutors should be able to provide satisfactory answers to the following questions. (1) Is there corroborating evidence to support the statement other than the testimony of another snitch? (2) Does the statement provide details of the crime or lead to evidence that could only be known by the perpetrator? (3) Could the incriminating evidence have been obtained from a source other than the accused, such as press accounts or legal proceedings? (4) Does the snitch or informant have a reputation for being dishonest? And (5) does the snitch or informant regularly provide incriminating evidence? There should be a presumption that the testimony of a jailhouse snitch or informant is unreliable, and the prosecutor should be required to overcome that presumption before a jury is allowed to hear the evidence. Any deal that police officers or prosecutors make with a snitch or informant should be recorded, preferably videotaped. Additionally, trial judges should inform jurors of the potential hazards of relying on the testimony of a jailhouse snitch or informant. Finally, the uncorroborated testimony of a jailhouse snitch or informant witness about the confession or admission of the defendant should never be the sole basis for imposition of a death penalty.

Improve Police Training

Training manuals should be developed and police who work on homicide cases should receive periodic training in the following areas: (1) the risks of false testimony by in-custody informants ("jailhouse snitches"), (2) the risks of false testimony by accomplice witnesses, (3) the dangers of tunnel vision or confirmatory bias, (4) the risks of wrongful convictions in homicide cases, (5) police investigative and interrogation methods, (6) police investigating and reporting of exculpatory evidence, (7) forensic evidence, (8) the risks of false confessions, and (9) consular rights and the notification obligations during the arrest and detention of foreign nationals.

Punish Police Misconduct

Depending on the seriousness of the misconduct, offending police officers should be reprimanded, suspended without pay, decertified (if applicable), or terminated. Particularly serious misconduct by police officers should be prosecuted in the federal courts.

Guide Prosecutors' Decisions to Seek the Death Penalty

Statewide written protocols should be developed to guide county prosecutors in making death penalty determinations. The guidelines should include the requirement that each county prosecutor establish within his or her office a committee to review homicide cases in which the death penalty may be sought, to assist the prosecutor in making the decision. The governor should appoint a statewide committee to review prior to trial death eligibility decisions made by prosecutors. Where the committee decides that death is not the appropriate sentence in the case, the prosecutor should not be authorized to seek the death penalty. Committee authorization of the death penalty should be required by statute and mandatory.

Improve Disclosure Requirements

The prosecutor should be required to file a certificate with the court at least 14 days before the date set for the trial guaranteeing that all material that is required to be disclosed to the defense has been disclosed. Also, any discussions with a witness or the representative of a witness about benefits, or potential benefits or detriments given to a witness by any prosecutor, police official, corrections official, or anyone else should be put in writing and disclosed to the defense prior to trial. Both of these requirements could occur in a case management conference before the trial judge. Following conviction, the prosecutor should have a continuing obligation to make timely disclosure to the defendant's counsel, or the defendant if not represented by counsel, of the existence of evidence known to the prosecutor that tends to negate the guilt of the defendant or mitigate the defendant's capital sentence.

Punish Prosecutor Misconduct

For extreme misconduct, prosecutors should be criminally prosecuted. At the least, statutes should be narrowed that grant prosecutors broad immunity from civil suits in cases of intentional misconduct. Another strategy is to create panels comprised of bar association members who would review complaints against prosecutors. For egregious cases of misconduct, prosecutors should be disbarred.

Better Training and Certification of Trial Judges in Capital Cases

Capital case training should be provided for all trial judges who preside over capital cases. The training should be required before a judge hears a capital case. A statewide bench manual covering capital cases should also be developed and used. A digest of relevant case law and other resources should be created and made available to trial judges and other participants in capital cases. The digest should contain information about relevant case law and other resources. Trial judges should be certified to hear capital cases by the state supreme court or the chief judges of judicial circuits. Certification should be based on experience and training. Only certified judges should hear capital cases.

Give Trial Judges Veto Power

The trial judge should have to indicate on the record whether he or she agrees with the jury's sentence of death. When the judge does not agree with the jury's death sentence, the defendant must not be sentenced to death. (In most cases, the defendant should be sentenced to LWOP.)

Eliminate Time Limits and Other Constraints on Claims of Actual Innocence

Claims of actual innocence in capital cases based on newly discovered evidence should be heard by a court of record any time after conviction, without regard for other post-conviction matters or timing. Also, state "closed discovery" laws should be repealed. Those laws prevent defense attorneys or journalists from reviewing evidence following a conviction, thus making the detection of miscarriages of justice even more difficult.

Improve the Clemency Process

To make officials more accountable in their decision making, clemency boards should hold public hearings to determine their recommendations to the governor. Governors should meet personally with attorneys and should be required to provide the public with an explanation of their clemency decisions. Better yet, to depoliticize the process, clemency decisions should not be made by governors but, instead, by respected three-judge panels.

Increase the Resources and Scope of Innocence Projects

Attorneys Barry Scheck and Peter Neufeld founded the first Innocence Project in 1992. It is a clinical law program for law students that operates out of the Benjamin N. Cardoza School of Law in New York City (The Innocence Project, n.d.). The Project provides pro bono legal services to inmates who are challenging their convictions based on DNA evidence. The Project has represented or assisted more than 100 cases in the United States, including several death penalty cases, where convictions have been reversed or overturned. As of this writing, a national network of Innocence Projects is operating in 40 states and the District of Columbia, including all but 5 death penalty states (Alabama, Arkansas, Montana, Oregon, and South Dakota). Because of limited resources, however, these Innocence Projects can assist only a small fraction of the inmates who seek help. Most of the Projects also do not help prisoners for which DNA evidence is not available to prove their innocence. With more resources, Innocence Projects could expand the scope of cases they handle to those that do not involve DNA evidence.

Collect Relevant Data

To provide a complete understanding of how a capital punishment system is working, each death penalty jurisdiction should collect detailed and relevant information and create a statistical database about all first-degree murder cases in that jurisdiction, and not just the death penalty cases. These data could be used for proportionality reviews, to effectively monitor the system, and for other research purposes.

Establish Innocence Commissions

Innocence Commissions should be established in death penalty states to provide a comprehensive review of the errors made in capital cases (Innocence

Project; Scheck & Neufeld, 2002). They should operate in much the same way as the National Transportation Safety Board does when it investigates airline crashes. They should address why the error occurred (e.g., was it an individual's mistake, official misconduct, or systemic error?) and suggest ways to correct the error and prevent it from reoccurring. To be effective, Innocence Commissions must have legal authority, subpoena power, ample resources for investigations, and freedom from political interference. The first Innocence Commission was established in North Carolina in 2002. California, Connecticut, Illinois, and Virginia are other death penalty states that have established Innocence Commissions.

Assistance and Indemnity

When wrongfully convicted inmates and especially death row inmates are released from prison, they almost always need immediate financial assistance. Most of them also need help with such things as obtaining a driver's license, opening a bank account, and getting meaningful employment. In addition, there is generally a need for counseling to overcome stress, depression, and anger caused by wrongful incarceration. Death penalty jurisdictions should create mechanisms or expand existing ones to help with these needs.

Rarely do victims of errors in capital cases receive indemnity from the state that wrongfully convicted them. Only 16 states and the federal government have statutory provisions for indemnifying the wrongly convicted (in capital and noncapital cases). For example, in California, an inmate can receive $100 a day for each day served; Texas provides $25,000 per year of incarceration, total not to exceed $500,000, plus one year of counseling; and Virginia offers 90 percent of the average Virginia income for up to 20 years, a $15,000 transition grant, and $10,000 in tuition to enroll in the state's community-college system (Table of Compensation Statutes, 2006). The federal government limits compensation to a maximum of $100,000 per year of incarceration (Death Penalty Information Center, 2007). Attorney expenses for preparing the necessary legal documents can take a third of the money. Getting the money from the state, even after it has been awarded, seldom is easy.

Moratorium

Short of total abolition some observers, including some respected individuals who support the death penalty in principle, have called for a moratorium on executions until some of the more egregious problems with its administration are fixed.

Conclusion

Errors in capital cases happen with regularity and frequency, and the special procedural safeguards provided in capital cases do not significantly reduce them. As Gross (1996, p. 497) maintains:

> The basic conclusion is simple. The steady stream of errors that we see in cases in which defendants are sentenced to death is a predictable consequence of our system of investigating and prosecuting capital murder. . . . But what about what happens after trial? Everybody knows that direct and collateral review are more painstaking for capital cases than for any others. Isn't it likely that all these mistakes are caught and corrected somewhere in that exacting process? The answer, I'm afraid, is No. At best, we could do an imperfect job of catching errors after they occur, and in many cases we don't really try. As a result, most miscarriages of justice in capital cases never come to light.

Consequences of making errors in capital cases, especially wrongful convictions, are the possibility, if not actuality, that innocent people are executed, innocent people are spending months or years on death row for crimes they did not commit, and sometimes the actual killer is allowed to remain free to victimize others.

The public is becoming increasingly aware of problems with administering capital punishment. For example, a May 2006 Gallup Poll found that 35 percent of adults nationwide thought that the death penalty is not applied fairly (60 percent believed it is applied fairly and 5 percent had no opinion).[5] Sixty-three percent of the respondents to a July 2000 *NBC News/Wall Street Journal* Poll favored the suspension of the death penalty until questions about its fairness can be studied. A December 2003 Harris Poll revealed that 95 percent of adults nationwide think that innocent people are sometimes convicted of murder. Perhaps even more telling, according to a May 2006 Gallup poll, 63 percent of adults nationwide believe that in the past five years a person has been executed who was, in fact, innocent of the crime with which he or she was charged. These poll results could be important because research shows that concerns about the administration of the death penalty, such as the possible execution of innocent people, are influential in changing death penalty opinions (see Bohm, 1989; Bohm et al., 1991; Bohm & Vogel, 1994, 2004; Bohm et al., 1993; Clarke et al., 2000–2001; Lambert & Clarke, 2001; Sandys, 1995).

However, policy makers will probably ignore or downplay the survey results and the substantial evidence of error in capital cases because they are reluctant to open Pandora's box. That is, if policy makers were to admit that errors in capital cases occur frequently and regularly, despite extraordinary safeguards that should minimize those errors, then they would have to admit the likelihood that many other criminal cases that do not receive nearly the scrutiny of capital cases must be infected with errors as well.[6]

No one expects an infallible system. However, given the fallibility of any system operated by human beings, policy makers should make every effort to reduce the likelihood of error in capital and other criminal cases. To paraphrase Thomas Jefferson: We should not be afraid to follow truth wherever it may lead, nor to tolerate any error as long as reason is left free to combat it. Implementing the remedies described here could significantly reduce the error. But following that course of action creates a dilemma for death penalty opponents because implementing the remedies and significantly reducing error may increase the legitimacy of the process and undermine the abolitionist effort. Still, there are other good reasons to oppose the death penalty besides the problem of error.

Notes

1. The modern era of capital punishment refers to the period following the Supreme Court's landmark decision of *Furman v. Georgia* (408 U.S. 238) in 1972. In that decision the Court held that the death penalty, as administered, constituted cruel and unusual punishment in violation of the Eighth and Fourteenth Amendments. The decision voided all existing death penalty statutes and the death sentences of all death row inmates. Almost immediately, states enacted new death penalty statutes designed to meet the Court's objections with pre-*Furman* statutes. The Court approved the new statutes in 1976 (*Gregg v. Georgia*, 428 U.S. 153) and executions resumed in 1977. For the view that there is no incontrovertible evidence that a factually innocent person has been executed in the modern death penalty period, see Committee on the Judiciary, 1982; Markman & Cassell, 1988; Sorensen, 2004. For the opposite view, see Bedau & Radelet, 1987; Bohm, 2007; Lehner, 1996; Radelet et al., 1992.
2. Eyewitness misidentification is the most important contributing factor to wrongful convictions in noncapital cases (Huff, 2002, p. 4; Huff et al., 1986; Scheck et al., 2001). For example, a study of recent DNA exonerations by the Innocence Project discovered that 82 percent of the wrongful convictions were at least in part a result of mistaken identification by an eyewitness or victim (Scheck et al. 2001, p. 95).
3. To help remedy that problem, some states, such as Florida, have created capital punishment defense agencies. The attorneys who work in the agencies handle only capital punishment cases, and, thus, are able to develop expertise. A problem is that most of the agencies are understaffed and underfunded, and, consequently, have only the resources to handle appeals.
4. Unless indicated otherwise, the remedies described in this section are from the Governor's Commission (2002), Scheck et al. (2001), and The Constitution Project (2005). Some of the same sources of error and remedies can also be found in Huff's (2002) discussion of wrongful convictions in all criminal cases (and not just capital cases).

5. Poll data in this section is from http://www.pollingreport.com/crime.htm#Death.
6. On the incidence of wrongful convictions in criminal cases, see Huff, 2002; Poveda, 2001; and Scheck et al., 2001.

References

Accusations cost chemist job. *The Orlando Sentinel* (September 26), p. A13.

Acker, J.R. & Lanier, C.S. (2003). Beyond human ability? The rise and fall of death penalty legislation. In J.R. Acker, R.M. Bohm, & C.S. Lanier (Eds.) *America's Experiment with Capital Punishment*, 2nd ed. (pp. 85–125) Durham, NC: Carolina Academic Press.

Acker, J.R. & Lanier, C.S. (2000). May God-or the governor-have mercy: Executive clemency and executions in modern death-penalty systems. *Criminal Law Bulletin* 36:200–237.

Acker, J.R. & Lanier, C.S. (1999). Ready for the defense? Legislative provisions governing the appointment of counsel in capital cases. *Criminal Law Bulletin* 35:429–477.

Alter, J. & Miller, M. (2000). A life or death gamble. *Newsweek* (May 29), pp. 23–27.

Andersen, K. (1983). An eye for an eye. *Time* (January 24), pp. 28–39.

Baldus, D.C. & Woodworth, G. (2003). Racial discrimination and the death penalty: An empirical and legal overview. In J.R. Acker, R.M. Bohm, & C.S. Lanier (Eds.) *America's Experiment with Capital Punishment*, 2nd ed. (pp. 501–551) Durham, NC: Carolina Academic Press.

Bedau, H.A. (Ed.) (1982). *The Death Penalty in America*, 3rd ed. New York: Oxford University Press.

Bedau, H.A. & Radelet, M.L. (1987). Miscarriages of justice in potentially capital cases. *Stanford Law Review* 40:21–179.

Blankenship, M.B., Luginbuhl, J., Cullen, F.T., & Redick, W. (1997). Jurors' comprehension of sentencing instructions: A test of the death penalty process in Tennessee. *Justice Quarterly* 14:325–346.

Bohm, R.M. (2007). *Deathquest III: An Introduction to the Theory and Practice of Capital Punishment in the United States*, 3rd ed. Cincinnati, OH: Lexis Nexis/Anderson.

Bohm, R.M. (1989). The effects of classroom instruction and discussion on death penalty opinions: A teaching note. *Journal of Criminal Justice* 17:123–131.

Bohm, R.M. & Vogel, B.L. (2004). More than ten years after: The long-term stability of informed death penalty opinions. *Journal of Criminal Justice* 32:307–327.

Bohm, R.M. & Vogel, R.E. (1994). A comparison of factors associated with uninformed and informed death penalty opinions. *Journal of Criminal Justice* 22:125–143.

Bohm, R.M., Clark, L.J., & Aveni, A.F. (1991). Knowledge and death penalty opinion: A test of the Marshall hypotheses. *Journal of Research in Crime and Delinquency* 28:360–387.

Bohm, R.M., Vogel, R.E., & Maisto, A.A. (1993). Knowledge and death penalty opinion: A panel study. *Journal of Criminal Justice* 21:29–45.

Bowers, W.J. & Foglia, W.D. (2003). Still singularly agonizing: Law's failure to purge arbitrariness from capital sentencing. *Criminal Law Bulletin* 39:51–86.

Bowers, W.J. & Steiner, B.D. (1999). Death by default: An empirical demonstration of false and forced choices in capital sentencing. *Texas Law Review* 77:605–717.
Bowers, W.J., Fleury-Steiner, B.D., & Antonio, M.E. (2003). The capital sentencing decision: Guided discretion, reasoned moral judgment, or legal fiction. In J.R. Acker, R.M. Bohm, & C.S. Lanier (Eds.) *America's Experiment with Capital Punishment*, 2nd ed. (pp. 413–467) Durham, NC: Carolina Academic Press.
Bowers, W.J. with Pierce, G.L. & McDevitt, J.F. (1984). *Legal Homicide: Death as Punishment in America, 1864–1982*. Boston: Northeastern University Press.
Bright, S.B. (2004). Why the United States will join the rest of the world in abandoning capital punishment. In H.A. Bedau and P.G. Cassell (Eds.) *Debating the Death Penalty: Should America Have Capital Punishment? The Experts on Both Sides Make Their Best Case* (pp. 152–182). New York: Oxford.
Bright, S.B. (2003). The politics of capital punishment: The sacrifice of fairness for executions. In J.R. Acker, R.M. Bohm, & C.S. Lanier (Eds.) *America's Experiment with Capital Punishment*, 2nd ed. (pp. 127–146). Durham, NC: Carolina Academic Press.
Bright, S.B. (1997). *Capital Punishment on the 25th Anniversary of* Furman v. Georgia. Atlanta, GA: Southern Center for Human Rights.
Bright, S.B. (1997b). Neither equal nor just: The rationing and denial of legal services to the poor when life and liberty are at stake. *Annual Survey of American Law 1997*:783–836.
Burnett, C. (2002). *Justice Denied: Clemency Appeals in Death Penalty Cases*. Boston: Northeastern University Press.
Clarke, A.W., Lambert, E., & Whitt, L.A. (2000–2001). Executing the innocent: The next step in the Marshall hypotheses. *Review of Law and Social Change* 26:309–345.
Committee on the Judiciary, U.S. Senate. (1982). Capital punishment as a matter of legislative policy. In H.A. Bedau (Ed.) *The Death Penalty in America*, 3rd ed. (pp. 311–318), New York: Oxford University Press.
Coyle, M., Strasser, F., & Lavelle, M. (1990). Fatal defense: Trial and error in the nation's death belt. *The National Law Journal* 12 (No. 40, June 11):30–44.
Coyne, R. & Entzeroth, L. (2001). *Capital Punishment and the Judicial Process*, 2nd ed. Durham, NC: Carolina Academic Press.
Davey, M. & Mills, S. (2003). Illinois governor sweeps inmates from death row. *The Orlando Sentinel* (January 12), p. A1.
Death Penalty Information Center. (2007). Available at http://www.deathpenaltyinfo.org.
Deiter, R.C. (1996). *Killing for Votes: The Dangers of Politicizing the Death Penalty Process*. Washington, DC: The Death Penalty Information Center. www.deathpenaltyinfo.org.
DNA Testing and the Death Penalty. (2002). American Civil Liberties Union. Available at http://www.aclu.org/DeathPenalty/DeathPenalty.cfm?ID=9315&c=65.
Dow, D.R. (2005). *Executed on a Technicality: America's Death Row*. Boston: Beacon Press.
Ferrero, E. (2006). Director of Communications, The Innocence Project. Personal Communication (September 27, 2006).
Frank, J. & Applegate, B.K. (1998). Assessing juror understanding of capital-sentencing instructions. *Crime and Delinquency* 44:412–433.

Governor's Commission on Capital Punishment. (2002). State of Illinois. Available at http://www.idoc.state.il.us/ccp/ccp/reports/commission_reports.html.
Gross, S.R. (1998). Lost lives: Miscarriages of justice in capital cases. *Law and Contemporary Problems* 61:125–152.
Gross, S.R. (1996). The risks of death: Why erroneous convictions are common in capital cases. *Buffalo Law Review* 44:469–500.
Haney, C. (2005). *Death by Design: Capital Punishment as a Social Psychological System*. New York: Oxford University Press.
Haney, C. (2003). Mitigation and the study of lives: On the roots of violent criminality and the nature of capital justice. In J.R. Acker, R.M. Bohm, & C.S. Lanier (Eds.) *America's Experiment with Capital Punishment*, 2nd ed. (pp. 469–500), Durham, NC: Carolina Academic Press.
Haney, C., Sontag, L., & Costanzo, S. (1994). Deciding to take a life: Capital juries, sentencing instructions, and the jurisprudence of death. *Journal of Social Issues* 50:149–176.
Harmon, T.R. (2001). Predictors of miscarriages of justice in capital cases. *Justice Quarterly* 18:949–968.
Harmon, T.R. & Lofquist, W.S. (2005). Too late for luck: A comparison of post-Furman exonerations and executions of the innocent. *Crime & Delinquency* 51:498–520.
Hastings, D. (2001). Facts disputed in execution case. *The Orlando Sentinel* (August 30), p. A3.
Hoffmann, J.L. (1995). Where's the buck?—Juror misperception of sentencing responsibility in death penalty cases. *Indiana Law Journal* 70:1137–1160.
Huff, C.R. (2002). Wrongful conviction and public policy: The American Society of Criminology 2001 presidential address. *Criminology* 40:1–18.
Huff, C.R., Rattner, A., & Sagarin, E. (1986). Guilty until proven innocent: Wrongful conviction and public policy. *Crime and Delinquency* 32:518–544.
Kobil, D.T. (2003). The evolving role of clemency in capital cases. In J.R. Acker, R.M. Bohm, & C.S. Lanier (Eds.), *America's Experiment with Capital Punishment*, 2nd ed. (pp. 673–692) Durham, NC: Carolina Academic Press.
Lambert, E. & Clarke, A. (2001). The impact of information on an individual's support of the death penalty: A partial test of the Marshall hypothesis among college students. *Criminal Justice Policy Review* 12:215–234.
Lehner, P. (1996). Abolition now!!! Available at http://www.abolition-now.com.
Liebman, J.S., Fagan, J., & West, V. (2000). A broken system: Error rates in capital cases, 1973–1995. Available at http://www.justice.policy.net/jpreport.html.
Markman, S.J. & Cassell, P.G. (1988). Protecting the innocent: A response to the Bedau–Radelet study. *Stanford Law Review* 41:121–160.
Mello, M. & Perkins, P.J. (2003). Closing the circle: The illusion of lawyers for people litigating for their lives at the fin de siecle. In J.R. Acker, R.M. Bohm, & C.S. Lanier (Eds.), *America's Experiment with Capital Punishment*, 2nd ed. (pp. 347–384). Durham, NC: Carolina Academic Press.
Miller-Potter, K.S. (2002). Death by innocence: Wrongful convictions in capital cases. *The Advocate: A Journal of Criminal Justice Education and Research* 24:21–29.
Poveda, T.G. (2001). Estimating wrongful convictions. *Justice Quarterly* 18:689–708.
Radelet, M.L., Bedau, H.A., & Putnam, C.E. (1992). *In Spite of Innocence: Erroneous Convictions in Capital Cases*. Boston: Northeastern University Press.

Sandys, M. (1995). Attitudinal change among students in a capital punishment class: It may be possible. *American Journal of Criminal Justice* 20:37–55.
Sandys, M. & McClelland, S. (2003). Stacking the deck for guilt and death: The failure of death qualification to ensure impartiality. In J.R. Acker, R.M. Bohm, & C.S. Lanier (Eds.) *America's Experiment with Capital Punishment*, 2nd ed. (pp. 385–411. Durham, NC: Carolina Academic Press.
Scheck, B.C. & Neufeld, P.J. (2002). Toward the formation of innocence commissions in America (2002). *Judicature* 86:98–105.
Scheck, B., Neufeld, P., & Dwyer, J. (2001). *Actual Innocence: When Justice Goes Wrong and How to Make It Right.* New York: Penguin Putnam.
Sorensen, J. (2004). The administration of capital punishment. *ACJS Today* 29:1–7.
Sundby, S.E. (2005). *A Life and Death Decision: A Jury Weighs the Death Penalty.* New York: Palgrave Macmillan.
Table of Compensation Statutes. (2006). Life after exoneration program available at http://www.exonerated.org/legal.php. (accessed June 24).
The Charlotte [NC] Observer, (1993). November 12, p. 8A.
The Constitution Project. (2005). Mandatory justice: The death penalty revisited (Washington, DC: The Constitution Project Death Penalty Initiative) available at http://www.constitutionproject.org/deathpenalty/article.cfm?messageID=136&categoryId=2
The Innocence Project. Available at http://www.innocenceproject.org/.
White, Welsh S. (1987). *The Death Penalty in the Eighties: An Examination of the Modern System of Capitol Punishment.* Ann Arbor: University of Michigan Press.
Williams, K. (2005). Ensuring the capital defendant's right to competent counsel: It's time for some standards. *The Wayne Law Review* 51:129–161.
Yardley, J. (2001a). Oklahoma takes close look at evidence in capital cases. *The Orlando Sentinel* (September 2), p. A5.
Yardley, J. (2001b). Oklahoma inquiry focuses on scientist used by prosecutors. *The New York Times* (May 2), p. A1.

Cases Cited

Bell v. Cone (2002) 535 U.S. 685.
Brady v. Maryland (1963) 373 U.S. 83.
Caldwell v. Mississippi (1985) 472 U.S. 320.
Chapman v. California (1967) 386 U.S. 18.
Herrera v. Collins (1993) 506 U.S. 390.

Scrutinizing the Death Penalty: State Death Penalty Study Commissions and Their Recommendations

2

JAMES R. ACKER

Contents

Introduction

The death penalty is an American tradition. In excess of 20,000 people have been lawfully executed on American soil since colonial times, including more than 7000 during the twentieth century (Banner, 2002; Bedau, 1997, p. 3). Thirty-seven states,[1] the federal government, and the U.S. military presently authorize capital punishment. At this writing, more than 3300 offenders are under sentence of death (Death Penalty Information Center, 2006; Snell, 2006). Despite the fact that all other Western industrialized countries have abolished the death penalty, the United States has stayed its course (Proctor, 2006–2007).

Capital punishment has endured in this country, although not without ambivalence. Abolition movements have periodically gained support and occasionally succeeded, especially during the years preceding the Civil War, World War I, and *Furman v. Georgia* (1972) (Haines, 1996, pp. 8–14). *Furman* brought a temporary halt to capital punishment nationwide, as the Supreme Court ruled that unregulated capital sentencing discretion, and its resulting arbitrariness, violated the Eighth Amendment's prohibition against cruel and unusual punishments. Today, although three-quarters of the states have capital-punishment legislation, fully one-quarter do not. Moreover, there are stark regional divides regarding the death penalty (Zimring, 2003, pp. 89–118). Strikingly, 11 Southern and border states are responsible for 85 percent of post-*Furman* executions, a geographical imbalance of unprecedented magnitude (Steiker & Steiker, 2006, pp. 1873–1874). Ten or fewer offenders were under death sentence in 15 of the 37 death penalty states at year-end 2005, including 7 states where fewer than five prisoners awaited execution (Snell, 2006, p. 5).

Public opinion polls reflect that most Americans endorse the death penalty. Support for capital punishment nevertheless dropped from 80 percent to 64 percent between 1994 and 2005, and it erodes markedly when respondents are asked whether they prefer death or life imprisonment without parole as punishment for murder (Bohm, 2003, pp. 44–46; Bowers et al., 1994). Concurrently, the number of death sentences imposed annually has plummeted, falling from 317 in 1996 to 125 in 2005. The 53 executions carried out in 2006 is the lowest yearly total in a decade, down from 98 in 1999, the post-*Furman* high water mark (Death Penalty Information Center, 2007; Sundby, 2006).

In 1997, the American Bar Association (ABA) called for a national moratorium on executions based on mounting concerns about the death penalty's fair administration, including the risk that innocent people might suffer capital punishment (American Bar Association, 1997). Although the ABA's call initially went unheeded, that trend was dramatically interrupted in January 2000 when Governor George Ryan ordered a halt to executions in Illinois following a series of highly publicized wrongful convictions in capital cases (Kirchmeier, 2002). Maryland and New Jersey imposed moratoria in 2002 and 2006, respectively. All three states commissioned an official study of their death penalty laws' administration while their executions bans remained in effect (Lanier and Acker, 2004, pp. 579–580; New Jersey Death Penalty Study Commission, 2007).

Official death penalty study commissions also sprang up in other states. Since 2000, one-third of the states with death penalty laws have ordered studies examining how capital punishment is administered within their borders, representing a remarkable demonstration of interest and concern about whether those laws are functioning as intended. When the United States Supreme Court upheld "guided discretion" death penalty legislation in 1976 (*Gregg v. Georgia*, 1976), approving the reinstatement of capital punishment following *Furman,* little was known about how the reform statutes would operate in practice. The Court quickly became immersed in a quagmire of vexing issues involving challenges to the new laws' application. Following an initial spate of rulings resulting in refinements in death penalty procedures, the justices substantially relaxed their scrutiny of capital punishment legislation by the mid-1980s (Acker, 1996; Steiker & Steiker, 1995). Thereafter, it became apparent that other branches of government would have to step into the breach to provide meaningful oversight of the operation of state capital punishment laws.

This chapter examines the government-commissioned studies to evaluate death penalty laws and their administration that have been carried out in 13 states since the turn of the 21st century. The studies differ in many important respects, including the source of their authority, the committees or individuals commissioned to complete them, and the scope of their inquiry. Yet, with varying degrees of comprehensiveness, all share a common purpose: to evaluate the effectiveness and/or fairness of state death penalty laws. After the studies' origins, participants, and charges are reviewed, their essential findings and recommendations are summarized. Concluding observations are provided about the studies' potential to help shape future death penalty laws and practices.

Death Penalty Study Commissions: Their Appointment, Composition, and Charges

Since 2000, official governmental studies have been commissioned in thirteen states to make findings and recommendations regarding the death penalty's administration. Studies have been carried out in Arizona, California, Connecticut, Illinois, Indiana, Kansas, Maryland, Nebraska, Nevada,

New Jersey, Pennsylvania, Tennessee, and Virginia.[2] Different government authorities commissioned the studies. Legislatures ordered that studies be carried out in four states (Connecticut, Nebraska, Nevada, and New Jersey) and studies were requested in four additional states by one branch of the legislature or a legislative committee (California, Kansas, Tennessee, and Virginia). Governors commissioned studies in three states (Illinois, Indiana, and Maryland). The state attorney general called for a study in Arizona, and the state supreme court directed that a study be carried out in Pennsylvania.

Responsibility for completing the studies and issuing reports varied. Special committees, of diverse composition, were appointed in seven states (Arizona, California, Connecticut, Illinois, Kansas, New Jersey, and Pennsylvania). Those committees ranged in size from eight members (Connecticut) to thirty-one (Arizona). They tended to be dominated by lawyers, including prosecutors, public defenders, and private attorneys. They frequently included current or former governmental officials, judges, and law enforcement officers, and occasionally involved representatives of religious and civic organizations. In four states, existing government councils or agencies carried out the work, including the Indiana Criminal Law Study Commission, the Nevada Legislative Commission Subcommittee, the Tennessee State Comptroller of the Treasury, and the Virginia General Assembly's Joint Legislative Audit and Review Commission's staff. Academic researchers were enlisted to complete the studies in two states. Professor David Baldus (of the University of Iowa College of Law) and colleagues conducted the Nebraska study, and Professor Raymond Paternoster (of the University of Maryland) and colleagues completed the Maryland study.

The scope of the studies, as defined by the charge of the authorizing authority, also varied; some mandates were general, others directed that several specific issues be investigated, and some were confined narrowly to one or a few select topics. Among the broader directives was the one issued to the Arizona Capital Case Commission, which was formed "to study key issues and make recommendations to try to ensure that the death penalty process in Arizona is just, timely, and fair to defendants and victims" (Office of the Attorney General, State of Arizona, 2002, p. 1). The California Commission on the Fair Administration of Justice, which addressed the state criminal justice system generally, including the "Fair Administration of the Death Penalty," was charged:

> To study and review the administration of criminal justice in California to determine the extent to which that process has failed in the past, resulting in wrongful execution or the wrongful conviction of innocent persons.
>
> To examine ways of providing safeguards and making improvements in the way the criminal justice system functions.

> To make any recommendations and proposals designed to further ensure that the application and administration of criminal justice in California is just, fair, and accurate. . . . (California Commission on the Fair Administration of Justice, 2007a)

Governor Ryan's Executive Order gave the Illinois Commission on Capital Punishment a similarly broad mandate, although it was coupled with specific directives:

> A. To study and review the administration of the capital punishment process in Illinois to determine why that process has failed in the past, resulting in the imposition of death sentences upon innocent people.
> B. To examine ways of providing safeguards and making improvements in the way law enforcement and the criminal justice system carry out their responsibilities in the death process—from investigation through trial, judicial appeal and executive review.
> C. . . .
> D. To make any recommendations and proposals designed to further ensure the application and administration of the death penalty in Illinois is just, fair and accurate. (Governor's Commission on Capital Punishment, 2002, p. 1)

Nebraska's inquiry "was undertaken pursuant to a decision of the Nebraska Legislature to support a study of Nebraska homicides with a focus on fairness" (Baldus et al., 2001, p. 23, n. 7), whereas the subcommittee's task in Nevada generally was "to study the death penalty and related DNA testing" (Legislative Commission's Subcommittee to Study the Death Penalty and Related DNA Testing, 2003, p. 3).

Several studies were initiated pursuant to more detailed charges. The legislation establishing the Connecticut Commission on the Death Penalty provided that the study "shall include but not be limited to" an examination of fourteen enumerated issues relevant to the state's death penalty law, including compliance with constitutional requirements, financial costs, charging or sentencing disparities involving racial and other factors, including location of crime, appellate and post-conviction review, executive clemency, innocence, victim impact evidence, and the causes and consequences of delay in carrying out death sentences (State of Connecticut Commission on the Death Penalty, 2003, App. A). Governor Frank O'Bannon directed the Indiana commission to address issues related to innocence, defense counsel, judicial review, race, financial cost, and to consider whether changes should be implemented in the state's capital sentencing statute (Janeway, 2002, p. 3).

The Kansas commission was instructed to focus on geographic and racial disparities, innocence, deterrence, and the treatment of murder victims' survivors; an earlier commission considered the financial costs of capital punishment (Kansas Judicial Council Death Penalty Advisory Committee, 2004a, pp. 4–5; Kansas Judicial Council Death Penalty Advisory Committee, 2004b, pp. 5–6). New Jersey's Commission was charged generally "with studying all aspects of the death penalty as currently administered in the State of New Jersey," and more specifically with considering whether capital punishment serves legitimate penological interests including deterrence, the comparative cost of the death penalty and life imprisonment, arbitrariness and discrimination, innocence, alternatives to capital punishment, and the death penalty's consistency with evolving standards of decency (New Jersey Death Penalty Study Commission, 2007, pp. 3–4).

The scope of four studies was more circumscribed. In Maryland, Governor Parris Glendening commissioned an empirical study "to examine whether or not the imposition of the death penalty in the state was affected by race (either of the offender, victim, or both) or geography (the jurisdiction where the crime occurred)" (Paternoster et al., 2003, p. 4). The Pennsylvania Supreme Court appointed the Committee on Racial and Gender Bias in the Justice System "to undertake a study of the state court system to determine whether racial or gender bias plays a role in the justice system" (Pennsylvania Supreme Court Committee on Racial and Gender Bias in the Justice System, 2003, p. 12). The Tennessee study focused narrowly on "the monetary costs to the taxpayers of Tennessee in connection with the state's administration of the death penalty" (Comptroller of the Treasury, State of Tennessee, 2004, p. 50). The Virginia General Assembly's Joint Legislative Audit and Review Commission (JLARC) asked the JLARC staff to study capital punishment in Virginia "in response to concerns about two key aspects" of the state's death penalty: "the use of prosecutorial discretion by Commonwealth Attorneys in the application of the State's death penalty statutes; and the fairness of the judicial review process for persons who have been sentenced to die" (Joint Legislative Audit and Review Commission of the Virginia General Assembly, 2002, Preface).

Issues, Findings, and Recommendations

The studies' findings and recommendations are cabined by the scope of their accompanying charges. Hence, they do not necessarily represent a complete portrait of the potential problems associated with state death penalty laws and their administration. However, some commissions found that issues they were assigned to explore implicated others, causing them to embrace matters not explicitly within their charge. For example, although the Pennsylvania commission was directed to focus on racial and gender bias, it determined that those issues "cannot be divorced from poverty." Consequently, it also studied "such issues as adequacy of court-appointed counsel for the poor and availability of essential resources for their defense" (Pennsylvania Supreme Court Committee on Racial and Gender Bias in the Justice System, 2003, pp. 200–201). With these constraints in mind, the aspects of capital punishment that were of greatest interest and concern to the study commissions are considered below, with accompanying findings and recommendations.

Penological Objectives

The studies largely ignored whether capital punishment in their states promoted such legislative objectives as general deterrence, retribution, and incapacitation. Only in Kansas and New Jersey were such issues considered. The reports in both states reviewed published studies about deterrence and assessed the related premises. Both studies expressed doubt about the death penalty's likelihood of inhibiting the commission of murder more effectively than life imprisonment, although neither claimed to be capable of resolving the debate (Kansas Judicial Council Death Penalty Advisory Committee, 2004a, p. 23; New Jersey Death Penalty Study Commission, 2007, p. 24).

Only the New Jersey commission considered retribution and incapacitation. It reported being divided about the legitimacy of retribution. "Of the commission members who felt that retribution is an appropriate penological intent, some felt that this intent is achieved by incarceration, so the death penalty is not indispensable for achieving it. Other members felt that the desire for retribution is trumped by the serious problems with the death penalty like cost, irreversible error, and inconsistency with evolving standards of decency" (New Jersey Death Penalty Study Commission, 2007, p. 30). The commission ultimately concluded that life imprisonment without parole (LWOP) incapacitates individuals from engaging in further acts of violence outside of prison and that this alternative sanction "would sufficiently ensure public safety and address other legitimate social and penological interests" (New Jersey Death Penalty Study Commission, 2007, p. 56).

Administrative Issues and Cost

Wrongful Convictions and Innocence

Governor Ryan's highly publicized moratorium on executions in Illinois and his formation of a special Commission on Capital Punishment was largely prompted by his concern that innocent people risked conviction and execution. Thirteen men had been released from Illinois' death row in little more than a decade amidst disturbing revelations of irregularities in police investigative techniques and other reasons to doubt the convictions' reliability. Anthony Porter, one of the wrongfully convicted, came within 48 hours of execution and owed his release as much to the determination of students and journalists as to the legal system (Governor's Commission on Capital Punishment, 2002, pp. 1 and 4; Warden, 2005). The Illinois commission thus devoted extensive consideration to law enforcement investigative procedures, evidentiary issues, and other factors associated with the threat that innocent people could face execution. Seven other state study commissions also examined issues associated with wrongful convictions and innocence.

The numerous recommendations in the Illinois commission's report addressing those issues encompass several aspects of capital murder investigations and trials. The commission urged that the police make a written record of all evidence, including potentially exculpatory evidence, and transmit all collected information to prosecutors; that custodial interrogations of murder suspects conducted at police facilities be videotaped and that interviews with other significant witnesses be electronically recorded; that line-ups and photo arrays be administered by officers who do not know the suspect's identity and that sequential rather than simultaneous presentation be made of suspects to identifying witnesses; that witnesses' measure of confidence in an identification be solicited and recorded; and that line-ups be videotaped when practicable. The commission additionally recommended that the police (as well as defense attorneys, prosecutors, and trial judges) receive training in those and related matters (Governor's Commission on Capital Punishment, 2002, pp. 19–64).

The Illinois commission further proposed that a state forensics laboratory be maintained independently of law enforcement, that a comprehensive DNA database be established and adequately funded, and that rules for post-conviction review of convictions be liberalized. It recommended that judges should conduct hearings on the reliability and admissibility of the testimony of in-custody informants prior to allowing juries to hear from such witnesses. The commission also endorsed legislation that would rule out the death penalty in cases based on the testimony of a single eyewitness or accomplice, or on the uncorroborated testimony of an in-custody informant concerning a defendant's purported confession. It further supported allowing discovery depositions in capital cases on leave of court, extending the rules of discovery to the penalty phase of a capital trial, and requiring case management conferences designed in part to ensure full compliance with discovery obligations, including the prosecution's duty to disclose exculpatory evidence. Nonfrivolous claims of actual innocence in capital cases could be raised at any time under the commission's recommendations (Governor's Commission on Capital Punishment, 2002, pp. 111–160).

Although the Illinois commission's recommendations in this area were by far the most exhaustive, many other states also addressed measures designed to minimize the threat of wrongful convictions. Arizona, California, and Connecticut recommended recording police interrogations, and the Kansas commission urged investigation of that reform. California and Connecticut proposed adopting "double-blind" and sequential line-up and photo identification procedures, and Kansas' commission again endorsed investigating those measures. The same three states proposed safeguards regarding the testimony of in-custody informants. Connecticut endorsed "open file" discovery of the prosecution's evidence, and Kansas urged investigation of such a policy. The study commissions in Arizona, Connecticut, and Nevada recommended mandatory preservation of biological evidence in anticipation of DNA analysis. The California commission encouraged the certification of forensic experts, and recommended independent investigation of laboratory errors, the creation of a government agency to develop and enforce standards governing scientific testing, report writing, and the proper boundaries of expert testimony, and better forensic training for attorneys and judges. It also recommended urgent attention to the problem of backlogs in DNA testing (California Commission on the Fair Administration of Justice, 2007b,c).

The Indiana Criminal Law Study Commission was charged, *inter alia*, to address "[w]hether safeguards are in place to ensure than an innocent person is not executed" (Janeway, 2002, p. 3). The Commission acknowledged the fallibility of the criminal justice system and concluded that "one may reasonably assume that the worst sentence, as with any other sentence, may 'inevitably be inflicted upon innocent men'" (Janeway, 2002, pp. 5–6). Its conclusion, in light of that premise, is somewhat perplexing. "After reviewing whether safeguards are in place to ensure that an innocent person is not executed, the Commission found a capital case system of 'super due process' comprised of multiple, integrated safeguards. Additional safeguards were discussed, with no consensus reached" (Janeway, 2002, unnumbered page).

New Jersey's commission did not equivocate. It was directed to address "[w]hether the penological interest in executing some of those guilty of murder is sufficiently compelling that the risk of an irreversible mistake is acceptable" (New Jersey Death Penalty Study Commission, 2007, p. 51). It responded unambiguously in the negative: "The penological interest in executing a small number of persons guilty of murder is not sufficiently compelling to justify the risk of making an irreversible mistake" (New Jersey Death Penalty Study Commission, 2007, p. 51). In keeping with that finding, the commission recommended that New Jersey rescind its capital punishment law.

Race and Arbitrariness

All 12 of the completed studies addressed the issues of race and/or arbitrariness, in the death penalty's administration. California's report almost certainly will encompass those issues as well, but the section on the "Fair Administration of the Death Penalty" remains pending. Several recommendations in this regard focused on prosecutorial discretion. Others looked to appellate courts to detect and correct problems associated with discrimination and arbitrariness. The reports in some states, including Arizona,

Connecticut, Kansas, Illinois, Nevada, and Pennsylvania, called for more comprehensive and systematic data collection to facilitate analysis of whether racial, ethnic, geographic, or other disparities characterize capital charging or sentencing decisions. The Connecticut, Nevada, and Pennsylvania commissions specifically recommended collecting and preserving demographic information about juries in their calls for data.

Studies carried out in four states found no evidence of race discrimination in capital cases. The Kansas committee qualified its finding with a recommendation that more information be gathered to allow for more definitive conclusions (Kansas Judicial Council Death Penalty Advisory Committee, 2004a, pp. 12–14). Professor Baldus' study of Nebraska produced "no significant evidence" of either race of defendant or race of victim biases (Baldus et al. 2001, p. 14), although the report found significant geographical charging disparities in the state. Those inconsistencies, however, were largely negated by lower death sentencing rates in Nebraska's three largest counties, where prosecutions were most commonly initiated (Baldus et al. 2001, pp. 18–21). The study also reported "significant disparities in treatment based on the socio-economic status of the victim" in murder cases (Baldus et al. 2001, p. 22). The New Jersey Death Penalty Study Commission concluded that "the available data do not support a finding of invidious racial bias in the application of the death penalty in New Jersey" (New Jersey Death Penalty Study Commission, 2007, p. 41), although it reserved judgment about inter-county variability in the death penalty's administration (New Jersey Death Penalty Study Commission, 2007, pp. 41–45).

The Virginia report found no evidence that race affected prosecutorial charging decisions once controls were imposed for other case factors (Joint Legislative Audit and Review Commission of the Virginia General Assembly, 2002, p. 27–44). However, it did uncover significant differences in capital prosecutions based on geography. "It is . . . clear that the most important factor influencing the decision of prosecutors to seek the death penalty . . . is the jurisdiction in which the murder occurred rather than the circumstances of the crime. . . . [P]rosecutors in the more highly populated localities are much less likely to seek the death penalty than their counterparts in less populated jurisdictions" (Joint Legislative Audit and Review Commission of the Virginia General Assembly, 2002, Preface and pp. 28–52).

Professor Paternoster's study in Maryland, on the other hand, found clear evidence of race of victim and geographical disparities in the application of the state's death penalty law. His report specifically concluded that, "even after taking into account jurisdiction and relevant case characteristics offenders who slay white victims are significantly more likely to be sentenced to death than those who slay all non-white victims" (Paternoster et al.,

2003, p. 33). Geographic variation in death penalty prosecutions also was pronounced. For example,

> the predicted probability that a death notice will be filed in a death eligible case ranges from a high of .620 in Baltimore County to a low of .046 in Baltimore City. This means that given the fact that a death eligible homicide has occurred, *the probability that a notification to seek death will be filed in Baltimore County is over 13 times higher than in Baltimore City, even after taking into account important case characteristics.* (Paternoster et al., 2003, p. 30, emphasis in original)

The reports completed by academic researchers (i.e., Professor Baldus's study of Nebraska's death penalty and Professor Paternoster's study of Maryland's) are distinctive in that they present detailed empirical findings and analysis, but make no corresponding policy recommendations. The study commissions in other states were not similarly constrained. Several of the commissions, including those in Connecticut, Illinois, Pennsylvania, and Tennessee, recommended implementing guidelines for prosecutors' capital charging decisions and/or compulsory centralized review of those decisions to help guard against arbitrariness.

Four commissions, those in Connecticut, Illinois, Nevada, and Pennsylvania, recommended that their state supreme courts engage in comparative proportionality review to attempt to identify capital sentences that were excessive when measured against punishments imposed in other, similar cases. Indiana's commission was unable to reach consensus about whether to recommend comparative proportionality review (Janeway, 2002, p. 113), whereas the New Jersey commission raised questions about the New Jersey Supreme Court's ability to complete such review successfully (New Jersey Death Penalty Study Commission, 2007, pp. 46–50). The Connecticut and Pennsylvania commissions additionally recommended that state "Racial Justice Acts" be adopted. Pursuant to such legislation, a statistical showing of statewide disparities in the administration of the death penalty would trigger a rebuttable presumption of impermissible discrimination in individual cases. Racial Justice Acts, which have been debated in Congress and implemented in Kentucky, were first proposed in response to the Supreme Court's decision in *McCleskey v. Kemp* (1987), in which the justices rejected the argument that aggregate statistics suggesting racial differences in the death penalty's administration support an inference of race discrimination in a discrete case (Arnold, 2005; Baldus et al., 1994; Schoeman, 1995).

The New Jersey commission made the most sweeping recommendation regarding the problem of arbitrariness and discrimination in capital punishment. "[T]he commission finds that despite the best efforts of the State, the risk remains that similar murder cases are being treated differently in the death penalty context thereby elevating the probability that the death penalty is being administered 'freakishly' and arbitrarily. Given the finality of the punishment of death, this risk is unacceptable" (New Jersey Death Penalty Study Commission, 2007, p. 50). The commission's recommendation to replace the death penalty with life imprisonment without parole obviated its consideration of specific corrective measures.

Perhaps not coincidentally, the recommendations of the standing (i.e., not death penalty specific), politically comprised committees in Indiana and Virginia regarding race and arbitrariness remained vague. The Indiana Criminal Law Study Commission devoted scant discussion to a state study that suggested, "if race plays a role in sentencing outcomes in Indiana, the race of the victim alone may play a more important role than the race of the offender" (Janeway, 2002, p. 123). It offered no firm conclusions in response to its charge to investigate "[w]hether Indiana imposes capital sentencing in a race neutral manner" (Janeway, 2002, p. 123).

Virginia's Joint Legislative Audit and Review Commission, after noting significant disparities in capital prosecutions throughout the state based on geography, remained noncommittal about remedies. It simply observed:

> These findings pose significant policy challenges for the General Assembly. In order for the system of capital punishment to be viable in Virginia, prosecutors must retain the discretionary authority they currently exercise in these cases. However, as shown in this study, this discretion will generate statewide outcomes that are not easily reconciled on the grounds of fairness. (Joint Legislative Audit and Review Commission of the Virginia General Assembly, 2002, Preface)

The study commission appointed by Arizona's attorney general also remained vague regarding possible race effects in capital cases. Some commission members concluded "that there does not appear to be a racial bias in the administration of the death penalty in Arizona. Other Commission members conclude that there may be a bias based on the race of the victim or that it is impossible to draw conclusions . . ." (Office of the Attorney General, State of Arizona, 2002, p. 26). The attorney general went on record as "not believ[ing that] the statistics . . . support an allegation of racial bias in the process" (Office of the Attorney General, State of Arizona, 2002, p. 27). The commission concluded weakly that "members unanimously agree that it is the responsibility of all participants in the criminal justice system to promote practices that ensure that race-neutral decisions are made regarding defendants and victims when deciding whether to seek or impose capital punishment, and that participants in the system should use the empirical data . . . in internal reviews and discussions regarding the death penalty process" (Office of the Attorney General, State of Arizona, 2002, p. 27).

Death Penalty Statutes: Scope, Sentencing Factors, and Alternative Punishments

Study commissions in three states recommended narrowing the scope of death penalty statutes. Another commission noted concerns about the breadth of an aggravating factor used in the state law and urged further study of its application. The most fundamental recommendation was made by the Illinois commission, which advocated a substantial reduction in the number of statutory aggravating factors used to determine death penalty eligibility. The twenty factors currently provided by law would give way, under the commission's recommendation, to five: murder of a peace officer or firefighter, murder committed in a correctional facility, multiple victim murders, torture murders, and murder committed to thwart the administration of justice (Governor's Commission on Capital Punishment, 2002, pp. 66–76). In recommending a narrower range of death eligible crimes, the commission sought to achieve greater consistency in charging and sentencing decisions while still being faithful to capital punishment's accepted penological justifications.

The Nevada commission focused attention on two arguably vague statutory aggravating circumstances, one involving "murder committed by a person who knowingly created a great risk of death to more than one person," and the other involving "murder committed upon one or more persons at random and without apparent motive." It ultimately recommended eliminating the former provision (Legislative Commission's Subcommittee to Study the Death Penalty and Related DNA Testing, 2003, p. 9). The Indiana commission was unable to reach a consensus about whether the number of aggravating factors in that state's death penalty statute was cause for concern. However, it did recommend that the law be amended to require that death penalty eligibility be limited to cases where "the defendant personally killed, intended to kill, or intended that a killing occur" (Janeway, 2002, p. 139).

Arizona's commission expressed concern that the statutory aggravating factor of killing in an "especially cruel, heinous or depraved manner" might be overused as well as vague. However, it only recommended that "additional study" be made of that factor's application (Office of the Attorney General, State of Arizona, 2002, p. 25). Kansas' study commission concluded that the state death penalty law was sufficiently narrow that changes in its scope were unnecessary (Kansas Judicial Council Death Penalty Advisory Committee, 2004a, p. 19).

Arizona's study commission recommended that the minimum age of death penalty eligibility be raised from 16 to 18. Indiana's commission considered a similar proposal but could not reach consensus. Study commissions in Arizona, Illinois, and Nevada recommended excluding the death penalty for mentally retarded offenders. Supreme Court decisions limiting capital punishment to offenders 18 years of age and older, and exempting the mentally retarded from death penalty eligibility rendered the commissions' recommendations on those matters moot (*Atkins v. Virginia*, 2002; *Roper v. Simmons*, 2005).

Three study commissions addressed mitigating factors relevant to state death penalty laws. The Illinois commission recommended that statutory mitigating factors be expanded to include an offender's history of extreme emotional or physical abuse, as well as the offender's reduced mental capacity. It further proposed that defendants be given the right of allocution at capital sentencing hearings (Governor's Commission on Capital Punishment, 2002, pp. 141–144). Nevada's commission urged adoption of a statutory mitigating factor encompassing the offender's mental illness or history of psychological disturbance, and advocated that courts be required to list "other" relevant unenumerated mitigating factors individually and submit them in writing to the sentencing jury (Legislative Commission's Subcommittee to Study the Death Penalty and Related DNA Testing, 2003, p. 10). The Arizona and Illinois commissions considered suggesting that residual or lingering doubt be listed as a statutory mitigating factor, but ultimately declined to make such a recommendation (Office of the Attorney General, State of Arizona, 2002, pp. 21–22; Governor's Commission on Capital Punishment, 2002, pp. 147). The Supreme Court later ruled that the Constitution does not require that residual doubt be considered as a mitigating factor (*Oregon v. Guzek*, 2006).

The study commissions in Illinois and New Jersey also addressed statutory alternatives to capital punishment. The Illinois commission recommended that if and only if the legislature followed another of the commission's recommendations—to limit death penalty eligibility to only five forms of aggravated murder—then the alternative punishment in all capital cases should be life imprisonment without the possibility of parole (Governor's Commission on Capital Punishment, 2002, pp. 155–156). When New Jersey's commission recommended that the state legislature abolish capital punishment, it simultaneously recommended life imprisonment without parole as the alternative punishment (New Jersey Death Penalty Study Commission, 2007, pp. 56–61). The state public defender, a member of the study commission, endorsed abolishing the death penalty, but protested that it was both misleading and inappropriate to suggest this ostensible trade-off between LWOP and capital punishment in first-degree murder cases. He argued that LWOP sentences almost certainly would far outnumber the death sentences imposed under New Jersey's current law and because prison sentences presumably would be imposed automatically, without weighing aggravating and mitigating factors, it was inaccurate to suggest that LWOP would simply be "replacing" capital punishment (New Jersey Death Penalty Study Commission, 2007, pp. 89–92).

Cost

Tennessee's State Comptroller of the Treasury was asked to study only the monetary costs associated with the state's death penalty. The study commissions in Connecticut, Indiana, Kansas, Nevada, and New Jersey also were charged with assessing the comparative costs of capital punishment and life imprisonment. The Tennessee report describes several aspects of capital cases, from investigation and trials through execution, that would be expected to enhance costs beyond those normally incurred in noncapital cases. However, it also notes that executions typically spare future incarceration costs in the magnitude of $680,000 to $774,000. It observes that several "indirect effects" of the death penalty resist quantification, including its impact on the families of both murder victims and offenders, and the speculative nature of capital punishment's effectiveness in deterring future murders,. In light of its charge, the report is conspicuous for not offering a general conclusion about the cumulative comparative costs of capital punishment and life imprisonment, resorting instead to calling for more comprehensive data collection (Comptroller of the State of Tennessee, 2004).

The Tennessee report was not alone in its inability to produce specific cost estimates for capital cases. The Connecticut and Nevada commissions similarly came to no conclusions and recommended that comprehensive studies be conducted based on more reliable data (State of Connecticut Commission on the Death Penalty, 2003, pp. 12–16; Legislative Commission's Subcommittee to Study the Death Penalty and Related DNA Testing, 2003, p. 20). The New Jersey commission concluded that: "The costs of the death penalty are greater than the costs of life in prison without parole, but it is not possible to measure these costs with any precision" (New Jersey Death Penalty Study Commission, 2007, p. 31). Indiana's commission also noted the considerable challenges associated with providing comparative cost estimates, but adopted the conclusions of an analyst who calculated that a "typical" capital case costs roughly 21 percent more than a "typical" LWOP case ($667, 560 versus $551,016) (Janeway, 2002, pp. 121–122ff).

The most detailed cost assessment was offered by the Kansas Judicial Council Death Penalty Advisory Committee (2004b), which was completed before life without parole was an available sentence in the state. The report thus compared capital cases to those resulting in life sentences with parole eligibility after 25 or 50 years. It estimated that the "median cost of a case in which the death sentence was given was $1.2 million, compared to the same estimated costs for a non-death penalty case of about $740,000" (Kansas Judicial Council Death Penalty Advisory Committee (2004b, p. 23). The committee noted that "there is really very little that states can do to contain or reduce death penalty cost" (Kansas Judicial Council Death Penalty Advisory Committee (2004b, p. 42), and projected that those costs "can be expected to continue to increase in the future" (Kansas Judicial Council Death Penalty Advisory Committee (2004b, p. 35).

Participants in Capital Trials: Defense Counsel, Prosecutors, Judges, Juries, and Victims

Defense Counsel

Seven of the study commissions addressed capital defense counsel, including minimum standards and qualifications, training requirements, and required resources. California's forthcoming report on the Fair Administration of the Death Penalty will likely do so, as well. The Arizona, Connecticut, Nevada, and Pennsylvania commissions urged creation of statewide capital defender offices or capital resource centers to manage capital trials, appeals, and post-conviction representation, and to provide back-up assistance to other attorneys who represent capital defendants. Commissions in states that did not already require capital defense counsel to meet minimum standards recommended threshold qualifications as well as continuing legal education and training obligations. Those recommendations frequently invoked the American Bar Association's *Guidelines for the Appointment and Performance of Defense Counsel in Death Penalty Cases* (2003) as a model. The Arizona, Nevada, and Pennsylvania commissions made recommendations of this nature, and the commissions in Illinois, Indiana, and Kansas affirmed the importance of already existing standards and training requirements.

All of the study commissions addressing defense counsel issues recognized the importance of adequate compensation and resources. Thus, the recommendations typically included ensuring the availability of investigators and experts, including mitigation specialists, and/or other assistance. The Illinois commission advocated the highest compensation for court-appointed counsel in capital cases, encouraging "regular reconsideration of the hourly rates authorized under the statute to reflect the actual market rates of private attorneys" (Governor's Commission on Capital Punishment, 2002, p. 179). Pennsylvania's commission was less specific, recommending "reasonable minimum compensation standards for capital counsel" (Pennsylvania Supreme Court Committee on Racial and Gender Bias in the Justice System, 2003, p. 220), and the Nevada commission advocated raising the presumptive fee cap for court-appointed counsel in capital cases from $12,000 to $20,000 (Legislative Commission's Subcommittee to Study the Death Penalty and Related DNA Testing, 2003, pp. 12–13). The Connecticut commission promoted higher hourly rates for special public defenders in capital cases, suggesting that the compensation rate for court-appointed counsel in federal cases provided a good benchmark. It further suggested that "accommodations are necessary for private attorneys in order to allow them to sustain the remainder of their practice during a lengthy trial" (State of Connecticut Commission on the Death Penalty, 2003, p. 42).

As with several other issues, Indiana's commission failed to reach consensus about the propriety of the current reimbursement rate of $90 per hour for defense counsel appointed in capital cases. Although noting that "the adequacy of the . . . rate was challenged by some Commission members," the report recommended that the Indiana Supreme Court should continue to set compensation levels (Janeway, 2002, pp. 82). The Kansas commission noted that "it appears that the cost of providing constitutionally effective counsel will continue to rise in the future. . . . These increasing costs may require study . . . so Kansas can continue to adhere to the ABA Guidelines" (Kansas Judicial Council Death Penalty Advisory Committee, 2004a, p. 16). The Arizona Capital Case Commission strongly recommended that the legislature appropriate additional funds for capital litigation resources and indicated that "it deeply regrets the Legislature did not address this need this year" (Office of the Attorney General, State of Arizona, 2002, p. 14). However, as one commission member commented:

> The Commission's Final Report . . . does not make any statements about what we as a state should do in the face of the failure of the legislature to act. I believe that the only reasonable response to a system that seeks to impose the death penalty, but is so underfunded as to be able to make the decision of who should live and who should die in a fair and equitable way, is either to eliminate that system or at least stop it until such time as adequate funding is provided. (Office of the Attorney General, State of Arizona, 2002, p. 30)

Prosecutors

Several state study commissions made recommendations about prosecutors that went beyond discovery policies and charging guidelines, as previously discussed. The Arizona, Connecticut, and Illinois commissions endorsed mandatory training for prosecutors who handle capital cases, much as they had recommended analogous training for defense counsel. The Connecticut commission also recognized that prosecutors, much like defense attorneys, are apt to encounter extraordinary costs in capital cases and that commensurate resources should be provided, including additional staff as needed (State of Connecticut Commission on the Death Penalty, 2003, pp. 42 and 68). The Illinois commission recommended that prosecutors file death penalty notices as soon as practicable, and in all cases within 120 days of arraignment (Governor's Commission on Capital Punishment, 2002, p. 90). To provide greater opportunity for conferences with defense counsel, the Arizona commission proposed that prosecutors be allowed more time to file death penalty notices than state law presently provided, or up to 60 days after arraignment (Office of the Attorney General, State of Arizona, 2002, p. 16).

Trial Judges

The Arizona, Illinois, and Nevada study commissions recommended that trial judges assigned to capital cases enroll in continuing legal education classes addressing death penalty issues. The Illinois commission stipulated that only death penalty-certified judges should be allowed to preside over capital trials, and recommended that the state supreme court appoint a standing committee comprised of trial and appellate judges with experience in capital cases to serve as a resource for trial judges handling death penalty cases (Governor's Commission on Capital Punishment, 2002, pp. 94–102). It further recommended that trial judges "should be reminded of their obligation . . . to report violations of the Rules of Professional Conduct by prosecutors and defense lawyers" (Governor's Commission on Capital Punishment, 2002, p. 191).

The Illinois and Nevada commissions recommended changes in trial judges' sentencing authority. The Illinois panel advocated that trial judges should be required to indicate on the record their agreement or disagreement with juries' sentencing verdicts and that they should be empowered to impose a sentence of life imprisonment when they disagreed with a jury's death penalty verdict (Governor's Commission on Capital Punishment, 2002, pp. 152–155). Under statutory provisions in effect when the Nevada commission issued its recommendations, three-judge panels were enlisted to decide the sentence in capital cases in which defendants pled guilty and when trial juries failed to arrive at a unanimous sentencing verdict. The Nevada commission expressed concerns about the fairness of those procedures, as well as their constitutionality in light of *Ring v. Arizona* (2002), which ruled that, absent a waiver, juries must decide all facts essential to support a death sentence. The commission recommended eliminating three-judge sentencing panels in cases involving hung juries, and that trial judges should either empanel a new sentencing jury in such cases or else sentence the defendant to life imprisonment without parole. It recommended retaining three-judge panels to impose sentence when defendants pled guilty to capital crimes (Legislative Commission's Subcommittee to Study the Death Penalty and Related DNA Testing, 2003, pp. 14–15).

Jury Issues

Study commissions in Illinois and Pennsylvania made several recommendations regarding jury instructions in capital cases. To supplement its numerous proposed reforms to help guard against wrongful convictions, the Illinois commission recommended that juries be specially instructed about factors affecting the reliability of eyewitness identification. It proposed that juries should receive cautionary instructions about the testimony of in-custody informants, and that recorded statements may be more reliable than unrecorded statements where recorded statements are lacking (Governor's Commission on Capital Punishment, 2002, pp. 129–133). It also recommended that instructions administered during the penalty phase of capital trials clarify the jury's obligation to weigh aggravating and mitigating factors and to decide whether death is an appropriate punishment (Governor's Commission on Capital Punishment, 2002, pp. 151–152). Both the Illinois and Pennsylvania commissions advocated that juries be specifically instructed about the alternative sentences to death including, where applicable, that a "life" sentence means life without the possibility of parole (Governor's Commission on Capital Punishment, 2002, pp. 144–147; Pennsylvania Supreme Court Committee on Racial and Gender Bias in the Justice System, 2003, p. 220).

In keeping with its charge, the Pennsylvania commission proposed several reforms designed to help purge capital juries of racial and gender bias. Its recommendations to the Pennsylvania Supreme Court included:

- . . . [R]equire the retention of the jury questionnaire utilized at trial, which indicates the race and gender of the jurors, for the duration of the defendant's incarceration.
- Require trial courts during *voir dire* in capital cases to explore fully, when requested by either party, views about race held by prospective jurors.
- Promulgate a rule that allows for reasonable latitude by defense counsel and the Commonwealth to explore all potential sources of racial bias in *voir dire* of prospective jurors.
- Require trial courts to charge capital juries, when requested by either party, that they may not consider the race of the defendant or victim in determining the appropriate sentence for the defendant.
- Promulgate a rule that should a *prima facie* case of discrimination in the use of peremptory challenges be established, reasons invoked for the exclusion of the juror that do not substantially relate to his or her qualifications, fitness, or bias shall be viewed as presumptively pretextual.
- Reduce the number of peremptory strikes in capital cases. (Pennsylvania Supreme Court Committee on Racial and Gender Bias in the Justice System, 2003, pp. 219–220)

The Nevada commission recommended implementing individual *voir dire* of prospective jurors, sequestering juries, and requiring written juror questionnaires in capital cases. It further proposed that defense counsel be allowed a final rebuttal argument in capital trials, deviating from the present policy entitling prosecutors to make both the first and last jury arguments (Legislative Commission's Subcommittee to Study the Death Penalty and

Related DNA Testing, 2003, pp. 13–14 and 16). Arizona's commission went on record as opposing a proposed amendment to the state rules of criminal procedure that would have allowed juries to begin their deliberations before receiving the trial judge's instructions, a proposal that eventually was not implemented (Office of the Attorney General, State of Arizona, 2002, pp. iv and 20).

Victims

Four study commissions addressed issues involving murder victims' survivors, including the use of victim impact evidence. Arizona's commission sought to ensure that victim impact evidence would be heard in a timely fashion. It proposed that murder victims' survivors be allowed to testify at the aggravation/mitigation hearing and that the trial judge not impose sentence earlier than one week following that hearing. Although the proposal was implemented into law, it became moot following Arizona's replacement of judge sentencing with jury sentencing in the wake of *Ring v. Arizona* (2002) (Office of the Attorney General, State of Arizona, 2002, pp. v and 21).

Connecticut law in effect (when that state's commission completed its work) provided that written victim impact statements should be included in a court file and that they "may" be read prior to imposition of sentence. Trial courts interpreted the law to preclude introduction of such statements during the penalty phase of capital trials, rendering them incapable of influencing sentencing decisions. After hearing testimony from several witnesses, including victims' representatives, the Connecticut commission recommended that victim impact statements continue to remain unavailable for sentencing purposes in capital cases. It further recommended that procedures be adopted to ensure that victims' survivors be apprised about those limitations to spare them from feeling misled or that they had been treated unfairly (State of Connecticut Commission on the Death Penalty, 2003, pp. 62–66). The commission commented on the emotional turmoil experienced by family members following the murder of a loved one:

> Most of the family members of victims of capital offenses who addressed this Commission and who were interviewed for this report said that their initial hope was that the judicial system would help to bring a sense of justice and healing into their lives. However, they found the opposite to be true. Once the judicial process began, the overwhelming feeling among those families was that the judicial process added to their distress and anxiety. Most of those who testified before the Commission said that their trust in the criminal justice system was damaged when sentences rendered by juries were not implemented in a fair, timely, and certain manner. (State of Connecticut Commission on the Death Penalty, 2003, p. 70)

The Kansas commission had been asked to address "[w]hether states that have the death penalty treat murder victim's [sic] families who oppose the death penalty the same as murder victims' families who favor the death penalty" (Kansas Judicial Council Death Penalty Advisory Committee, 2004a, pp. 24). After hearing from a representative of Murder Victims Families for Reconciliation and drawing on its members' own experiences with capital litigation, the commission reported finding "no evidence of discriminatory treatment in Kansas of murder victims' families who oppose the death penalty" (Kansas Judicial Council Death Penalty Advisory Committee, 2004a, p. 26).

New Jersey's Death Penalty Study Commission also addressed victims' issues. It concluded that "[t]he alternative of life imprisonment in a maximum security institution without the possibility of parole would sufficiently ensure public safety and address other legitimate social and penological interests, including the interests of the families of murder victims" (New Jersey Death Penalty Study Commission, 2007, p. 56). The commission heard testimony from numerous individuals about what victims' families endure following the murder of a relative or spouse. It recommended that "[s]ufficient funds should be dedicated to ensure adequate services and advocacy for the families of murder victims" (New Jersey Death Penalty Study Commission, 2007, p. 62). It concluded "that any cost savings resulting from the abolition of the death penalty [should] be used for benefits and services for survivors of victims of homicide" (New Jersey Death Penalty Study Commission, 2007, p. 67).

Appeals, Post-Conviction Review, and Clemency

As noted previously, several study commissions recommended that their state supreme courts should engage in comparative proportionality review of capital sentences and that comprehensive data should be collected to enable them to carry out that function in the interest of guarding against arbitrariness and discrimination. Other reforms were recommended in efforts to eliminate unnecessary delays in appellate and post-conviction review of capital convictions and sentences. For example, the Arizona commission proposed rule changes designed to expedite appeals, recommended that judges be required to consider victims' interests as well as defendants' before ruling on requests for time extensions, and suggested that county-level files be maintained in capital cases to minimize delays in preparing petitions for post-conviction review (Office of the Attorney General, State of Arizona, 2002, pp. 19–20 and 22–23). Connecticut's commission proposed that technological innovations be introduced and that additional staff and attorneys be made available to prosecutors and public defenders to help prevent unnecessary delay in capital appeals and post-conviction proceedings (State of Connecticut Commission on the Death Penalty, 2003, pp. 47–53 and 66–68). Illinois' commission recommended that time limits be established in capital cases for requesting post-conviction relief and conducting evidentiary hearings (Governor's Commission on Capital Punishment, 2002, pp. 169–171).

The Virginia General Assembly's Joint Legislative Audit and Review Commission identified "the fairness of the judicial review process for persons who have been sentenced to die" as one of the principal issues to be studied (Joint Legislative Audit and Review Commission of the Virginia General Assembly, 2002, Preface). The ensuing report noted that Virginia death penalty cases had a low reversal rate (18 percent) compared to the national average (68 percent) identified by Liebman et al. (2000). The Virginia Supreme Court found reversible error in capital cases in 8 percent of direct appeals (9/132), and in just 2 percent of appeals in the state post-conviction review process (1/56). The federal courts had vacated an additional 4 percent of state capital convictions or sentences (4/111). Never had the Virginia Supreme Court invalidated a death sentence under its statutory mandate to engage in comparative proportionality review. The report noted that the Virginia Supreme Court invoked the doctrine of procedural default to decline to review 33 percent of the issues presented on post-conviction review in capital cases. Federal district courts did not reach the merits of 35 percent of issues presented, and the Fourth Circuit Court of Appeals refused to consider 20 percent of claims because of procedural defaults (Joint Legislative Audit and Review Commission of the Virginia General Assembly, 2002, pp. 53–78). Although presenting those findings, the report stopped short of making a specific recommendation.

> [T]he substance of these findings indicate [sic] that appellate review for death row inmates in Virginia has been expedited by the courts and that many claims raised by these inmates are not considered on their merits through application of the doctrine of procedural default. In addition, when Virginia's State courts procedurally bar certain claims from review, the federal courts are restricted from consideration of these assignments of error as well . . . . Whether Virginia's rules on procedural default should be loosened, at least in capital cases, is a decision for the General Assembly and the Virginia Supreme Court. They must strike the proper balance between the desire for finality and efficiency in capital cases and the ideal of fairness in the criminal process. (Joint Legislative Audit and Review Commission of the Virginia General Assembly, 2002, p. 78)

Nevada's commission was not so equivocal regarding the issue of procedural default and the courts' refusal to entertain claims not properly preserved for review. It recommended that the Nevada Supreme Court be urged to consider amending its rules to provide: "Due to the unique severity of capital sentences and the complexity of capital litigation, the Supreme Court of Nevada shall not apply procedural default rules to bar consideration of constitutional issues on direct appeal or in collateral proceedings" (Legislative Commission's Subcommittee to Study the Death Penalty and Related DNA Testing, 2003, p. 12).

The clemency process in capital cases received only modest attention by state study commissions. In Connecticut, where clemency authority resides in a Board of Pardons rather than the governor, the commission suggested no procedural changes. However, it recommended that the legislature act "to require an affirmative vote of a majority of the five members of the Board of Pardons in order to commute a death sentence to a sentence of life imprisonment without parole" (State of Connecticut Commission on the Death Penalty, 2003, p. 56). To allow ample time for and more orderly review of clemency petitions, the Illinois commission recommended that clemency petitions must be filed with the governor within 30 days of the exhaustion of appeals and the Illinois Supreme Court's scheduling the date of an execution (Governor's Commission on Capital Punishment, 2002, pp. 173–174).

The Virginia study observed that 38 percent of the clemency petitions filed in capital cases in Virginia since 1977 presented claims of innocence, and that governors had granted clemency in 17 percent (4/24) of those cases. It further pointed out that Virginia's "21-day rule"—which bars requests for a new trial based on newly discovered evidence made more than 21 days after a trial court's imposition of a death sentence (except when based on DNA evidence)—puts a premium on the clemency process as a mechanism for correcting wrongful convictions (Joint Legislative Audit and Review Commission of the Virginia General Assembly, 2002, pp. 78–83). Virginia's governor has the authority to request the parole board to conduct an investigation of issues raised in clemency petitions, but is not required to take such action. The largely confidential nature of the clemency process heightened concerns about the reliability and fairness of the executive's consideration of clemency petitions. The report concluded:

> These problems could be addressed through legislative changes that established a more structured process involving the Parole Board or some other State entity that would be charged with reviewing and investigating each clemency petition submitted by an inmate on death row. Following this effort, the relevant authority could be required to make a public report to the Governor outlining the issues that were considered in the review and provide a recommendation regarding clemency to the Governor. The final decision on the petition would remain with the Governor. This board might also be required to maintain a complete file of clemency petitions for reference purposes, as this function is not currently provided by any other state office or agency. (Joint Legislative Audit and Review Commission of the Virginia General Assembly, 2002, p. 83)

Executions

Perhaps surprisingly, in light of the considerable controversy surrounding medical ethics and implementation of execution by lethal injection, no state study commission considered methods or protocols for carrying out death sentences, or made recommendations regarding other execution procedures. However, former Governor Jeb Bush ordered a halt to executions and appointed an official commission in late 2006 to study lethal injection in Florida after questions arose about whether state executions using that method had gone awry. The commission's report was issued March 1, 2007 (Governor's Commission on Administration of Lethal Injection, 2007).

The only execution-related matters addressed by any of the study commissions involved the Arizona commission's recommendation involving death sentenced inmates who are adjudged incompetent for execution. Under current policies, incompetent prisoners were spared execution only as long as efforts to treat them failed to restore competency. Relying on a practice followed in Maryland, a majority of Arizona's commission endorsed permanently removing a prisoner from risk of execution following an initial determination of incompetency for execution (Office of the Attorney General, State of Arizona 2002, pp. 8 and 23–24).

Moratoria

Executions were suspended in Illinois, Maryland, and New Jersey pending completion of the commissioned studies. The Arizona and Pennsylvania commissions considered whether to recommend moratoria following issuance of their reports, a move designed to allow consideration of their findings and recommendations before additional executions were carried out. They arrived at different answers. Some members of the Arizona commission "argued that the likelihood of error in capital cases, together with uncertainty resulting from the *Ring [v. Arizona]* decision, warranted . . . a moratorium. . . . A majority of Commission members, including the Attorney General, disagreed and declined to recommend a moratorium" (Office of the Attorney General, State of Arizona, 2002, p. 27). The Pennsylvania commission came to the opposite conclusion. It urged the responsible authorities in each branch of government—the Pennsylvania Supreme Court, the legislature, and the governor—to order a moratorium on executions pending completion of comprehensive studies regarding the influence of race in capital cases, and until policies and procedures were implemented to ensure that the death penalty was being administered fairly and impartially (Pennsylvania Supreme Court Committee on Racial and Gender Bias in the Justice System, 2003, pp. 219–221).

Discussion and Conclusion

The recent proliferation of government-commissioned studies of state death penalties is noteworthy in its own right. This unprecedented showing of official interest in the workings of capital punishment lends itself to different interpretations. It could signify, on the one hand, mounting uneasiness about capital punishment's utility and operation or, alternatively, confidence that a public examination of the death penalty will reaffirm its value and essential fairness. The study commission reports might stimulate needed reforms in the death penalty process, or they could prove to be palliatives resulting at best only in cosmetic changes or, even worse, function as smokescreens that obscure and deflect attention from fundamental defects in capital punishment's administration. An analysis limited to the pages of the studies cannot address the reasons leading to their formation or the purposes they ultimately may serve. Such a review nevertheless can offer insights about capital punishment commissions' processes and work products, and indirectly about the death penalty itself.

For instance, it is apparent that the person responsible for examining a state's death penalty system can influence both the scope and content of the study. The reports of the study commissions in Indiana (the Indiana Criminal Law Study Commission) and Virginia (the staff of the Virginia General Assembly's Joint Legislative Audit and Review Commission), as well as the report of the Tennessee State Comptroller of the Treasury, are conspicuous for their comparatively inconclusive and/or vague findings, and their equivocal or noncommittal recommendations. Each report was authored by a committee or official occupying a permanent position within state government, an arrangement that provides little independence or insulation against official backlash compared to specially formed committees that are not made up exclusively of political insiders. However, the Nevada Legislative Commission Subcommittee, which shared similar characteristics, arrived at concrete findings and made several substantial recommendations.

The Maryland and Nebraska studies were unique in that they were not completed by political officials or special committees, but by academic researchers. Not surprisingly, each study was distinguished by an empirical focus on a circumscribed range of issues (race and arbitrariness). And, again not surprisingly, each report included detailed findings and analysis of factual data, devoid of policy recommendations.

Study commissions tended to be dominated by lawyers. Only Arizona's included an empirical researcher, which is startling in light of the largely empirical nature of the issues considered. Of course, study commissions can and frequently did enlist research staff to facilitate their work. The Connecticut commission, however, lamented that its appointed members served as volunteers, had barely more than a year to respond to fourteen complex issues, and that "[n]o funding was appropriated for purposes of conducting the study" (State of Connecticut Commission on the Death Penalty, 2003, pp. 1 and 4–5).

By design, some studies fell short of a comprehensive examination of the state's death penalty and its administration. Tennessee's study was confined to the costs of capital punishment, and the Virginia's committee's charge focused on prosecutorial discretion and the judicial review process. The Pennsylvania commission was formally charged to examine issues relating to racial and gender bias, although its recommendations encompassed other matters, including the quality and resources available to capital defense counsel. It justified this broader inquiry because its members perceived a connection between race and gender bias and other aspects of criminal justice administration.

Although it is noteworthy that studies were carried out in thirteen states, it also is significant that official studies were not commissioned elsewhere. The most conspicuous omission is Texas, which is far and away the leader in post-*Furman* executions (between 1977 and 2006, Texas carried out 379 executions, compared to second-place Virginia's 98). In fact, among the eleven leading execution states, only Virginia carried out a study of its death penalty. In addition to Texas, the other top executing states that did not study their death penalty systems included Oklahoma, Missouri, Florida, North Carolina, Georgia, South Carolina, Alabama, Louisiana, and Arkansas (Death Penalty Information Center, 2007). The American Bar Association's Death Penalty Moratorium Implementation Project has planned or has completed studies of the death penalty's operation in many of those and other jurisdictions, "to examine the extent to which ... [their] death penalty systems comport with minimum standards of fairness and due process" (American Bar Association, 2007).

Although the studies collectively addressed several issues important to the death penalty's administration, coverage was not exhaustive. There was a notable lack of interest in exploring the deterrent efficacy of capital punishment—only the Kansas and New Jersey commissions did so—and only in New Jersey were the death penalty's other penological justifications of retribution and incapacitation addressed. Other important death penalty issues received scant attention or were not addressed at all, including protocols for lethal injection and other methods of execution; administrative rules governing executions, involving matters such as publicity and the presence of witnesses and spiritual advisors; conditions of confinement on death row; the prevalence and causes of "volunteers," that is, death sentenced prisoners who give up available judicial review; and the death- and life-qualification of capital jurors, to mention several.

At the same time, some of the reports included eye-opening recommendations and perspectives. The Nevada commission's bold suggestion that the state supreme court should not invoke the doctrine of procedural default to bar consideration of claims in capital cases qualifies as one such recommendation. One member of New Jersey's commission, the representative of the New Jersey Office of the Public Defender, offered illuminating perspectives about why life imprisonment without parole should not be considered a "replacement" for the death penalty if capital punishment is abolished in that state pursuant to the commission's recommendation. The Illinois commission, whose work is distinguished by its thoroughness and thoughtfulness, coupled an unorthodox suggestion with cogent observations about other cases processed within the criminal justice system.

> The Commission strongly urges consideration of ways to broaden the application of many of the recommendations made by the Commission to improve the criminal justice system as a whole.... The Commission's mandate was to review the capital punishment system in Illinois and report to the Governor on ways in which the system can be made more just, fair and accurate.... It became readily apparent during many of the discussions on particular points, however, that recommendations that were being made with respect to the capital punishment system could apply with equal force to other cases in the criminal justice system.... (Governor's Commission on Capital Punishment, 2002, pp. 187–188)

By devoting particular attention to capital punishment within studies that address the administration of criminal justice generally, the California and Pennsylvania commissions were similarly attuned to the stark reality that if problems are discernible in capital cases, which represent a minute sample of criminal prosecutions, they must certainly inhere in other, less highly visible cases. The stakes may not be as high, but other criminal cases are far more numerous and also involve vitally important interests. Even though most state studies, their findings, and their recommendations were limited to the death penalty context, the reports and what they reveal are reminders that procedural reforms are also needed to prevent and correct grave injustices that can and do occur in cases throughout the criminal justice system.

Notes

1. New York frequently is counted as a 38th state with the death penalty. However, the New York Court of Appeals ruled that state's death penalty law unconstitutional in *People v. LaValle* (2004), and New York does not presently have a valid capital-punishment statute.

2. This paper does not review the commission formed in Massachusetts to study death penalty issues (Massachusetts Governor's Council on Capital Punishment 2004) because Massachusetts does not authorize capital punishment. Nor does it include a New York Assembly report that was based on public hearings but did not involve a study commission (New York State Assembly 2005). Because consideration is limited to state study commissions, the paper does not review findings regarding the federal death penalty's administration (United States Department of Justice 2000). Reports issued later than May 2007 also are not captured.

References

Acker, James R. (1996). The Death Penalty: A 25-Year Retrospective and a Perspective on the Future. *Criminal Justice Review* 21:139–160.

American Bar Association. (2007). *American Bar Association Death Penalty Moratorium Implementation Project.* Available at http://www.abanet.org/moratorium/assessment project/home.html. Website consulted March 3, 2007.

American Bar Association. (2003). *Guidelines for the Appointment and Performance of Defense Counsel in Death Penalty Cases.* Chicago: American Bar Association. Available at http://www.abanet.org/legalservices/downloads/sclaid/indigentdefense/deathpenaltyguidelines2003.pdf. Website consulted March 3, 2007.

American Bar Association. (1997). Recommendation and Report. Reprinted in (1998) Appendix. *Law and Contemporary Problems* 61 (no. 4):219–231.

Arnold, Justin R. (2005). Race and the Death Penalty After *McCleskey*: A Case Study of Kentucky's Racial Justice Act. *Washington and Lee Journal of Civil Rights and Social Justice* 12:93–107.

Baldus, David C., George Woodworth, Gary L. Young, & Aaron M. Christ. (2001, amended 2002). *Final Report—The Disposition of Nebraska Capital and Non-Capital Homicide Cases (1973–1999): A Legal and Empirical Analysis.* Lincoln, NE: Nebraska Commission on Law Enforcement and Criminal Justice. Available at http://www.nec.state.ne.us/documents/other/homicide.htm. Website consulted Feb. 19, 2007.

Baldus, David C., George Woodworth, & Charles A. Pulaski, Jr. (1994). Reflections on the 'Inevitability' of Racial Discrimination in Capital Sentencing and the 'Impossibility' of its Prevention, Detection, and Correction. *Washington and Lee Law Review* 51:359–419.

Banner, Stuart. (2002). *The Death Penalty: An American History.* Cambridge, MA: Harvard University Press.

Bedau, Hugo Adam, Ed. (1997). *The Death Penalty in America: Current Controversies.* New York: Oxford University Press.

Bohm, Robert M. (2003). American Death Penalty Opinion: Past, Present, and Future, in *America's Experiment with Capital Punishment: Reflections on the Past, Present, and Future of the Ultimate Penal Sanction* 27–54, in James R. Acker, Robert M. Bohm, & Charles S. Lanier, Eds. Durham, NC: Carolina Academic Press.

Bowers, William J., Margaret Vandiver, & Patricia H. Dugan. (1994). A New Look at Public Opinion on Capital Punishment: What Citizens and Legislators Prefer. *American Journal of Criminal Law* 22:77–149.
California Commission on the Fair Administration of Justice. (2007a). Charge. Available at http://www.ccfaj.org/charge.html. Website consulted Feb. 15, 2007.
California Commission on the Fair Administration of Justice. (2007b). Report and Recommendations Regarding Forensic Science Evidence. Available at http://www.ccfaj.org/rr-problems-official.html. Website consulted May 30, 2007.
California Commission on the Fair Administration of Justice. (2007c). Emergency Report and Recommendations Regarding DNA Testing Backlogs. Available at http://www.ccfaj.org/rr-problems-official.html. Website consulted May 30, 2007.
Comptroller of the Treasury, State of Tennessee. (2004). *Tennessee's Death Penalty: Costs and Consequences*. Nashville: State of Tennessee Comptroller of the Treasury. Available at http://www.comptroller.state.tn.us/orea/reports/deathpenalty.pdf. Website consulted Feb. 21, 2007.
Death Penalty Information Center. (2007). Number of Executions by State and Region Since 1976. Available at http://www.deathpenaltyinfo.org/article.php?scid=8&did=186. Website consulted March 3, 2007.
Death Penalty Information Center. (2006). *The Death Penalty in 2006: Year End Report*. Washington, DC: Death Penalty Information Center.
Governor's Commission on Administration of Lethal Injection. (2007). *Final Report with Findings and Recommendations: Presented to the Honorable Charlie Crist, Governor of Florida*. Available at http://www.law.berkeley.edu/clinics/dpclinic/Lethal%20Injection%20Documents/Florida/lethalinjectionfinalreport.pdf. Website consulted May 30, 2007.
Governor's Commission on Capital Punishment. (2002). *Report of the Governor's Commission on Capital Punishment*. Springfield: State of Illinois. Available at http://www.idoc.state.il.us/ccp/ccp/reports/index.html. Website consulted Feb. 16, 2007.
Haines, Herbert H. (1996). *Against Capital Punishment: The Anti-Death Penalty Movement in America, 1972–1994*. New York: Oxford University Press.
Janeway, Kathryn (Reporter). (2002). *The Application of Indiana's Capital Sentencing Law: Findings of the Indiana Study Criminal Law Study Commission*. Indianapolis: Indiana Criminal Justice Institute. Available at http://www.in.gov/cji/special-initiatives/clsc.html. Website consulted Feb. 17, 2007.
Joint Legislative Audit and Review Commission of the Virginia General Assembly. (2002). *Review of Virginia's System of Capital Punishment*. Richmond, VA: Commonwealth of Virginia. Available at http://jlarc.state.va.us/reports/rpt274.pdf. Website consulted Feb. 22, 2007.
Kansas Judicial Council Death Penalty Advisory Committee. (2004a). *Report of the Kansas Judicial Council Death Penalty Advisory Committee on Certain Issues Related to the Death Penalty*. Topeka, KA: State of Kansas. Available at http://www.kscourts.org/council/death_penalty_rpt11-12-04.pdf. Website consulted Feb. 19, 2007.
Kansas Judicial Council Death Penalty Advisory Committee. (2004b). *Report of the Kansas Judicial Council Death Penalty Advisory Committee*. Topeka, KA: State of Kansas. Available at http://www.kscourts.org/council/report_death.pdf. Website consulted Feb. 19, 2007.

Kirchmeier, Jeffrey L. (2002). Another Place Beyond Here: The Death Penalty Moratorium Movement in the United States. *University of Colorado Law Review* 73:1–116.

Lanier, Charles S. & James R. Acker. (2004). Capital Punishment, the Moratorium Movement, and Empirical Questions: Looking Beyond Innocence, Race, and Bad Lawyering in Death Penalty Cases. *Psychology, Public Policy, and Law* 10:577–617.

Legislative Commission's Subcommittee to Study the Death Penalty and Related DNA Testing. (2003). *Death Penalty and Related DNA Testing.* Carson City, NV: Nevada Legislature. Available at http://www.leg.state.nv.us/lcb/research/03InterimReports/Bulletin03-05.pdf. Website consulted Feb. 20, 2007.

Liebman, James S., Jeffrey Fagan, & Valerie West. (2000). *A Broken System: Error Rates in Capital Cases, 1973–1995.* Available at http://www2.law.columbia.edu/instructionalservices/liebman/. Website consulted March 3, 2007.

Massachusetts Governor's Council on Capital Punishment. (2004). *Report of the Governor's Council on Capital Punishment.* Available at http://www.law.lib.state.ma.us/docs/5-3-04Governorsreportcapitalpunishment.pdf. Website consulted February 28, 2007.

New Jersey Death Penalty Study Commission. (2007). *New Jersey Death Penalty Study Commission Report.* Trenton, NJ: State of New Jersey. Available at http://www.njleg.state.nj.us/committees/dpsc_final.pdf. Website consulted Feb. 20, 2007.

New York State Assembly. (2005). *The Death Penalty in New York.* Available at http://assembly.state.ny.us/comm./Codes20050403.pdf. Website consulted February 28, 2007.

Office of the Attorney General, State of Arizona. (2002). *Capital Case Commission Final Report.* Phoenix: State of Arizona. Available at http://www.azag.gov/CCC/FinalReport.html. Website consulted Feb. 14, 2007.

Paternoster, Raymond, Robert Brame, Sarah Bacon, Andrew Ditchfield, David Biere, Karen Beckman, Deanna Perez, Michael Strauch, Nadine Frederique, Kristin Gawkoski, Daniel Zeigler, & Katheryn Murphy. (2003). *An Empirical Analysis of Maryland's Death Sentencing System with Respect to the Influence of Race and Legal Jurisdiction: Final Report.* College Park, MD: University of Maryland.

Pennsylvania Supreme Court Committee on Racial and Gender Bias in the Justice System. (2003). *Final Report of the Pennsylvania Supreme Court Committee on Racial and Gender Bias in the Justice System.* Harrisburg, PA: Pennsylvania Supreme Court. Available at http://www.courts.state.pa.us/Index/supreme/BiasCmte/FinalReport.pdf. Website consulted February 21, 2007.

Proctor, Greta. (2006–2007). Reevaluating Capital Punishment: The Fallacy of a Foolproof System, the Focus on Reform, and the International Factor. *Gonzaga Law Review* 42:211–255.

Schoeman, Paul. (1995). Easing the Fear of Too Much Justice: A Compromise Proposal to Revise the Racial Justice Act. *Harvard Civil Rights-Civil Liberties Law Review* 30:543–576.

Snell, Tracy. (2006). *Capital Punishment, 2005.* Washington DC: United States Dept. of Justice, Bureau of Justice Statistics.

State of Connecticut Commission on the Death Penalty. (2003). *Study Pursuant to Public Act No. 01-151 of the Imposition of the Death Penalty in Connecticut.* Hartford: State of Connecticut. Available at http://www.opm.state.ct.us/pdpd1/CDP/CDP-FinalReport.htm. Website consulted Feb. 16, 2007.

Steiker, Carol S. & Jordan M. Steiker. (2006). A Tale of Two Nations: Implementation of the Death Penalty in 'Executing' versus 'Symbolic' States in the United States. *Texas Law Review* 84:1869–1927.

Steiker, Carol & Jordan Steiker. (1995). Sober Second Thoughts: Reflections on Two Decades of Constitutional Regulation of Capital Punishment. *Harvard Law Review* 109:355–438.

Sundby, Scott E. (2006). The Death Penalty's Future: Charting the Crosscurrents of Declining Death Sentences and the McVeigh Factor, *Texas Law Review* 84:1929–1972.

United States Department of Justice. (2000). *The Federal Death Penalty System: A Statistical Survey (1988–2000).* Washington DC: United States Department of Justice. Available at http://www.usdoj.gov/dag/pubdoc/dpsurvey.html. Website consulted February 28, 2007.

Warden, Rob. (2005). Illinois Death Penalty Reform: How It Happened, What It Promises. *Journal of Criminal Law and Criminology* 95:381–426.

Zimring, Franklin E. (2003). *The Contradictions of American Capital Punishment.* New York: Oxford University Press.

Cases Cited

Atkins v. Virginia (2002) 536 U.S. 304.

Furman v. Georgia (1972) 408 U.S. 238.

Gregg v. Georgia (1976) 428 U.S. 153.

McCleskey v. Kemp (1987) 481 U.S. 279.

Oregon v. Guzek (2006) 546 U.S. 517.

People v. LaValle (2004) 817 N.E.2d 341 (N.Y.).

Ring v. Arizona (2002) 536 U.S. 584.

Roper v. Simmons (2005) 543 U.S. 551.

Themes of Wrongful Executions in the Post-*Furman* Era*

3

TALIA ROITBERG HARMON

Contents

Introduction

Recent public opinion polls suggest that although a majority of Americans favor the death penalty, support has significantly declined since 1994 (Saad, 2005). The issue of potential executions of the innocent may be partly responsible for this result. A study conducted by Unnever and Cullen (2005) found that support for capital punishment was significantly lower among respondents who believed that an innocent person had been executed in the past five years. Recent developments throughout the country and media attention devoted to the issue may have played a significant role in the change in public opinion. In fact, it was concern about wrongful convictions that figured most prominently in Illinois Governor George Ryan's decision to declare a moratorium on executions in 2000 and, more dramatically, in his decision to empty Illinois' death row through a blanket commutation in January 2003 (Wilgoren, 2003). Additionally, numerous states have formed commissions to study innocence cases, including Pennsylvania, California, North Carolina, and New Jersey (Raffaele, 2006; Robertson, 2006; Weinstein, 2006a,b). In early January 2007, the New Jersey commission recommended abolition of the state's death penalty and replacement with the alternative sentence of life without parole. Among the reasons cited for this decision was the "risk of executing the innocent" (DeFalco, 2007; Santi, 2006). Finally, Judge Carolyn Dineen King of the U.S. Court of Appeals for the Fifth Circuit publicly expressed serious concerns about the risk of executing the innocent. She stated that "profoundly troubling is the risk that an innocent man will be executed." Her assessment of the death penalty is that it "remains a human endeavor with a consequent risk of error that may not be remediable" (King, 2006).

Much of the recent research on wrongful capital convictions has focused on exonerations (Radelet et al., 1992, 1996; Liebman, 2000, 2002). One notable exception was the groundbreaking study conducted by Bedau and Radelet in 1987. In their study spanning 1900–1985, they identified more than 350 potentially wrongful capital convictions, including 23 wrongful executions. Bedau and Radelet introduced a neutral observer standard to determine whether a conviction was wrongful. More specifically, they identified cases where "a majority of neutral observers, given the evidence at our disposal, would judge the defendant in question to be innocent" (Bedau & Radelet, 1987, p.47). Criticism of the standard used to define innocence in the Bedau and Radelet study and dispute surrounding the specific claims of the 23 wrongful executions followed (see Markman & Cassell, 1988). As a result, much of the research since 1987 has focused on the exonerated innocent. It is important to continue studying the exoneration of death row inmates, however, it is equally important to undertake the difficult and controversial task of identifying and analyzing potentially wrongful executions. Although this population is much harder to identify because of a lack of formal legal recognition that an error occurred, it is problematic to rely exclusively on the courts to validate claims of innocence by recognizing their own errors (Harmon & Lofquist, 2005). Moreover, the results of an analysis of potential wrongful executions may have even more dramatic and serious implications for the continued use of capital punishment in this country.

This study is a continuation of the analyses conducted by Harmon and Lofquist (2005) and Lofquist and Harmon (2008). Harmon and Lofquist (2005) conducted a quantitative analysis that compared two groups of factually innocent capital defendants in the post-*Furman* era: those who were executed and those who were exonerated. Through the use of a logistic regression model, they found the following variables were significant predictors of case outcomes: allegations of perjury, multiple types of evidence, prior record, type of attorney at trial, and race of the defendant. This study utilized 16 wrongful executions in the statistical analysis, but did not undertake a careful qualitative examination of the themes associated with these cases or a comparison of the wrongful executions to the population of executions more generally.

In their 2008 study, Lofquist and Harmon identified 16 wrongful executions in the post-*Furman* era and provided brief vignettes describing each case. This study expands on that analysis by identifying themes associated with 18 potentially factually innocent capital defendants who were executed in the post-*Furman* era.[1] More specifically, this study identifies the following: the evidence that suggests the defendants were factually innocent, the main causes of the wrongful convictions, and the factors that led to the executions despite significant doubt related to the guilt of the defendants. This study also provides a summary of the geography, the timeframe, and the race of the executed innocents and their victims. Finally, this study compares these results to the population of executions more generally to identify any significant differences between the two populations. The implications of the results are discussed.

Methodology

The methodology used in this study was the same as the approach taken by Harmon and Lofquist (2005) and Lofquist and Harmon (2008). Potential wrongful executions were identified on the basis of compelling evidence that the executed individuals were factually uninvolved in any element of the murder for which they were convicted and executed. Examining more than 1000 post-*Furman* executions to identify those with compelling claims of factual innocence is an unavoidably cumbersome process. In the absence of pre-existing legal authority to help narrow the scope of the inquiry, there is little choice but to examine the entire population of executions and the claims of innocence associated with many of those cases, and attempt to evaluate them to identify meritorious claims. This was the approach taken by Bedau and Radelet in their original research (Bedau & Radelet, 1987).

Bedau and Radelet began with extensive searches of newspapers, scholarly materials, and government publications, looking for innocence claims. Next, they added claims brought to their attention as a result of announcements they placed in the association newsletters of criminologists, capital defense attorneys, and abolitionists. After gathering this initial group of cases, they collected appellate opinions, newspaper sources, archived information, and information provided, where possible, by parties to each case. They then evaluated this information and made their determinations of innocence. Although this approach is certainly imprecise and open to criticism, no clear alternative, short of rejecting all but legally sanctioned claims of innocence, is available.

Following Bedau and Radelet's approach, the present research proceeded along similar multiple paths. The starting point was an exhaustive review of the existing literatures (scholarly, popular, activist, and electronic) on post-*Furman* claims of executions of the innocent. This effort produced approximately 60 cases involving independent claims (made by someone other than the defendant) of factual innocence. At the same time, contact was made with death penalty scholars, activists, and defense attorneys in every state with a post-*Furman* execution and they were asked to identify cases with which they were familiar that involved a credible innocence claim. This produced a list of 45 cases. Closely examining each of these cases—particularly through newspaper accounts, appellate opinions, and published sources—allowed elimination of some cases that did not meet the narrow standards used to define innocence in this research, usually as a result of the determination that the executed individual was an accomplice to the capital murder.

This process resulted in 29 cases. Questionnaires were sent to those individuals (usually defense attorneys, but also scholars and activists) most closely involved with each case. These questionnaires queried the views of the respondent about the innocence claim made regarding the case, as well as factors that contributed to the original wrongful conviction and to the failure to detect this error prior to execution. The results of this effort, as well as additional scrutiny of each case and examination of available clemency petitions, were 18 cases presenting compelling claims of factual innocence.

Although these are the cases that met the standards for compelling claims of factual innocence that we established, it is unlikely that each person identified herein was in fact factually innocent of the crime for which he was executed. These are complex cases, frequently involving individuals whose prior criminal records or troubled personal lives brought them to the attention of the police, and whose trial and post-conviction counsel were inadequate to counter the state's claims and unable to make effective use of a complicated legal process. At the same time, it is at least as unlikely that all of the more than 1000 individuals executed since 1977 were factually involved in the crimes for which they were executed.

Qualitative Results

Evidence That Casts Doubt about the Defendant's Guilt

Two common types of new evidence that cast doubt about the defendant's guilt included evidence that pointed to another suspect and evidence that supported an alibi.

Strong Evidence Pointing to Another Suspect

In several of the cases, new evidence discovered after the conviction indicated that another suspect might have committed the murder. The Wilburn Henderson case (Arkansas, 1998) illustrates this common theme. Prior to Henderson's execution, exculpatory evidence surfaced over the years that pointed to other suspects in the robbery–murder. The main suspect was Bob O'Neal, the victim's husband. In 1991, a federal appeals court reversed Henderson's conviction because of significant doubt about Henderson's guilt. The court ruled that his trial counsel failed to follow up on leads that pointed to other suspects, particularly Bob O'Neal. The court stated that "at least three other persons, particularly Bob O'Neal, had motive, opportunity, and ability to kill Willa Dean O'Neal" and that the "evidence against Bob O'Neal was substantial" (*Henderson v. Sargent*, 1991, pp.710–711). While Henderson was on death row, O'Neal wrote a letter to the state asserting that Henderson was wrongfully convicted (Mills et al., 2000).

Another case that provides an example of this theme is Leo Jones (Florida, 1998). One of the main pieces of evidence against Jones was a rifle that was found in his apartment; it was the same type as the murder weapon. Jones claimed that the rifle belonged to his friend, Glen Schofield (*Jones v. Florida*, 1996). Schofield, a drug dealer with a prior record of violence and on parole for manslaughter, was initially a suspect in the murder (Rauch, 1998). After Jones' conviction, ten inmates came forward and said that Schofield had boasted to them about the murder. Six additional new witnesses came forward claiming they saw Schofield running from the crime scene with a rifle. They stated that they did not come forward sooner because they were afraid of Schofield. Schofield offered the police several alibis prior to Jones' execution. The defense investigated these alibis, one of which led to Schofield's former girlfriend. Schofield stated that he was with her on the night of the murder. However, she claimed that she was not with him that evening and that he told her to confirm the alibi and tell the authorities he was with her (Rauch, 1998). Another alibi that Schofield presented was that he was with a male and a female friend. The male friend was tracked down, and he claimed that he was with Schofield on the night of the murder and that he actually saw Schofield shoot the victim (*Jones v. Florida*, 1988). Schofield is currently serving 30 years in prison for murder, prison escape, and possession of a firearm (Silva, 1998, p. 16).

Strong Alibi

Another theme that emerged after examination of the cases was the post-conviction discovery of evidence that supported an alibi. For example, in the case of Timothy Baldwin (Louisiana, 1984), after the defendant's trial, a receipt was discovered from a motel 70 miles from the crime scene. This evidence showed that the defendant checked into the motel before midnight. The murder occurred at 11 pm (Rose, 1996). Howard Marsellus, chair of the Louisiana Pardon Board at the time of Baldwin's execution, claimed that his efforts to investigate this alibi prior to Baldwin's execution were met with threats: "I decided I had to repeat that drive to see if whether it was possible, . . . [a]nd then I got an anonymous phone call. It was put to me that the road went through wild bayou country and that if I should happen to disappear, nobody would know" (Rose, 1996, p. 8). Marsellus decided not to make the trip.

The case of Willie Darden (Florida, 1988) also illustrates this theme. Two new witnesses came forward after the defendant's conviction and sentence and confirmed the defendant's innocence claim (Ingle, 1990). Christine Bass, who lived at the location of Darden's car problems, stated that he was in front of her house at the time of the murder; she was not called to testify at trial. This account was corroborated in part by Reverend Sam Sparks, who claimed that he went to the victim's widow to console her following the murder. This information assists in establishing the time of the murder and, in combination with Bass's account, suggests that Darden was innocent (Ingle, 1990, p. 262).

Causes of the Wrongful Convictions

Prior research indicates that the following factors are the main causes of erroneous convictions: witness perjury, police misconduct, state suppression of evidence, ineffective counsel, and mistaken eyewitness identification (Harmon, 2001; Bedau & Radelet, 1987; Huff et al., 1996).

Witness Perjury

One of the leading causes of errors in capital cases is witness perjury (Bedau & Radelet, 1987; Gross, 1996). It is common for co-defendants to lie in order to avoid the death penalty. Other witnesses may commit perjury in exchange for favors, immunity, or other deals.

The case of Walter Blair (Missouri, 1993) illustrates this theme. The state's main witnesses against Blair at trial were Ernest Jones and Blair's girlfriend Sharon Jones (no relation) (see *Blair v. Armontrout*, 1990). They testified that

Blair had discussed details of the contract killing before and after the commission of the murder. Evidence later surfaced that Ernest Jones was granted immunity for any part he may have played in the murder in exchange for his testimony against Blair. He also received probation on pending charges of assault, burglary, and possession of a controlled substance (*Blair v. Armontrout*, 1990). After Blair's conviction and death sentence, seven new witnesses came forward indicating that Ernest Jones confessed to killing the victim and framing Blair. Tina Jackson, Ernest Jones' girlfriend, also testified for the state at trial and implicated the defendant in the murder. However, she later recanted her testimony and claimed that Ernest Jones had coerced her and her sister, Sharon Jones, into committing perjury and testifying falsely against Blair (Blair, 1993).

The Bernard Bolender case (Florida, 1995) also exemplifies this problem. One of the co-defendants in the case, Joseph Macker, pled guilty to second-degree murder in exchange for a life sentence and became the state's main witness against Bolender (*Bolender v. Singletary*, 1995). Macker claimed that the defendant tortured the victims and killed one of them. During post-conviction proceedings, Bolender alleged that the state withheld several items of evidence that raise doubt regarding Macker's credibility: most important, Macker had confessed to the killings, and evidence in police files indicated Macker was an "alleged liar, briber, violent extortionist, and corrupter of public officials" (*Bolender v. Singletary*, 1995, p. 879). Other new evidence included six witnesses who stated that Macker confessed to the murders and disclosed that he framed Bolender. Bolender's attorney, Mark Olive, stated, "Bolender was innocent based on statements from former cellmates who say co-defendant Joseph Macker, now free, admitted [to] framing Bolender" (*Orlando Sun Sentinel*, 1995, p. 8A).

Another case that illustrates this theme is that of Billy Conn Gardner (Texas, 1995). Gardner was executed for a robbery–murder in a high school cafeteria. The main witness against Gardner at trial was Melvin Sanders, who stated that he approached Gardner with the idea of robbing the cafeteria and they agreed that Gardner would commit the robbery and Sanders would be the getaway car driver. Although Melvin Sanders was "an accomplice as a matter of law," he was given a deal to testify against the defendant (*Gardner v. Texas*, 1987, p. 678). He received immunity in the capital murder case, probation on the robbery charge, and dismissal of [a] firearms charge (Wiseman, 1996).

The Griffin case (Missouri, 1995) also illustrates the pervasive problem of perjury. The evidence introduced against Griffin at trial consisted primarily of Robert Fitzgerald's testimony (*Missouri v. Griffin*, 1983). Fitzgerald was a federally protected witness with a lengthy criminal record; he was given a deal in exchange for his testimony (Griffin, 1995). Pending felony credit card fraud charges were dismissed after he testified against Griffin. While in prison, Fitzgerald recanted his testimony and admitted that he committed perjury at the defendant's trial (Griffin, 1995).

Police Misconduct/False Confessions

Police misconduct, specifically, coerced confessions are a common cause of error in capital cases (Drizin & Leo, 2004; Gross, 1998). As noted above with regard to perjury, Walter Blair alleged that several incriminating statements Blair made to the police were coerced. He alleged that an officer put a gun to his head until he confessed, and he was threatened that his girlfriend would be charged with murder if he did not confess to the murder (*Blair v. Armontrout*, 1990).

Other types of police misconduct included fabrication and destruction of evidence. The Farris case (Texas, 1999) illustrates this type of misconduct. Farris argued that county law enforcement officers interfered with preserving the crime scene. Marijuana that was found in the possession of a deputy—perhaps unlawfully—was either concealed or destroyed. A captain initially claimed in a sworn affidavit that he "flushed" the marijuana; he subsequently changed his story and claimed that the marijuana resurfaced. The captain was indicted for perjury and fabrication of false evidence in the Farris case. After the defendant's conviction, the charges against him were dismissed and the record of the incident destroyed (Sanders, 1999). More than 60 crime scene photographs and plaster casts of tire tracks, evidence that "could have provided direct proof of who was at the scene," disappeared prior to trial and were never seen by the defense (Bonner and Rimer, 2000, p. 30).

State Suppression of Evidence

In many cases of wrongful conviction, the state suppresses evidence that may cast doubt about the defendant's guilt. The suppressed evidence may weaken the credibility of state witnesses or point to another suspect who may have committed the murder. The case of Bennie Demps (Florida, 2000) demonstrates this type of misconduct. New evidence discovered more than 20 years after the murder suggests Demps may have been innocent. More specifically, a report that was suppressed by the state revealed that the victim implicated another inmate, not Demps, as his assailant (Pellemans, 2000). This report was written by a chief prison inspector and investigator to the director of the Florida Department of Corrections (Sewell, 1976). Additional documents suppressed by the state included a letter written by a prison official who supervised the murder investigation. This letter condemned the state's main witness for lying in another investigation, and Demps' attorneys could have used it to challenge the witness's credibility at trial (Mills et al., 2000).

Another striking example of suppressed evidence occurred in the case of David Wayne Spence (Texas, 1997). Police reports suppressed by the state included incriminating evidence that implicated an early suspect in the investigation, Terry Harper, a convicted felon with a lengthy prior violent record (*Spence v. Scott,* 1996). Other police reports indicated that approximately 20 witnesses saw the victims on the night of the murders. None of these witnesses identified Spence or anyone resembling him. However, several of the witnesses saw Harper with the victims (State of Denial, 2002). Other police reports revealed that one of the victims may have been a drug dealer and was a known associate of Harper (*Spence v. Scott*, 1996).

Ineffective Attorneys

The problem of ineffective counsel in capital cases has been well documented (Bright, 1992, 1994; Huff et al., 1996). Many of the defendants in these cases were represented by inexperienced counsel who did not conduct even minimal investigations prior to trial. For example, Timothy Baldwin, whose case was discussed previously as an example of a strong alibi, had a court-appointed trial attorney who Baldwin argued was ineffective (*Baldwin v. Blackburn,* 1981). His lawyer had "never handled a capital case" (Ingle, 1990, p. 212). Moreover, there were 20 character witnesses "from a sheriff to a Catholic priest" who were never called to testify on the defendant's behalf at trial (Ingle, 1990, p. 222).

In the Darden case mentioned above as an example of a strong alibi, Darden's trial attorneys had no experience handling a capital case. Mid-trial, a one-day postponement was granted after a senior partner in the defense went out and got drunk with prosecution witnesses (*US News and World Report*, 1988). Indicative of these problems, Justice Blackmun wrote a dissenting opinion in a Supreme Court decision denying Darden federal habeas corpus. He raised serious concerns over the fairness and reliability of Darden's trial (*Darden v. Wainwright*, 1986).

Finally, the case of Gary Graham (Texas, 2000) provides a good example of this theme. Graham's trial attorney called no witnesses at the guilt phase of the trial, instead he simply pointed to the two witnesses who failed to identify Graham as the killer (*Graham v. Johnson*, 1999). In his closing argument, he suggested that the state's key witness deserved a standing ovation for her bravery in testifying against Graham (Rimer and Bonner, 2000). Over the years, the lawyer was reprimanded several times by the Texas Bar Association for professional misconduct. He was also jailed during jury selection in another capital murder trial for failing to file court papers on time. Many clients have filed complaints against him; one claimed that he smelled of alcohol during meetings. At one time, he owned eleven bars (Rimer and Bonner, 2000).

Eyewitness Misidentification

The problem of mistaken eyewitness identification is pervasive in wrongful convictions (Borchard, 1932; Huff et al., 1996; Gross, 1998). The case of

Ruben Cantu (Texas, 1993) exemplifies this type of problem. Juan Moreno was the main witness against the defendant and testified that Cantu shot and killed Pedro Gomez and shot and injured him. The central issue in the case involved the eyewitness identification by Moreno. The police showed Moreno photographs of suspects on four separate occasions. The defendant was included in three of the four photo arrays. Moreno did not identify the defendant until the last or fourth photo array. He claimed that he was too afraid to identify the defendant sooner (*Cantu v. Texas*, 1987). In 1987, the Texas Court of Criminal Appeals ruled that the police used a suggestive identification procedure. More specifically, they claimed that "the procedure of showing Juan [Moreno] several arrays on different occasions all containing appellant's photograph is a suggestive procedure. Such procedure tends to highlight a particular defendant since the witness sees the same face repeatedly. Such reoccurrence of one particular face might suggest to the witness that the police think the defendant is the culprit" (*Cantu v. Texas*, 1987, p. 252). However, the court ruled that the suggestive procedure did not "give rise to a substantial likelihood of irreparable misidentification" and therefore ruled against the defendant (p. 252.) In 2006, three witnesses came forward claiming that Cantu was innocent, including Moreno (Editorial, 2006).

The Darden case, which was mentioned as an example of both a strong alibi and ineffective counsel, also illustrates this theme. The main witnesses at Darden's trial were the victim's wife, Helen Turman, and Philip Arnold, a sixteen-year old who was injured during the robbery. Both of these witnesses identified Darden as the assailant (*Darden v. Wainwright*, 1986). Significant problems were associated with each of these identifications. Immediately after the murder, Helen Turman told the police that she could not identify the suspect. However, at the preliminary hearing, she identified the defendant. Interestingly, he was the only black male in the courtroom at the time. While in the hospital, Arnold was given a photo array with six suspects. Although Arnold picked the defendant's picture, it was one of two that had the notation "Sheriff's Department, Bartow, Florida," on the bottom of it (*Darden v. Wainwright*, 1986, p. 199). This was a suggestive procedure because the witness knew that the defendant had been in police custody and therefore had a prior record.

Another noteworthy case that involved eyewitness identification is the case of Roy Roberts (Missouri, 1999). The state's theory was that Roberts held the victim down while two other inmates fatally stabbed him (*Roberts v. Bowersox*, 1998). The state's case against Roberts was based upon four eyewitness identifications (*Missouri v. Roberts*, 1986). These included three corrections officers and an inmate (*Roberts v. Missouri*, 1989). Evidence was subsequently discovered that raises doubt about the accuracy of the eyewitness testimony of the four state witnesses. Roberts weighed more than 300 pounds at the time of the murder, but the initial report by the Department of Corrections regarding the killing did not refer to him and implicated two other inmates in the murder (*Roberts v. Bowersox*, 1999). Given Roberts' weight, it is strange that he was not identified initially (*In re Roberts*, 1999).

Factors That Led to the Executions Despite Doubts about the Defendant's Guilt

Two factors that led to the executions despite doubts about the defendant's guilt are procedural bars to courts or new evidence not entertained by the courts and political pressure to execute.

Procedural Bars to Courts/New Evidence Not Entertained by the Courts

In several cases, defendants were procedurally barred from presenting their appeal and were effectively denied access to the courts. As a result, no appellate court ever heard the merits of their cases. For instance, Bolender alleged that the state withheld several items of evidence that challenged the credibility of the state's main witness. All of these claims were procedurally barred under the abuse of writ doctrine, preventing the appellate courts from considering their merits (*Bolender v. Singletary*, 1995).

Another example involved the Farris case (Texas, 1999). In 1990, the Texas Court of Criminal Appeals upheld Farris's conviction and death sentence, despite noting that "the circumstantial and forensic evidence offered at trial not only failed to connect Farris with the killing of Rosenbalm, but also failed in nearly all material respects to confirm the testimony" of Vance Nation and Jimmy Daniels, the state's two main witnesses (*Farris v. Texas*, 1990, p. 495). The court affirmed the conviction based upon Farris's alleged confession to Daniels. In 1994, the Texas Court of Criminal Appeals overruled their prior decision and held that "Farris was wrongly decided and is expressly overruled" based upon a jury issue (*Riley v. State*, 1994, pp. 297–298). However, a procedural bar denied Farris access to the appellate courts; the state or federal courts did not consider the merits of his appeal even though his case was overruled (*In re Farris*, 1999). His attorney expressed the peculiarity of Farris's legal situation in stating: "Incredible as it may seem, this man may be executed even though he has a court decision in his hand saying his sentence should be overturned" (Ward, 1999, p. B2).

Political Pressure to Execute

In many of the cases, there was significant political pressure, particularly on governors, not to grant clemency, despite doubts about the defendant's guilt. For example, in the Timothy Baldwin case discussed earlier, Howard Marsellus, the Louisiana Pardon Board Chair, stated that he had serious

Table 3.1 Summary of Qualitative Results[a]

Name of Variable	Frequency	Valid Percentage
Evidence of innocence		
Strong alibi	5	28
Evidence pointing to another suspect	8	44
Causes of wrongful convictions		
Witnesses perjury	9	50
Police misconduct	4	22
Coerced confessions	3	17
Suppression of evidence	4	22
Ineffective attorneys	9	50
Mistaken eyewitness identification	6	33
Factors that led to execution despite doubts about guilt		
Procedural bars to the courts	4	22
Political pressure identified	2	11

[a] $N = 18$. In some of the executions, multiple variables were present in the same case.

doubts about Baldwin's guilt, but gave in to political pressure by voting for his execution (Rose, 1996).

The Roberts case illustrates this theme. In January 1999, Missouri Governor Mel Carnahan granted clemency to another death row inmate, Darryl Mease, at the request of Pope John Paul II, whose papal visit to St. Louis coincided with Mease's execution date (Alter, 1999). Because Roberts' execution was scheduled shortly thereafter, he was forced to present a compelling claim of innocence and clemency at a time when such claims were least likely to be considered. Facing a Senate race against conservative Republican John Ashcroft, a strong supporter of the death penalty, critics contend that Carnahan was too concerned about being portrayed as soft on crime to grant clemency (Alter, 1999).

Table 3.1 summarizes the results of the qualitative analysis.

Quantitative Results

Beyond the themes of these 18 cases, there are a number of observations to be made about them in the aggregate. At the outset, it is important to issue a caveat to the reader. These comparisons should be made and interpreted with some caution because of the relatively small number of executions of the innocent and the high levels of uncertainty about the actual composition of this population. The addition or subtraction of a few cases may have substantial effects on the geographic, temporal, and racial distributions of these cases. At the same time, because the cases being examined represent the population of executions of the innocent (at least as determined by the research), rather than a random sample of all executions, any differences between race patterns of all executions and those of executions of the innocent are interpreted as real, rather than as a statistical artifact.

The Geography of Executions of the Innocent

The geographic distribution of executions of the innocent closely parallels the larger geography of the death penalty and of executions (Lofquist, 2002). The state most active in executing—Texas—also has the largest number of executions of the innocent. It is also noteworthy that every execution of the innocent has occurred inside the traditional Southern death belt. The South, whether defined narrowly as extending from Virginia to Texas and including the eleven states of the Confederacy (Virginia, North Carolina, South Carolina, Georgia, Texas, Alabama, Mississippi, Louisiana, Texas, Arkansas, and Tennessee), or more broadly to include some or all of the following, Oklahoma, Missouri, Kentucky, Maryland, and Delaware, is distinct in its commitment to the death penalty (Lofquist, 2002).

This geographic pattern of executions of the innocent is significant, although not surprising, in that it accords with historic and contemporary patterns of commitment to the death penalty and other forms of lethal violence, such as lynchings and imprisonment (Tolnay & Beck, 1995). Indeed, there are close parallels between patterns of death penalty intensity—an aggregate measure of death penalty use encompassing rates of death sentencing, appellate retention, and nonconsensual executions—and executions of the innocent (Lofquist, 2002). This suggests that executions of the innocent are a byproduct of commitments to the death penalty so strong that due process protections are fatally weakened. Table 3.2 shows the geographic distribution of executions of the innocent.

Executions of the Innocent over Time

In 1991, legal scholar Mark Tushnet began his review of Welsh White's *The Death Penalty in the Nineties*, by stating that "[s]ometime in the 1990s, an innocent person will be executed" (Tushnet, 1991, p. 261). His implication was that changes in death penalty law and capital jurisprudence documented by White, particularly related to habeas corpus, had eroded protections against wrongful convictions and executions of the innocent to the point that they could no longer be prevented. Tushnet was already too late in his prediction.

Looking more closely at the data, two observations may be made. First, the larger numbers and more regular occurrence of executions of the

Table 3.2 The Geographic Distribution of Executions of the Innocent

State	Frequency	Percentage of All Executions ($N = 1060$)	Frequency	Percentage of Executions of the Innocent
Arkansas	27	2.5	1	5.5
Florida	64	6.0	4	22.2
Louisiana	27	2.5	1	5.5
Mississippi	8	.75	1	5.5
Missouri	66	6.2	3	16.6
Texas	381	35.9	7	38.9
Virginia	98	9.2	1	5.5
Total	671	63.05	18	100

Table 3.3 The Temporal Distribution of Executions of the Innocent

Year	Number of Executions of the Innocent	Number of Total Executions	Percentage of Innocent Executions
1984	1	21	4.8
1987	1	25	4.0
1988	1	11	9.1
1989	1	16	6.3
1993	2	38	5.2
1995	4	56	7.1
1997	1	74	1.4
1998	2	68	2.9
1999	2	98	2.0
2000	2	85	2.4
2004	1	59	1.7

innocent beginning in 1995 provide some support for Tushnet's hypothesis by suggesting that the especially aggressive and punitive anti-crime rhetoric of that era (Gross, 2000; Bright, 1995), culminating with the Anti-Terrorism and Effective Death Penalty Act of 1996 and including the "deregulation of death" that began earlier in the 1980s (Weisberg, 1984), contributed to an environment that allowed more executions of the innocent. Second, and more tentatively, it may be that the high levels of public, media, and political attention to wrongful convictions in the last few years have contributed to fewer executions of the innocent since 2000. Table 3.3 shows the temporal distribution of executions of the innocent.

Table 3.4 Racial Distribution for Executions of the Innocent

Race of Defendant	Executed Innocents Frequency (Valid Percentage)	All Other Executions Frequency (Valid Percentage)
White	9 (50%)	600 (58%)
Black	7 (39%)	350 (34%)
Latino	2 (11%)	68 (6.5%)
Native American	—	15 (1.4%)
Asian	—	7 (.7%)
Missing	—	2
Total	18 (100%)	1042
Race of Victim	**Executed Innocents Frequency (Valid Percentage)**	**All Other Executions Frequency (Valid Percentage)**
White	14 (78%)	833 (80%)
Black	2 (11%)	134 (13%)
Latino	2 (11%)	53 (5%)
Native American	—	2 (.2%)
Asian	—	16 (1.5%)
Missing	—	4
Total	18 (100%)	1042

Race and Executions of the Innocent

Most interesting are the data regarding the race of the offenders and victims in executions of the innocent. When compared to all executions, a pattern emerges in which the racial inequalities at work in the death penalty operate somewhat differently, but still discriminatorily, in executions of the innocent. It is well established that the racial pattern of executions operates most discriminatorily to place those who kill whites, whatever their race, at substantially greater risk of execution. The racial identity of offenders, however, has little effect on the likelihood of execution (Baldus et al., 1986, 1994; Gross and Mauro, 1989; Baldus and Woodworth, 1998).

In executions of the innocent, a different pattern is found. There is a greater emphasis on race of offender as a location of racial disparity. More specifically, whereas 58 percent of executions are of whites, 50 percent of executions of the innocent are of whites. Black offenders account for 34 percent of those executed and 39 percent of executions of the innocent. Latino offenders account for 6.5 percent of those executions and 11 percent of executions of the innocent.[2] Differences between race of victim in executions and race of victim in executions of the innocent are negligible.[3] Whites are victims in 80 percent of executions and 78 percent of executions of the innocent, and blacks are victims in 13 percent of executions and 11 percent of executions of the innocent. Table 3.4 shows the racial distribution for executions of the innocent.

Conclusion

The qualitative analysis identified specific themes associated with the wrongful executions. Two of the most prevalent types of new evidence that cast doubt about the guilt of the defendants included evidence implicating another suspect and evidence that supported an alibi. The main factors related to the wrongful convictions included the following: witness perjury, police misconduct, prosecutorial misconduct, ineffective counsel, and mistaken eyewitness identification. It is noteworthy that both witness perjury and ineffective counsel were the most frequent types of error that contributed to a wrongful conviction. Factors that led to the executions of the innocent despite doubts about the defendants' guilt were new evidence that was not considered by the courts and political pressure to execute the defendants.

The quantitative analysis suggests that executions of the innocent are a significant problem in the traditional southern death belt. They are a regular occurrence, and there seem to be a disproportionate number of black and minority offenders among the executed innocents when compared to all post-*Furman* executions. The implications of these results are simple. First, the potential risk of executing the innocent is disturbingly high, and these fatal errors seem to occur frequently. Second, these mistakes tend to happen because of systemic problems with the death penalty, particularly in southern states, such as perjury of witnesses, ineffective attorneys, racial discrimination, and political pressure. Finally, the results of this study should be considered by policy makers in the continued debate over the efficacy of capital punishment.

Notes

* I would like to give special thanks to William S. Lofquist for his contributions to this research.

1. The case of Roger Coleman was removed from this study and three new cases were added that came to light after the Lofquist and Harmon publication in 2008. The added cases are: Carlos De Luna (Texas), Cameron Willingham (Texas), and Ruben Cantu (Texas). The rest of the cases are those of Timothy Baldwin (Louisiana), Walter Blair (Missouri), Bernard Bolender (Florida), Willie Darden (Florida), Bennie Demps (Florida), Troy Farris (Texas), Billy Conn Gardner (Texas), Gary Graham (Texas), Larry Griffin (Missouri), Wilburn Henderson (Arkansas), Edward Earl Johnson (Mississippi), Leo Jones (Florida), Roy Roberts (Missouri), David Wayne Spence (Texas), and Dennis Waldon Stockton (Virginia).
2. No Asian or American Indian minorities were identified among the executed innocent. I calculated bivariate relationships between the two race-independent variables (race of the defendant and race of the victim) and the dependent variable, executed innocents versus general executions. Both of these results

were not statistically significant. However, it is possible that the race of the defendant was not significant because of the small size of the population of executed innocents (n = 18).

3. In cases when there were multiple victims with mixed races, they were classified as white victim cases (see Liebman et al., 2002; Harmon, 2004).

References

Alter, J. (1999). How sure is sure enough? *Newsweek* (March 22), p. 37.

Baldus, D., Pulaski, Jr., C., & Woodworth, G. (1986). Arbitrariness and discrimination in the administration of the death penalty: A challenge to state supreme courts. *Stetson Law Review* 15:133–261.

Baldus, D. & Woodworth, G. (1998). Race discrimination and the death penalty: An empirical and legal overview. In J.R. Acker, R.M. Bohm, & C.S. Lanier (Eds.) *America's Experiment with Capital Punishment*, 2nd ed. (pp. 501–551) Durham, NC: Carolina Academic Press.

Baldus, D., Woodworth, G., & Pulaski, Jr., C. (1994). Reflections on the 'inevitability' of racial discrimination in capital sentencing and the 'impossibility' of its prevention, detection and correction. *Washington & Lee Law Review* 51:359–426.

Bedau, H.A. & Radelet, M.L. (1987). Miscarriages of justice in potentially capital cases. *Stanford Law Review* 40 (November):21-91-173.

Bonner, R. & Rimer, S. (2000). A closer look at five cases that resulted in executions of Texas inmates. *New York Times* (May 14), p. 30.

Borchard, E. (1932). *Convicting the Innocent: Sixty-Five Actual Errors of Criminal Justice*. New Haven, CT: Yale University Press.

Bright, S.B. (1995). The politics of crime and the death penalty: Not 'soft on crime,' but hard on the Bill of Rights. *Saint Louis University Law Review* 39: 479–503.

Bright, S.B. (1994). Counsel for the poor: The death sentence not for the worst crime but for the worst lawyer. *Yale Law Journal* 103:1835–1912.

Bright, S.B. (1992). In defense of life: Enforcing the Bill of Rights on behalf of poor, minority. *Missouri Law Review* 57:849–870.

DeFalco, B. (2007). New Jersey legislative commission recommends abolition of state's death penalty. *Associated Press* (January 2).

Drizin, S. & Leo, R. (2004). The problem of false confessions in the post-DNA world. *North Carolina Law Review*. 82: 891–1007.

Editorial. (2006). Mistrust: Court's decision to leave a wrongful execution inquiry with a tainted DA clouds Texas justice. *Houston Chronicle* (September 5).

Gross, S.R. (2000). Still arbitrary, still unfair – But do we care? *Ohio Northern University Law* Review 26:517–527.

Gross, S.R. (1998). Lost lives: Miscarriages of justice in capital cases. *Law and Contemporary Problems* 61:125–152.

Gross, S.R. (1996). The risks of death: Why erroneous convictions are common in capital cases. *Buffalo Law Review* 44:469–500.

Gross, S. & Mauro, R. (1989). *Death & Discrimination: Racial Disparities in Capital Sentencing*. Boston: Northeastern University Press.

Harmon, T.R. (2004). Race for your life: An analysis of the role of race in erroneous capital convictions. *Criminal Justice Review* 29: 76–96.

Harmon, T.R. (2001). Predictors of miscarriages of justice in capital cases. *Justice Quarterly* 18: 949–968.

Harmon, T.R. & Lofquist, W.S. (2005). Too late for luck: A comparison of post-Furman exonerations and executions of the innocent. *Crime and Delinquency* 51: 498–520.

Huff, R.C., Rattner, A. & Sagarin, E. (1996). *Convicted but Innocent*. Thousand Oaks, CA: Sage.

Ingle, J. (1990). *Last Rights: 13 Fatal Encounters with the State's Justice*. Nashville: Abington Press.

King, C.D. (2006). For Catholics, 'there can be no morally acceptable justification for vengeance,' says speaker at red mass. *South Texas Catholic News*, (October 20), retrieved on 1/31/07 at: http://www.goccn.org/stc/articles/article.cfm?article=550.

Liebman, J.S., Fagan, J., & West, V. (2000). *A broken system: error rates in capital cases: 1973–1995*. Available at http://www2.law.columbia.edu/brokensystem2/. Website consulted February 1, 2007.

Liebman, J. S., Fagan, J., Gelman, A., West, V., Davies, G., & Kiss, A. (2002). A broken system, part II: Why there is so much error in capital cases, and what can be done about it. Available at http://www2.law.columbia.edu/brokensystem2/. Website consulted February 1, 2007.

Lofquist, W.S. (2002). Putting them there, keeping them there, and killing them: An analysis of state level variations in death penalty intensity. *Iowa Law Review* 87:1505–1557.

Lofquist, W.S. & Harmon, T.R. (forthcoming) 2008. Fatal errors: compelling claims of executions of the innocent in the post-Furman era. In R. Huff & M. Killias. *Wrongful Convictions: International Perspectives on Miscarriages of Justice*. Philadelphia: Temple University Press.

Markman, S.J. & Cassell, P.G. (1988). Protecting the innocent: A response to the Bedau-Radelet study. *Stanford Law Review* 41:121–160.

Mills, S., Possley, M., & Armstrong, K. (2000). Shadow of doubt haunts executions. *Chicago Tribune* (December 17), p. 1.

Orlando Sun Sentinel. (1995). Appeals still open as execution nears. (July 18), p. 8A.

Pellemans, M. (2000). Facing execution, inmate's killer claims innocence. *Tampa Tribune* (June 7), p. 2.

Radelet, M.L., Bedau, H.A., & Putnam, C.E. (1992). *In Spite of Innocence: Erroneous Convictions in Capital Cases*. Boston: Northeastern University Press.

Radelet, M.L., Lofquist, W.S., & Bedau, H.A. (1996). Prisoners released from death rows since 1970 because of doubts about their guilt. *Cooley Law Review* 13:907–966.

Raffaele, M. (2006). Panel to study wrongful convictions. *Associated Press* (November 28).

Rauch, J. (1998). Death by mistake. *National Journal* (May 30) pp. 1224–1231.

Rimer, S. & Bonner, R. (2000). Texas lawyer's death row record a concern. *New York Times* (June 11), p. A1.

Robertson, G.D. (2006). Easley backs innocence commission. *Associated Press*. (August 3, 7:29:57).

Rose, D. (1996). Dead man stalking. *The (London) Observer* (April 21), p. 8.

Saad, L. (2005). Support for death penalty steady at 64%. *The Gallup Poll* (December 8), pp. 456–457.
Sanders, B. (1999). Execution of Farris would be mistake. *Ft. Worth Star Telegram*, January 10. p.1
Santi, A.D. (2006). New Jersey lawmakers vote to suspend executions as death penalty study proceeds. *Associated Press* (January 10).
Sewell, C. (1976), September 7. Interoffice Memorandum (on file with author).
Silva, M. (1998). Man convicted of killing cop dies in electric chair. *Houston Chronicle* (March 25), p. 16.
State of denial: Texas justice and the death penalty, Chapter 9, "A bitter harvest," Available at http://www.texasdefender.org/study/chapter9.html. Website consulted May 3, 2002.
Tolnay, S.E. & Beck, E.M. (1995). *A Festival of Violence: An Analysis of Southern Lynchings, 1882–1930*. Urbana: University of Illinois Press.
Tushnet, M.V. (1991). The politics of executing the innocent. *University of Pittsburgh Law Review* 53:261–269.
Unnever, J.D. & Cullen, F.T. (2005). Executing the innocent and support for capital punishment: implications for public policy. *Criminology and Public Policy* 4:3–38.
US News and World Report. (1988). The symbolic death of Willie Darden. (March 28), p. 9.
Ward, M. (1999). Inmate faces execution today despite ruling. *Austin American-Statesman* (January 13), p. B2.
Weinstein, H. (2006a). Moratorium on executions is urged: Author of state's death penalty initiative and other prosecutors send a letter to the assembly backing a bill seeking a two-year suspension. *Los Angeles Times* (January 10), p. B3.
Weinstein, H. (2006b). Panel seeks to curb false confessions: Officials urge a law that would require taping of jailhouse interrogations and a warning to juries if a suspect's statement wasn't recorded. *Los Angeles Times* (July 26), p. B3.
Weisberg, R. (1984). Deregulating death. *Supreme Court Review* 1983:305–395.
Wilgoren, J. (2003). Citing issue of fairness, governor clears out death row in Illinois. *New York Times* (January 12), p.1.
Wiseman, C. (1996). Representing the condemned: A critique of capital punishment. *Marquette Law Review* 79: 731–758.

Cases Cited

Baldwin v. Blackburn, 653 F2d 924 (1981).
Blair v. Armontrout, 916 F2d 1310 (1990).
Blair, Walter, 1993. Application for Commutation.
Bolender v. Singletary, 898 F. Supp 876 (1995).
Cantu v. Texas, 738 SW2d 249 (1987).
Darden v. Wainwright, 477 US 168 (1986).
Farris v. Texas, 819 SW2d 490 (1990).
Gardner v. Texas, 730 SW 2d 675 (1987).
Graham v. Johnson, 168 F3d 762 (1999).

Griffin, L., 1995. Clemency Petition.
Henderson v. Sargent, 926 F2d 706 (1991).
In re Roy Roberts, clemency petition (1999).
In re Troy Farris, clemency petition (1999).
In re Troy Farris, supplement clemency petition (1999).
Jones v. Florida, 528 So. 2d 1171 (1988).
Jones v. Florida, 678 So. 2d 309 (1996).
Missouri v. Griffin, 662 SW2d 854 (1983).
Missouri v. Roberts, 709 SW2d 857 (1986).
Riley v. State, 889 SW2d 90 (1994).
Roberts v. Bowersox, 137 F3d 1062 (1998).
Roberts v. Bowersox, 1999 US App. Lexis 3757 (1999).
Roberts v. Missouri, 775 SW2d 92 (1989).
Spence v. Scott, 80 F3d 989 (1996).

Making It Work: Compensation for the Wrongfully Convicted

4

CATHLEEN BURNETT

Contents

Introduction

Nationally, a growing number of persons have been exonerated and released after serving years in prison for crimes they did not commit. The Death Penalty Information Center reports that, to date, 126 persons have been released from death rows with evidence of their actual innocence. More often than not, these persons exit the institution with just a bus ticket and suit of clothes. Ironically, if they had been guilty and then released from prison they would at least have a parole officer with whom to meet to assist in finding a job and finding shelter. Unfortunately, there are no good options for assisting these exonerated persons with reintegration back into society because the legal system is set up not to take responsibility for their predicament and hence not accept the obligation to assist in their restoration (Burnett, 2005).

The problem may be quite significant. These 126 persons released from death rows with evidence of actual innocence are likely the tip of the iceberg. Conservative estimates are that about one percent of criminal convictions are likely to be wrongful convictions (Huff, 1996, p. xiv; Berlow, 1999; Forst, 2004, p. 5). Although that rate is small and likely a socially acceptable risk in some venues, when applied to all those convicted of felonies, one percent represents about 10,000 persons wrongfully incarcerated every year (Forst, 2004, p. 5), a circumstance that adversely affects them as well as their families. Only a few of these individuals are fortunate to win exoneration and release. The Life After Exoneration Program knows of more than 400 exonerees nationwide. Although these persons resist the label of victim, they nonetheless are victims of a criminal justice system intent on convicting the bad guys in the name of protecting society.

The social contract that characterizes the relationship between government and its citizens provides legitimacy to the government to control and regulate its citizens while accepting the responsibility to protect the welfare of all its citizens. An argument can be made that because we have a criminal justice system with significant powers, the state government acting on behalf of all society has an inherent obligation to provide for the welfare of those who erroneously have been caught up in our punishment system. Because the state government has "set the criminal justice system in motion for the public good" (Rosenn, 1976), then the government should be obligated to correct any mistakes that occur. The state has the ability to share the costs of correcting errors among its entire population (Bernhard, 1999), whereas the individual victim should not be expected to shoulder that burden. Fairness demands that the state accept as its responsibility caring for these victims of the criminal justice system. Without having their needs addressed, these persons are let down by society a second time.

Literature Review

A recent LAEP (2005) study of 60 exonerees nationwide confirmed that exonerees have considerable difficulty rebuilding their lives.

- Half were living with family members.
- Two-thirds were not financially independent.
- One-third lost custody of their children as a result of their wrongful incarceration.
- At least one fourth suffer from post-traumatic stress disorder.

Unlike the September 11th victims in whose losses the entire nation participated and to whom we generously (by September 22, 2001) responded by establishing a compensation fund that merely required an application to be filed with a special master (Feinberg, 2004), the wrongfully convicted, for the most part, have been left to fend for themselves. Acknowledging the wrongfully convicted threatens belief in the integrity of the criminal justice system by pointing to its fallibility; acknowledging the 9/11 victims carries none of that negative baggage. In addition, there generally is some residual doubt about an exonerated inmate's actual innocence and worthiness; there is no such doubt about the 9/11 victims. Ironically, the legal doctrine of eminent domain, permitting the taking of property for public benefit, requires compensation, whereas the taking of an innocent person's liberty does not (Rosenn, 1976).

Three Types of Responses to Assist the Wrongfully Convicted

Generally, there are three types of responses that might be available to assist the wrongfully convicted upon release—lawsuits, private legislation, and private donations—but each has its flaws in effectively dealing with this issue (Burnett, 2005). Only 21 states have actual statutes to deal with this problem. (A compilation of relevant state statutes is available from the Life After Exoneration Program website at http://www.exonerated.org).

Lawsuits require that the wrongfully convicted hire an attorney to file a claim in which the burden of establishing innocence is the first hurdle. A second hurdle is finding an attorney to take the case within a given time limit. Persons readjusting to civilian life have enough on their hands and may not be able to think clearly about pursuing this option. In addition, the former prisoner might be reluctant to enter a courtroom again. Subjecting an exonerated inmate to another adversarial process might revictimize him or her and give the appearance of blaming the victim for his or her circumstance. Fault-based lawsuits are inadequate because they do not compensate victims for mistakes made "in good faith" (see Huff et al., 1996). States that rely on DNA evidence as absolute proof of innocence do not assist those exonerated who have no DNA proof. (Only 15 of the 126 on the DPIC list were released based on DNA evidence.)

When private legislation is available, it assumes that compensation is a discretionary action rather than an obligation of the state government. As such, there is no urgency to offer compensation to those wrongfully convicted and delay creates damaging injustice.

Private donations rarely achieve the amounts necessary to cover or sustain the costs of reintegration. This approach requires organization and trusted stewardship on the former prisoner's behalf and serves to continue his or her dependency upon others, in essence, begging for help.

An Administrative Response to the Wrongfully Convicted

Rather than promoting one or all of these approaches that draw on the legal system to correct the injustice of a wrongful conviction, a simple administrative response could be more easily employed. Once an individual has been recognized as actually innocent through the official system, then the actual need for redress and compensation should be a simple task, indeed, a clerical task, once the prisoner has been released from custody. Because the release has come about through strong evidence of innocence under one of several widely accepted criteria, there is no need for further litigation. There is no need for revictimizing the wrongfully convicted individual.

Following the model of the response to the 9/11 victims, the challenge to aid the wrongfully convicted former prisoner can be addressed by a simple administrative program that deals restoratively with the needs of the wrongfully convicted without the focus on finding someone to blame for the unfortunate situation. Elsewhere I have described this program in which a caseworker is assigned to accompany the released exoneree for a period of time, assisting in identifying needs and resources to address those needs (Burnett, 2005). Application is made to the government to fund the restoration of the individual. Funding is not automatic because it is keyed to the individual's needs. Therefore, application must be made to establish what needs exist. Others of course would be drawn into the process in which the goal is to create a future out of the present, rather than dwelling on the past.

The Missouri Problem

Although Missouri has had three persons exonerated and released from death row and 21 others exonerated who have had lesser sentences (Center on Wrongful Convictions, 2007), few of these individuals (and none of the death row prisoners) have been exonerated through DNA evidence. Yet, current Missouri law only deals with individuals who are determined to be "actually innocent" through DNA evidence (Section 650.055.9 Mo. Rev. Stat.). According to Missouri statutes:

> The individual may receive an amount of fifty dollars per day for each day of postconviction incarceration . . . Petition for the payment of said restitution shall be filed with the sentencing court within one year of the release from confinement. . . . All restitution paid pursuant to this subsection shall be paid from moneys in the DNA profiling analysis fund [collected from a criminal case surcharge of $15]. . . . If insufficient moneys remain in the fund on June thirtieth of each fiscal year to pay restitution to such persons, the department shall pay each individual who has received an order awarding restitution a pro rata share of the amount such person is owed. The remaining amounts owed to such individual shall be paid from the fund on June thirtieth of each subsequent fiscal year, provided moneys remain in the fund on June thirtieth, until such time as the restitution to the individual has been paid in full. However, no individual awarded restitution under this subsection shall receive more than thirty-six thousand five hundred dollars during each fiscal year.

> No interest on unpaid restitution shall be awarded to the individual. *If there are no moneys remaining in the DNA profiling analysis fund, then no payments shall be made under this subsection* [emphasis added].

The problem for Missourians who have been determined to be "actually innocent" without DNA evidence is that they are not covered by the statute and must sue the state for compensation for their wrongful conviction. Should they fail to find someone to blame and fail in convincing a court of the blame, they would come away from the courthouse empty-handed, destitute, and at-risk of reoffending.

The Project

Having written a 2005 article in which I proposed a simple administrative solution to the problem of effectively reintegrating the wrongfully convicted, the next step in making a difference is to turn the proposal into legislation. Although there have been several exonerees in Missouri, this legislation may not ever apply to any of them. Several have won awards through lawsuits, one died (Dick Dexter), one remains incarcerated (Eric Clemmons), and one is currently in mediation and litigating a lawsuit. The transition from journal article to legislation is a frustrating process when dealing with wrongful convictions. In early 2005, I gave a draft of a bill (see Appendix A) to a lawyer with experience with these clients to look over. He said he passed it along to a legal staff member in the General Assembly. I never heard back from either of them.

Next, I met with my state senator and his assistant in the fall of 2005 and gave them my draft of the bill. They said they would work on it, but I didn't pursue them, and they never got back to me. I sent a copy of the article and the draft bill to my newly elected legislators just before Thanksgiving 2006. Early in January 2007, I called to make appointments with my new legislators.

I met with my representative on Friday, January 12, at a neighborhood restaurant for coffee, and she took my draft bill and 2005 article. This was the second copy given to her. I gave her a basic description of the bill and why it was needed. As a social worker, she liked my approach of viewing the whole person, adding that she likes to talk about individuals' strengths. She said she would show it to the House staff who are the legal eyes to "perfect" it, make a copy, and talk with my senator about it. We both recognized that passing bills could be a three- to four-year proposition if you are lucky, but she said, "You have to begin sometime!" She ended our meeting by saying she would get back in touch with me in a couple of weeks. It has been three months and I have not heard from her.

In the meantime, I revised the needs assessment instrument by simplifying the categories of need (Appendix C). I met with a forensic economist, who works with lawyers in personal injury cases, assisting juries in their determination of awards to plaintiffs. He reviewed my list of factors (Appendix B) and focused on the issue of lost income.

Reviewing the Instrument

A local list of exonerees is available from the Midwestern Innocence Project. I will get those names and contact information and ask for appointments to talk to them about the instrument and their willingness to review it. Basically, I want to see if I have anticipated all the needs that might arise for individuals and then see what would be the range of money and support required to assist their reintegration into society. Then a comparison can be made between their experiences and the outcomes predicted by this proposal.

Barriers to Implementation

The key to implementing this proposed legislation is the state's commitment to recognize and fulfill the needs assessment profile. It is the right thing to do for the long-term viability of the community. A healthy community protects the welfare of all its citizens and thereby thrives when all can participate to reach their potential. The question is whether the moral leadership exists to do the right thing in the short term. There are several barriers that need to be overcome.

1. *Competition for scarce resources:* State budgets are always tight, some years more so than others. This legislation requires that the state pay what is owed as a priority obligation, not as an afterthought. Thus, the legislature must designate sufficient funds to cover the uncertain and unexpected occurrence of a wrongful conviction and imprisonment. In Missouri, the plan is housed in the attorney general's office and would be part of the requested budget appropriation.
2. *Acknowledging fallibility:* Missouri officials need to acknowledge that the criminal justice system is fallible because it is a system that is administered by human beings, as Chief Justice Rehnquist wrote in *Herrera v. Collins* (1993). Acknowledging and fixing mistakes will bring integrity back to state authority, rather than diminish it. To date, Missouri officials have denied that mistakes have been made, despite strong evidence to the contrary.
3. *Political will:* Many government officials today believe that the government should not help those in need, but rather it should simply allow the fittest to survive. This philosophy prescribes that government

not intervene or provide programs to assist those most in need. This position needs to be confronted and challenged as unresponsive and contrary to what most citizens believe is right.

4. *Blaming the victim:* Relatedly, many people, both government officials and individual citizens, "blame the victim," which allows them to relinquish responsibility for the wrongfully convicted's welfare.
5. *Increase visibility:* Because the numbers of wrongfully convicted are relatively small, this issue has low visibility. The media need to widely distribute the stories of the wrongfully convicted to make the public aware of the problem and embarrass officials into doing the right thing.

Future Political Opportunities

The proposed administrative solution to the challenge of reintegrating exonerees can certainly be adapted to all former prisoners. However, this proposal begins with the small number of individuals to whom society owes support by having made the ultimate error. The basic program depends upon some legal entity releasing an inmate who has been ruled to be innocent of the charge or charges for which he or she had been convicted. There is no need to relitigate the matter. Simply enter the court's or governor's order of record and proceed to assess needs. This plan does not waste time dwelling on the past by requiring that proof of responsibility or blame be established through a legal proceeding. It merely begins with the official document proclaiming that the individual was wrongly incarcerated and then deals with helping the exonoree make the transition to a productive future.

However, such legislation faces an uphill battle and it will likely take several years to educate government officials and the public that such a plan is morally necessary and practically needed.

Appendix A: A Draft Act

To amend chapter 537, RSMo by adding thereto one new section relating to compensation for wrongful imprisonment.

Be it enacted by the General Assembly of the state of Missouri, as follows:

Section A Chapter 537, RSMo, is amended by adding thereto one new section, to be know as section 537.780, to read as follows:

537.780.1. Notwithstanding the provisions of any other law, any person convicted and subsequently imprisoned for one or more crimes which such person did not commit may, under the conditions hereinafter provided, apply for compensation to the State Attorney General's Office and the Committee on Compensation for Wrongful Conviction.

537.780.2. The person, hereinafter referred to as the "claimant," shall be eligible if

(1) he or she was convicted and sentenced to death; and released by the state; and
(2) he or she was pardoned by the governor on grounds not inconsistent with actual innocence, or
(3) the conviction was vacated or reversed on grounds consistent with actual innocence, and
(4) he or she was found not guilty in a retrial or
(5) the government refused to retry the claimant when re-trial was granted or
(6) any other judicial or executive order has been issued indicating that the claimant is not guilty of the offense, and
(7) all appeals have been exhausted or
(8) an order of release has been entered by the court.

537.780.3. A state caseworker works with the claimant's attorney to arrange emergency assistance for 30 days upon release from the correctional institution. Within 30 days of release, the state caseworker in conjunction with claimant (who may have the assistance of an advocate) will complete an Assessment of Loss and Needs and a Community Integration Plan. A hearing will be held before the Committee on Compensation for Wrongful Conviction to approve the recommendations of the caseworker for compensation. Claimant may appeal the Committee's award to the Victim's Compensation Board of the Department of Corrections.

537.780.4(1) Compensation shall include reasonable and necessary expenses in order to integrate claimant into society. This will be determined by the Loss and Needs Assessment and the Community Integration Plan. There is no limit to the amount of the award.

537.780.4(2) In addition to the damages awarded pursuant to subdivision (1) of this subsection, the claimant shall be entitled to receive reasonable attorney fees.

537.780.5(1) A person shall not be eligible to file a claim for compensation pursuant to the provisions of this section if the sentence for the crime of which the person was mistakenly convicted was served concurrently with the sentence for the conviction of another crime.

537.780.6. The provisions of this section providing compensation funds and attorney fees shall be made through the Attorney General's Office.

Appendix B: Compensation and Needs Assessment

For a Hypothetical Exonerated **Amount**

A. As a result of incarceration from the time of arrest:
  1. Direct Financial losses:
     a. Payments to department of corrections: victim compensation fund: Public defenders: signed note for Funeral expenses for crime victim Other? Income tax refund held
     b. Lost wages (**including social security contributions**) for each year based on an average of three years prior to incarceration or **median family income, based on aggregate state statistics, for each year of wrongful incarceration, whichever is greater.**
     c. Inability to give **child support** (per child)
     d. Loss of Home (see below)
     e. Loss of car (see below)
  2. Health injuries/medical treatment in prison— (see below)
  3. Suffering in jail/prison
     a. Physical: assaults in custody (included in A2)
     b. Psychological: threats/deprivations/terror, fear, prison conditions, family separations and losses, coping with miscarriage of justice, bitterness, *Grief process for death of wife, death of father*, and b*roken relationships* (see below) All Attorney's fees and court costs associated with criminal defense and efforts to prove innocence

B. Upon Release Start-up money for:
Shelter for one year
  Or if home was lost, replacement value of home (including furniture)—
Job training
  Or 4 year college education at Missouri institution of choice
Clothing
Transportation (purchase of vehicle)
Driver's education fees
Unscheduled time for adjustment to "free" life. Money to live without a job for 6–12 months. No deductions for any charitable donations received.
Mentoring/Coaching
  Training in Basic Skills for daily living: banking, cooking, shopping on a budget, maintaining an apartment/home
  Computer classes
  Classes to assist in job search—resume writing, interviewing, identifying potential jobs and assistance in filling out applications
  Job search
  Support group

Complete physical and dental examination and Insurance Coverage for health care (up to 10 years)
Psychological counseling (up to 10 years)
Dealing with Notoriety; Grief, anger, death of friends while incarcerated, Family relationships/counseling;
Post-traumatic stress disorder, Personality change, Dispressive disorder, Panic disorder
Paranoid symptoms, Alcohol/drug dependence, safety needs, etc.
Humiliation and loss of dignity—restoration. We know that former prisoners have strong stigma to overcome.

> Expungement of record and an Official Apology from the governor's office should also be arranged by the state staff person.
>
> The award shall not be offset by any expenses incurred by the state while in custody. It should also be tax-free.

Appendix C: Payment for Needs

As a result of incarceration from the time of arrest:

Direct Financial losses:	
Payments to department of corrections:	$ 15
Victim Compensation Fund	
Public Defenders: signed note for	$5,000
Funeral expenses for crime victim	$6,000
Income Tax withheld	variable
Other?	
Child support (per child)	variable
All attorney's fees and court costs associated with criminal defense and efforts to prove innocence	variable

Upon Release Start-up Money for Re-Integration:

Shelter for one year: Rent $12,000 OR if home was lost, present value of mortgage and equity value of home	variable
Furniture	$60,000

Job training OR 4 year college education at state institution of choice (includes tuition, fees and books)	$20,000
Computer classes	$ 2,500
Clothing	$ 5,000
Transportation (purchase of vehicle and insurance)	$25,000
Driver's education fees	$ 500
Money to live without a job for 6–12 months	$30,000
Medical insurance coverage for dental, eye and health care (up to 10 years)	$14,000
Psychological counseling (up to 10 years)	$45,000
Money for a mentor or coach, if needed.	$15,000

References

Berlow, Alan. (1999). The wrong man, *The Atlantic Monthly* (November: 66–91).

Bernhard, Adele. (1999). When Justice Fails: Indemnification for Unjust Conviction. *University of Chicago Law School Roundtable* 6:73–112.

Burnett, Cathleen. (2005). Restorative justice and wrongful capital convictions: A simple proposal. *Journal of Contemporary Criminal Justice* 21: 272–289.

Center on Wrongful Convictions. (2007). Northwestern University Law School. Chicago, IL. 60611. Available at http://www.law.northwestern.edu/wrongfulconvictions/exonerations/moIndex.html. Website consulted January 5, 2008.

Feinberg, Kenneth R. (2004). Final report of the Special Master for the September 11th Victim Compensation Fund of 2001, Washington DC: Department of Justice (November).

Forst, Brian. (2004). *Errors of Justice: Nature, Sources and Remedies.* UK: Cambridge University Press.

Huff, C. Ronald, Arye Rattner, and Edward Sagarin. (1996). *Convicted but Innocent: Wrongful Conviction and Public Policy.* Thousand Oaks, CA: Sage.

Life After Exoneration Program Available at http://www.exonerated.org. Website consulted January 5, 2008.

Rosenn, K. (1976). Compensating the innocent accused, *Ohio State Law Journal* 37:705–728.

Cases Cited

Herrera v. Collins (1993) 506 U. S. 390.

A Painless Cocktail? The Lethal Injection Controversy

5

GAVIN LEE

Contents

Introduction

The study of the various lethal injection protocols in the United States is of vital importance to the criminal justice system. Lethal injection has been used in 84.5 percent of the 1089 executions (as of August 10, 2007) carried out since the execution of Gary Gilmore in 1977 which saw the return of capital punishment to the United States (Death Penalty Information Center, 2007). Lethal injection is currently the primary method of execution in 36 of the 37 death penalty states (Death Penalty Information Center, 2007). Only Nebraska does not have lethal injection as an option, something that may change in the near future as a result of legislative action. Despite its widespread use (and political expediency), lethal injection is one of the most controversial issues in an already very controversial area of criminal justice policy. To understand the current controversies, it is necessary to examine the somewhat confusing manner in which lethal injection became the preferred method of execution in the United States.

In Search of a More Humane Method of Execution

Except for the ten years between 1968 and 1977, capital punishment has been employed in the United States, and for most of that time, death penalty states have attempted to employ a humane method to put capital offenders to death (Bohm, 2007). This is not because of some misplaced sympathy for capital offenders, but rather because of the U.S. Supreme Court's interpretation of the Eighth Amendment prohibition of cruel and unusual punishment. Since the latter part of the 19th century, the U.S. Supreme Court ("the Court") has prohibited punishments that involve "torture," "unnecessary cruelty," or "lingering death . . . something more than the mere extinguishment of life" (see *Wilkerson v. Utah*, 1878; *In re Kemmler*, 1890). Five execution methods apparently have met these criteria: hanging, firing squad, electrocution, lethal gas, and lethal injection. The modifier "apparently" is used here because, despite dozens of horribly botched executions (Death Penalty Information Center, 2007), the Court has never ruled as unconstitutional any of the five aforementioned execution methods.

In 1972, in the landmark case of *Furman v. Georgia*, the Court struck down all capital punishment statutes in the United States on Eighth and Fourteenth Amendment grounds, not because of the methods employed but because of the arbitrary and capricious nature of their application. In response to the *Furman* decision, most state legislatures rewrote their death penalty statutes to address the problems cited by the Court. Four years later, in *Gregg v. Georgia* (1976), the Court held that, with certain modifications (such as guided discretion, bifurcated trials, and automatic appellate review), executions could resume (Bohm, 2007). With the *Gregg* decision, the United States entered the "modern age" of capital punishment.

The Creation of a Lethal Cocktail

To make their executions more "humane" in the modern age of capital punishment, the state of Oklahoma examined various alternatives to its previous method of electrocution. State Representative Bill Wiseman (R-Tulsa) was aware that electrocution was losing public support as an execution method because of high-profile botched executions and the inherent visible violence of the procedure (such as the flesh being burned off the condemneds' bodies or the bodies themselves catching fire). To this end, Wiseman sought the assistance of doctors and other scientists to look for a more socially acceptable method. In addition, the state faced financial issues with respect to its capital punishment procedure and this may also have played a role in its rationale to examine new execution methods. It was reported that "it would cost the state $62,000 to repair the electric chair and $300,000 to build a gas chamber and [Senator Bill Dawson-R] had been informed that . . . lethal injection . . . would be substantially cheaper" (Denno, 2002, p. 95).

Representative Wiseman was initially unsuccessful in the search for a physician, primarily because most doctors were unwilling to play a part in developing a procedure that was designed to extinguish human life, an idea anathema to both the medical ethos and the Hippocratic Oath (Ward, 2006). However, two doctors did play prominent roles in the birth of Oklahoma's (and later other states') lethal injection statute: Dr. Jay Chapman, Chief Medical Examiner for the State, and Dr. Stanley Deutsch of Oklahoma's Medical School's Anesthesiology Department. Both Senator Dawson and Representative Wiseman initially contacted Dr. Chapman for help in their endeavor. Dr. Chapman agreed, despite informing the legislators that he was by no means an expert in either the fields of anesthesia or toxicology. This lack of expertise, however, did not appear to bother Chapman, who subsequently said (with regard to the medical authorities' animus toward physician participation in executions), "To hell with them: let's do this" (Denno, 2007, p. 11, fn.92).

Déjà Vu

At this point it should be noted that, in 1953, the Royal Commission on Capital Punishment had examined lethal injection as a potential execution method to be used in the United Kingdom (Report of the British Royal Commission, 1953). The Commission did not recommend lethal injection because of the possibility that executioners might not possess the necessary medical expertise to deal with the different physiologies of condemned persons, resulting in potential problems with venous access and dosing levels. The Royal Commission also concluded that the injections would probably have to be delivered into the muscle as opposed to the vein, leading to a slower and more painful death. The conclusion seems prescient when one considers the constitutional challenges to current lethal injection procedures.

Lethal injection was also rejected in the late 19th century by a New York state commission charged with determining and recommending "the most humane and practical method [of execution] known to modern science" (cited in Bohm, 2007, p. 155). Based on the commission's recommendation, the New York State Legislature chose to replace hanging with electrocution. The commission rejected lethal injection because of the medical profession's protests. Doctors were afraid the public would associate death with the hypodermic needle and medical practice (Bohm, 2007, p. 156).

Oklahoma's Lethal Injection Protocol

Perhaps oblivious to the concerns of both the Royal Commission and the New York state commission, Dr. Chapman and Representative Wiseman proceeded to craft their proposed lethal injection protocol on a pad of paper. In a later interview, Dr. Chapman stated that the protocol was "a lethal quantity of an ultra-short acting barbiturate or other similar drug in combination with a chemical paralytic to cause death." He further stated that "[he] didn't care which drug killed the prisoner, as long as one of them did" (Human Rights Watch, 2006). Chapman and Wiseman did not want to be explicit regarding the drugs used in the procedure, because they were concerned about unforeseen issues or the availability of any suggested drug. At about the same time, Senator Dawson had a telephone conversation with Dr. Deutsch and requested that Deutsch provide him with a lethal injection procedure. Dr. Deutsch responded in a letter dated February 28, 1977, wherein he suggested "'an ultra-short acting barbiturate' (for example, sodium thiopental) in 'combination' with a 'nueromuscular [sic] blocking drug' (for example, pancuronium bromide) to create a 'long duration of paralysis'" (Denno, 2007, p. 11, fn. 101). Dr. Deutsch also stated in his letter that he believed that this method of "anesthetizing condemned inmates would be a 'rapidly pleasant way of producing unconsciousness' leading to death" (Human Rights Watch, 2006, p. 14).

Denno (personal communication) is unsure as to which doctor actually had more input in the final Oklahoma protocol, as once it was completed it appeared remarkably similar to Dr. Deutsch's original suggestion. With respect to his original two-drug protocol, Dr. Chapman said in an interview, "I didn't do any research. I just knew from having been placed under anesthesia myself, what we needed. I wanted to have at least two drugs [sodium thiopental and a paralytic agent] that would kill the prisoner, to make sure that if one didn't kill him, the other would" (Human Rights Watch, 2006, p.15).

A Third Lethal Drug Is Added

The reasons that potassium chloride, which induces cardiac arrest, was added as a third drug is not clearly understood. However, Chapman, when asked the reason for the addition of the third chemical, and why that chemical was potassium chloride, answered, "Why not. . . . You wanted to make sure the prisoner was dead at the end, so why not just add a third drug. I didn't do any research . . . it's just common knowledge. Doctors know potassium chloride is lethal. Why does it matter why I chose it?" (Human Rights Watch, 2006, p. 15).

Despite Dr. Chapman's stated rationale, the origins of the use of potassium chloride as a third drug are a matter of some debate. Denno (2007) posits that the drug may have been included because potassium chloride was listed in Oklahoma's two-drug statute as one of three named paralytic agents, along with tubocurarine and succinylcholine chloride. It is noteworthy that the paralytic agent that is actually used in executions, pancuronium bromide (also known as Pavulon), is absent from the statute. Denno (2007) also suggests a second possibility for the use of potassium chloride as a third drug in a "two-drug" cocktail: the advice of a man named Fred Leuchter.

Enter Fred Leuchter

Fred Leuchter described himself as an engineer; however, according to the Anti-Defamation League's website, Leuchter "had graduated from Boston University in 1964 with only a B.A. in history, and had never taken an engineering licensing test in Massachusetts" (Anti-Defamation League, 2007). In 1991, Leuchter admitted to misrepresenting himself as an engineer in his dealings with various correctional facilities. With criminal charges pending, Leuchter agreed to "cease and desist from using the title 'engineer' in connection with his execution equipment. . . ." (Anti-Defamation League, 2007). Leuchter claims to have become involved in America's capital punishment methods because of "the deplorable conditions of the hardware that's in most of the state's prisons, which generally results in torture prior to death" (Morris, 1999).

He began his death penalty career in Tennessee, where he was hired to repair that state's electric chair. Afterward, as a result of his Tennessee work and work in other electrocution states, he was contacted by the State of New Jersey to devise a mechanized method to deliver lethal injections to inmates. The machine which he designed passed the state's medical staffs' inspection and during his presentation to the New Jersey Department of Corrections the Deputy Commissioner exclaimed, "[S]top the meeting. You designed the [electrocution] helmet, the one they [North Carolina] just used? . . . OK . . . Do the necessary paperwork, and see that Mr. Leuchter gets the contract" (Morris, 1999).

At the time Leuchter was awarded the New Jersey contract, the state specified sodium thiopental and potassium chloride as the two drugs in its lethal injection statute. This may be why potassium chloride is included in the "mix" of lethal chemicals now used in the protocols of most other states. A disturbing fact surrounding Leuchter's involvement is that due to the paucity of literature available about the lethality of potassium chloride, Leuchter garnered secondary data regarding the drug's lethality from experiments carried out on pigs. He then extrapolated those findings to calculate a dosage for use in human executions (Denno, 2002).

Leuchter promised in his promotional literature to the Missouri Department of Corrections that his injection machine "would 'insure a problem free execution'." The machine itself was designed to deliver the chemicals in the following manner.

> A total of eight disposable syringes are utilized in this system delivering . . . [a] pre-injection 10cc antihistamine, one half hour prior to execution . . . pre-injection 8cc 2% Sodium Pentathol (5 grams/250ml . . .) five minutes prior to transmittal of subject to the death chamber . . . [a] [m]achine injection 15cc Sodium Pentathol 2% Solution delivered over a ten second time period . . . one minute wait . . . [a] [m]achine injection 15cc Pancuronium Bromide 2ml/2mg/ml over a ten second time period . . . one minute wait . . . [a] [m]achine injection 15cc Potassium Chloride (KCl Injectable solution) . . . two minute wait . . . execution over. (Lethal Injection Machine Manual State of Missouri, 1988)

The same document contains the following: "DISCLAIMER . . . Fred A. Leuchter Associates, Inc. assumes no liability for the intended or actual use of this device." During the 1980s, several states used Leuchter's machine, and variations of it, until Leuchter was discredited for, among other things, being a holocaust denier. This ended his execution business.

Early Concerns about Lethal Injection

On April 20, 1977, the lethal injection bill was passed in the Oklahoma house; it had passed in the state senate on March 2, 1977 (Oklahoma Lethal Injection Statute, Ch. 1014). However, it did not take long for the controversy to begin; a controversy that has never really ceased. According to Denno (2007), Dr. Chapman was interviewed by *The Daily Oklahoman* and, considering the recent passing of the law, began making troublesome assertions. For example, "Dr. Chapman . . . said . . . if the death-dealing drug is not administered properly, the convict may not die and could be subjected to severe muscle pain." He also stated that the drugs should be administered by someone "knowledgeable in drug injection" (Denno, 2007, p. 13). Furthermore, the article asserted that state legislators were not entirely happy with the drugs to be used, but felt that "when they have to use the [lethal] injection law, new and better drugs may be available" (Denno, 2007, p. 14).

This sentiment among Oklahoma lawmakers almost defies belief. To create legislation knowing it to be potentially and seriously flawed seems reckless at the very least. All of this was not lost on officials of the Oklahoma Department of Corrections, who, in 1978, observed that the lethal injection protocol "might need 'a few modifications or refinements'" (Denno, 2007, p.15). It may well have been these concerns that led to Chapman's formal addition of potassium chloride to the protocol in 1981 (Denno, 2007).

As can be seen from the information above, the nation's first lethal injection protocol would appear to have been created in a confusing, convoluted, and untested manner, by an individual who was unqualified and unsure of the efficacy of his suggestions which later became law. If this is not troublesome enough, the original Oklahoma protocol called for "continuous" IV anesthesia, whereas Chapman said in *The Daily Oklahoman* interview that "one big push of drugs" would be made. In medical terms this is known as a "bolus" and would appear to contradict the written statute, which called for the opposite of what Chapman stated in his interview.

In sum, the three chemicals typically used in lethal injection executions are:

1. Sodium thiopental, an anesthetic that is designed to put the inmate to sleep
2. A paralyzing agent, pancuronium bromide (also known as Pavulon) that is designed to suffocate the inmate by paralyzing the diaphragm
3. Potassium chloride, the second killing drug, designed to induce cardiac arrest

If the anesthetic works, the inmate falls asleep, and the effects of the next two drugs are not felt, resulting in a painless death. The problem occurs when the anesthetic does not work by virtue of either a poorly trained team not allowing enough time for the anesthetic to take effect or a poor IV line insertion. Regarding the latter, some executioners have failed to "hit" a vein thereby negating the effect of the anesthetic. If the sodium thiopental does not work, the procedure leaves the inmate suffocating from the second drug and subsequently suffering the excruciating experience of potassium chloride coursing through the blood stream. In addition, the paralyzing agent renders the inmate unable to communicate his agony to his executioners (Denno, 2007).

Mistakes of this sort are fairly common because unskilled prison staff instead of trained medical personnel generally conduct lethal injection executions. The reason trained medical staff do not conduct most executions is because the medical profession's governing bodies have issued guidelines stipulating that taking part in executions is unethical for doctors, nurses, or E.M.T.s. The medical board in North Carolina, for example, has stated that it will consider sanctions for doctors who participate in executions (other than certifying death). This has led the North Carolina Attorney General's office to sue the medical board claiming they have no control over doctor's activities in a "non-medical" procedure (*CBS Evening News*, 2007).

Early Legal Challenges to Lethal Injection

The Oklahoma lethal injection statute was almost immediately adopted by Texas on May 12, 1977, and in September of that year two inmates, Howard Lincoln and Kenneth Granviel, were scheduled for execution by lethal injection. These two inmates both challenged the proposed method of their execution on the grounds that the new method Texas had adopted violated the Eighth Amendment's prohibition against "cruel and unusual punishment." They claimed that the standard of the Eighth Amendment "must draw its meaning from the evolving standards of decency that mark the progress of a maturing society" (citing *Trop v. Dulles*, 1958). Granviel was eventually executed by lethal injection in 1996, and Lincoln's sentence was commuted (Amnesty International, 1998). These early legal challenges to the process are noteworthy because they foreshadowed the hundreds of Eighth Amendment challenges to lethal injection that would be brought over the next 30 years.

The above inference is made due to the fact that it is most unlikely that two states adopted 2 such similar protocols within such a close time frame.

Lethal Injection Employed

Charles Brooks was executed by the state of Texas on December 7, 1982. He was the first person in United States' history to be executed by lethal injection. His execution ushered in a new era in the history of capital punishment. Because Texas carried out the first lethal injection executions, most, if not all, of the other death penalty states that switched to lethal injection simply "Xeroxed" the protocol and adopted it as their own. In fact, many states were carrying out lethal injection executions without any written protocol.

Since the execution of Brooks, Texas has carried out 400 lethal injection executions (as of this writing) of which at least ten executions have been botched (Radelet, 2006). For example, in some cases, executioners have been unable to find suitable veins in which to insert the IVs. Sometimes the search for a suitable vein has taken more than two hours, during which the inmate has suffered a violent reaction to the procedure evidenced by "gasping . . . coughing . . . rearing up against the leather restraints [and muscular] spasms" (Radelet, 2006). Again, one wonders how many times these obvious signs of suffering have been masked by the paralyzing effect of pancuronium bromide. In other states, the venous access problem has been resolved by the execution team performing a procedure known as a "cut-down." This involves an incision being made deeper into the inmate's tissue in order to find a suitable vein for IV insertion. Cut-downs have allowed executioners to insert IVs in the legs, arms, wrists, groin, and even directly into the neck of the condemned, as in the case of Michael Eugene Wilkins in South Carolina in 1997 (Radelet, 2006).

The Current Lethal Injection Controversy

State and Court Responses

The lethal injection "issue" is currently causing so much consternation that the states of Tennessee, Missouri, California, South Dakota, Florida, Ohio, Kentucky, New Jersey, Maryland, North Carolina, Delaware, and Arkansas have recently put holds on all executions by either gubernatorial, judicial (both state and federal), or legislative intervention until the problems with lethal injection can be resolved (The Death Penalty Information Center, 2007).

In California, U.S. District Court Judge Jeremy Fogel declared California's death penalty protocol unconstitutional on Eighth Amendment grounds (*Morales v. Tilton,* 2002). Judge Fogel instructed the state to resubmit a new version of "Operation 770" (California's lethal injection protocol) after what Denno (2007, p. 2) describes as the "longest and most thorough evidentiary hearing ever conducted on any execution method." Fogel ruled that "Operation 770" was unconstitutional "as implemented." In his opinion, he stated that the protocol used by California had "inconsistent and unreliable screening of execution team members" and that it "lack[ed] . . . meaningful training, supervision, and oversight of the lethal injection team" (at 935). Fogel responded in anger to one correctional officer's statement regarding errors in a lethal injection execution. The officer testified, "Shit does happen." Fogel was surely referring to this comment when he wrote of "shockingly indifferent reactions by team members when describing troublesome executions" (*Morales v. Tilton*, 2005).

Missouri was instructed not to carry out any further executions until U.S. District Court Judge Fernando Gaitan was satisfied that the new execution protocols did not violate the Eighth Amendment (The Death Penalty Information Center, 2007). The doctor in charge of Missouri's executions, Dr. Alan Doerhoff, was dyslexic, and admitted under oath that he had "difficulty reading numbers." For a medical practitioner responsible for ensuring the administration of the correct dosage of lethal chemicals, such a disability is troubling at the very least. (*Taylor v. Crawford,* 2005). At the time of writing, Dr. Doerhoff is working at the U.S. Government Lethal Injection Facility in Terre Haute, Indiana. The U.S. Eighth Circuit Court of Appeals overturned Judge Gaitan's ruling on June 4, 2007. In response, Missouri Attorney General Jay Nixon immediately sought execution dates for ten of the states' death row inmates. The original plaintiff is now challenging the Eighth Circuit's ruling on the grounds that "the panel focused too narrowly on the protocol rather than on how it is implemented and any accidents or mistakes that may result" (*The Kansas City Star*, 2007). The plaintiff's counsel argued, "The humaneness of executions depends as much

Table 5.1 Decisions Circuit Court Judges in Capital Cases, by the President Who Appointed Them

President Making Appointment	% of Votes Against Defendant	% of Votes For Defendant
Jimmy Carter (D)	11	89
Ronald Reagan (R)	75	25
George H. W. Bush (R)	93	7
William Clinton (D)	30	70
George W. Bush (R)	87	13

on the Department of Corrections' implementation of the protocol as on the protocol itself" (*The Kansas City Star*, 2007). This argument may be heard by the Eighth Circuit Court of Appeals *en banc*, as opposed to the three-judge panel that considered the original appeal (*The Kansas City Star*, 2007).

The problem of panels hearing execution cases instead of the full court is amply shown in the state of Ohio. *The Cincinnati Enquirer* examined this "judicial lottery" in April, 2007. Four inmates were recently granted stays by a three-judge panel in order to challenge lethal injection on Eighth Amendment grounds, and two other inmates were denied this opportunity by a different three-judge panel. Requests for stays are rarely heard *en banc*. *The Enquirer* interviewed retired Sixth Circuit Judge Nathaniel Jones who said, "It's a roll of the dice. When I look at a line up of a panel in this kind of case, you can almost go to the bank on what the result is going to be. . . . [I]t looks very much like a lottery. Literally, if someone lives or dies depends on the panel they get." Many people would contend that this level of blatant arbitrariness is unacceptable in criminal justice, let alone capital punishment.

The Enquirer also found that the president who appoints judges to the Sixth Circuit has a significant influence on their capital punishment decisions. Table 5.1 clearly shows that judges appointed by Republican presidents are more likely to vote against the defendant in a capital case, whereas judges appointed by Democrats are more likely to vote for the defendant in a capital case.

Judge Boyce Martin neatly summed up this rather bizarre situation in *Alley v. Little* (2006):

> [T]he dysfunctional patchwork of stays and executions going on in this country further undermines the various states' effectiveness and ability to properly carry out death sentences. We are currently operating under a system wherein condemned inmates are bringing nearly identical challenges to the lethal injection procedure. In some instances stays are granted while in others they are not and the defendants are executed, with no principled distinction to justify such a result.

In another case dealing with the same judicial concerns, U.S. District Court Judge Gregory Frost stated:

> [T]his court is now confronted with two different unreported decisions by two different appellate panels, both concerned with the same issues of law and both reaching wholly opposite, unexplained results.... This court's inability to discern the appellate rationale for denying *or* granting a stay does not promote confidence in the system, does not promote consistency in court decisions, and does not promote the fundamental value of fairness that underlies any conception of justice. (The Death Penalty Information Center, 2007)

In contrast, another federal judge has ruled that all inmates on Delaware's death row can be part of a class action lawsuit challenging the constitutionality of Delaware's lethal injection process. This has led to a *de facto* moratorium in that state, which, until recently, was also the situation in Arkansas, for the same reason. Indiana and Oklahoma have rewritten their protocols to avoid U.S. Eighth Amendment challenges that these states suspect might be coming from death row inmates. Even the U.S. government, which had four executions scheduled for 2006, had these dates stayed by the U.S. District Court for the District of Columbia because of the various challenges to the federal government's lethal injection procedure. On the other hand, Tennessee lawmakers have voted to form a commission to study their states' lethal injection protocols but are continuing to allow executions to be carried out while the commission is formed, deliberates, and subsequently delivers its findings (The Death Penalty Information Center, 2007).

The Execution of Angel Nieves Diaz

Many recent studies support the potential unconstitutionality of lethal injection. Denno (1997) and Radelet (2006) discovered 61 botched post-*Furman* executions of which 33 involved lethal injections. One of the most infamous and recent cases of a botched lethal injection was that of Angel Nieves Diaz on December 13, 2006, in Florida. (Death Penalty Information Center, 2007). Mr. Diaz took 34 minutes to die and was seen to be struggling for breath, moving, attempting to speak, and grimacing in pain for the first 24 minutes of the procedure. At his autopsy the medical examiner discovered 11- and 12-inch blisters on his right and left arms, respectively. The problem was that when the execution technician inserted the IV, he pushed the needle through the vein into the surrounding soft tissue. Because this mistake delayed the absorption of the lethal chemicals, Mr. Diaz was administered a second dose.

This botched execution caused such a furor around the world that on December 15, 2006, then-Governor Jeb Bush imposed an immediate moratorium on executions and ordered a commission to be formed to examine the administration of lethal injection in the state of Florida. The moratorium was declared after a press release from the Florida Department of Corrections in which spokeswoman, Gretl Plessinger, was reported to have said that the need to give Mr. Diaz a second dose of lethal chemicals was part of the protocol and expected because he was suffering from liver disease. Plessinger's assertion was curious because the medical examiner that performed the autopsy stated before the commission that he did not see evidence of liver disease in Mr. Diaz. Professor Gravenstein, Chair of the School of Anesthesiology at the University of Florida, provided another troublesome piece of testimony regarding the liver disease claim. Gravenstein stated that none of the drugs administered to Mr. Diaz during the lethal injection procedure would have had their efficiency affected by a diseased liver.

Nevertheless, Governor Bush reiterated Gretl Plessinger's "pre-existing medical condition" excuse in a press release on the day of Mr. Diaz's execution. Both Bush and the Department of Corrections have yet to provide a satisfactory response to the conflicting testimony about whether a second dose of lethal chemicals was needed because of Mr. Diaz's "pre-existing medical condition." Were these public servants incorrect, misled, or simply being mendacious in the face of a public relations disaster?

An anesthesiologist, Dr. David Varlotta, D.O. (a member of the Florida commission), in a presentation before the Florida Society of Anesthesiologists in June 2007, gave further evidence as to what happened at the execution of Angel Nieves Diaz. Dr. Varlotta stated that only 17 states required the presence of a physician during the proceedings, and the states of Illinois and Kentucky specifically forbade the presence of a physician. In many cases the physician is only present to certify death and cannot, or will not, intervene if something untoward or unexpected goes awry during the execution. He also asserted that some witnesses reported that Diaz was conscious for up to 15 minutes, asked, "What's happening?," at least twice, and was observed trying to breathe for at least 24 minutes of the 34-minute execution procedure. The longest previous Florida lethal injection execution lasted 17 minutes before the pronouncement of death. He also set out a timeline of the execution events (taken directly from Dr. Varlotta's PowerPoint presentation):

- Left IV "A"
  - The injection began in the left arm "A"
  - All of the sodium pentothal delivered
  - 25/100 mg of pancuronium
  - Executioner reported he could no longer push on the syringe
  - Advised by a "highly qualified medical individual" to switch to the right IV
- Right IV "B"
  - 75/100 mg of pancuronium
  - All of the KCl [potassium chloride]

    - No change in the heart rate
    - Began a second round of chemicals
    - Gave additional KCl through the left IV
- Coroner's Testimony
    - IVs were through the back wall of the vein on both sides and protruding from skin at a 45 degree angle
    - Large chemical burns on both arms
    - Large fluid filled bullae [Bullae is the plural of bulla. A bulla is a blister more than 5 mm (about 3/16 inch) in diameter with thin walls that are full of fluid.]
    - Skin necrosis [death of tissue in the body]
- Suspicious/Unexplained Evidence
    - Pulmonary edema [swelling or fluid accumulation in the lungs]
    - Jugular venous distention
    - Coronary artery heart disease
    - **NO** significant liver disease [my emphasis]
- Implications
    - All of the chemicals injected into subcutaneous [under the skin] tissue
    - Local burning
    - [Caused by] sodium pentothal and KCl [potassium chloride]
    - If "B" IV functioning [second line, right arm]
    - [Mr. Diaz would have been] awake and paralyzed when heart stopped

The ramifications of Dr. Varlotta's presentation are chilling. Although no one can be sure that line "B" was working, there is no reason to believe otherwise because the problem reported by the executioner seemed to be mainly associated with Line "A."

Following are some of the Florida commission's findings in the case of Angel Nieves Diaz:

- The execution team failed to ensure that the IV line was in Mr. Diaz's arm throughout the execution.
- The execution team did not follow protocol with respect to delivering the chemicals into Mr. Diaz's body.
- The protocols failed to state necessary actions when things went awry.
- The team was very poorly trained.
- In the absence of protocols for unexpected occurrences there was a lack of a leader when these unexpected occurrences did happen.
- The warden was not informed that the executioners were having problems delivering the anesthetic into Mr. Diaz.

Anesthetic Awareness

Whether lethal injection violates the Eighth Amendment's prohibition of cruel and unusual punishment depends significantly on the problem of anesthetic awareness. Anesthetic awareness is the phenomenon of being mentally alert (and terrified) while supposedly under full general anesthesia. Under this condition, the condemned inmate is paralyzed, unable to speak, and totally helpless to communicate his or her awareness.

Carol Weihr, who testified before the Florida Gubernatorial Commission on the Administration of Lethal Injection (a commission at which this author also testified), described the issue and experience of anesthetic awareness to me in February 2007. Ms. Weihr had her right eye removed, and the anesthetic did not work. Because of the paralytic agent (Pavulon) that was administered to her, she was unable to alert the surgical team to her plight and was very painfully aware of the entire procedure. Ms. Weihr said that the potassium chloride felt like the "fires of hell flowing through my veins" (Weihr, 2007).

Ms. Weihr's terrifying experience begs the question: how many of the more than nine hundred inmates executed by lethal injection have experienced anesthetic awareness? For obvious reasons, the answer is unknown. However, recent studies in clinical or hospital settings indicate that incidences of anesthetic awareness are reported between 28,000 and 46,000 times per year in the United States, alone (http://www.anesthesiaawareness.com, accessed June 2007). Because these incidences of anesthetic awareness occur in clinical or hospital settings with highly trained medical staff and oftentimes a highly trained anesthesiologist in the room monitoring the patient constantly, which most certainly is not the case in lethal injection executions, one might expect the rate of anesthetic awareness incidences to be much higher in cases of lethal injection executions.

A study published in the British medical journal *The Lancet* in 2005 provides support for that expectation (see Koniaris et al., 2005). After examining the blood drawn from 49 prisoners executed by lethal injection, the researchers reported that 43 of them had anesthetic levels conducive to possible suffering during the execution, and, as noted above, the prisoners would not have been able to communicate their suffering to their executioners because of the paralyzing drug pancuronium bromide. Thus, concerns about whether lethal injection executions constitute "cruel and unusual punishment" in violation of the Eighth Amendment seem well founded.

As noted previously, the problem of anesthetic awareness is exacerbated by the fact that the individuals inserting the IV lines may have little or no medical training. The Florida executioner who dispatched Angel Nieves Diaz had one "execution" training session in the year 2000 and no further instruction as of March 2007. When asked by the Florida commission whether he had ever received medical training of any kind, he replied, "No" (Anonymous executioner of Angel Diaz, testifying before the Florida commission, February 2007). Dr. Mark Heath, a professor of anesthesia at Columbia University, when testifying before the Florida commission, stated that he would only allow a third-year resident to insert an IV line into a patient in a clinical environment (verbal testimony before the Florida Commission, February, 2007).

According to several other testifying medical doctors, the blisters on the arms of Mr. Diaz were classic signs of sodium thiopental entering muscle/flesh, as opposed to the bloodstream, meaning that little or no anesthetic was delivered to his central nervous system before the suffocating drug and the caustic potassium chloride were introduced into his bloodstream. According to Dr. Heath, the executioner was doing "exactly the wrong thing" when he switched to the line in Mr. Diaz's left arm and went to the second drug in the protocol, pancuronium bromide. These same doctors came to a general consensus that the inmate probably died in agony.

So what was the outcome of the Florida commission's report? A few minor changes in procedure, such as better training, were made but the problematic three-drug cocktail was left untouched. These minor changes seemed to satisfy new Florida governor Charlie Crist, who in July 2007 set the first post-moratorium execution date for the child rapist and murderer Mark Schwab (Crist, 2007). Unfortunately, the minor changes that were made are unlikely to have the desired results.

In a study of lethal injection execution records from California and North Carolina, researchers concluded that better training would not fix the problem because the problem was with the drugs used (Zimmers et al., 2007). The researchers maintained that even with the suggested huge overdose of sodium thiopental, there was still a possibility that the inmate might spontaneously awaken. The researchers remarked,

> Our findings suggest that current lethal injection protocols may not reliably effect death through the mechanisms intended, indicating a failure of design and implementation. . . . Thus the conventional view of lethal injection leading to an invariably peaceful and painless death is questionable. (Zimmers et al., 2007)

The authors further observed:

> [L]ethal injection for judicial execution was designed and implemented with no clinical or basic research whatsoever . . . no ethical or oversight groups have ever evaluated the protocols and outcomes of lethal injection . . . there are no published clinical or experimental data regarding the safety and efficacy of the three-drug cocktail. (Zimmers et al., 2007)

Conclusion

In May 2007, the state of Ohio executed Christopher Newton and it took them 90 minutes and more than ten attempts to find a vein. Newton's execution, along with the execution of Angel Nieves Diaz and the other noted botched lethal injection executions discovered by Denno (1997) and Radelet (2006), shows that similar errors are made in other jurisdictions that use this method of execution. This is not surprising because most of the executing jurisdictions simply copied Oklahoma's flawed protocol and use medically untrained staff. Dr. Chapman, himself, has gone on record as saying that if he were asked to create a protocol now he would not arrive at the same method. "Never in my wildest dreams," remarked Dr. Chapman, "did I foresee this procedure being carried out by untrained medical personnel" (Dr. Jay Chapman's communication with Dr. Mark Heath entered into testimony before the Florida Commission).

> The evidence is clear that the lethal injection protocol, as presently constituted, violates the Eighth Amendment's prohibition of cruel and unusual punishment. Too many capital offenders executed by lethal injection have experienced "torture," "unnecessary cruelty," and "lingering death . . . something more than the mere extinguishment of life" (see *Wilkerson v. Utah*, 1878; *In re Kemmler*, 1890). At the very least, moratoriums on lethal injection executions should be imposed or continued until the problems with lethal injection executions described in this chapter are corrected.

It is clear that additional medical research is needed, as opposed to gubernatorial commissions that seem to be designed to appease the public and subsequently have their findings ignored. This research should be specific to the three-drug protocol used nationwide and should be carried out by independent scientists. Sadly, as we have seen in many cases over the past 18 months, without the political will to listen, change, and admit error, then research, commissions, and working groups are a waste of both time and money.

Addendum

On September 25, 2007 the United States Supreme Court granted *certiorari* in the case of *Baze v. Rees* resulting in a seemingly *de facto* death penalty moratorium across all death penalty jurisdictions.

References

Amnesty International. (1998). Lethal injection: The medical technology of execution, http://www.web.amnesty.org/library/Index/engACT500011998 (retrieved July 2007).

Anti-Defamation League, www.adl.org. (retrieved Aug. 2007).

Bohm, R.M. (2007). *Deathquest III: An Introduction to the Theory and Practice of Capital Punishment in the United States.* Cincinnati: Anderson.

CBS Evening News. (2007). Doctors vs. executions in North Carolina (May 8, 2007) at http://www.cbsnews.com/stories/2007/05/08/eveningnews/main2777288.shtml.
Cincinnati Enquirer. (2007). The 6th Circuit considers death penalty appeal cases from Ohio, Kentucky, and Tennessee (April 15) at http://news.enquirer.com.
Crist, Governor C. (2007). Letter to Warden Randall Bryant of Florida State Prison authorizing the execution of Mark Dean Schwab between 11/12/2007 and 11/19/2007 (July 18). Available at http://www.dc.state.fl.us.
Death Penalty Information Center. (1997). Available at http://www.deathpenaltyinfo.org. Website consulted June 2007.
Denno, D. (1997). Getting to death: Are executions constitutional? *Iowa Law Review* 82: 319–464.
Denno, D. (2007). Personal communication.
Denno, D. (2002). When legislatures delegate death: The troubling paradox behind state uses of electrocution and lethal injection and what it says about us. *Ohio State Law Journal* 63:1–260.
Denno, D. (2006). Death bed. *Triquarterly Journal* 124: 141–168.
Denno, D. (2007). The lethal injection quandary: How medicine has dismantled the death penalty (working paper).
Human Rights Watch. (2006). *So long as they die: Lethal injections in the United States* at http://hrw.org/reports/2006/us0406/. Website consulted June 2007.
Koniaris, L.G., T.A. Zimmers, D.A. Lubarsky, and J.P. Sheldon. (2005). Inadequate anaesthesia in lethal injection for execution. *The Lancet* 365 (accessed through http://www.sciencedirect.com).
Lethal Injection Manual State of Missouri. (1988). Fred A. Leuchter Associates, Inc., Lethal Injection System, Operation and Instruction Manual (October 15) at http://www.angelfire.com/fl3/stark/injection.html.
Morris, E. (1999). *Mr. Death: The Rise and Fall of Fred Leuchter, Jr.* Fourth Floor Productions.
New challenge to Missouri's lethal injections. (2007). *The Kansas City Star* (July 2) at www.kansascity.com.
North Carolina Corrections Department sues to restart executions. (2007). Available at http://www.jurist.law.pitt.edu. Website consulted August 2007.
Oklahoma Lethal Injection Statute, Ch. 1014.
Radelet, M. (2006). *Some examples of botched post Furman executions*, at http://www.deathpenaltyinfo.org/article.php?scid=8&did=478 (retrieved July 2007).
Report of the British Royal Commission on Capital Punishment by Command of Her Majesty the Queen. H.M.'s Stationary Office. September 1953.
Ward, M. (2006). Death penalty's drug cocktail rooted in Texas. *Austin American-Statesman* (May 28) at http://www.deathpenaltyinfo.org.
Weihr, C. (2007). Personal communication (February).
Weinstein, H. (November 15, 2007). Doctors barred by Missouri helps in federal executions. *Los Angeles Times*. Available at http://www.latimes.com. Website consulted December 2007.
Zimmers, T.A., J. Sheldon, D.A. Lubarsky, F. Lopez-Munoz, L. Waterman, R. Weisman, and L.G. Koniaris. (2007). *Lethal injection for execution: Chemical asphyxiation?* At www.plosmedicine.com (retrieved June 2007).

Cases Cited

Alley v. Little, No. 06-5650 (6th Cir., May 16, 2006) (Martin, J., dissenting from denial of a rehearing *en banc*).

Baze v. Rees, 07-5439 (2007).

Furman v. Georgia, 408 U.S. 238 (1972).

Gregg vs. Georgia, 428 U.S. 153 (1976).

In re Kemmler, 136 U.S. 436 (1890).

Morales v. Tilton, C06 219 JFRS (2002), C06 926 JFRS (2005).

Trop v. Dulles, 356 U.S. 86 (1958).

Wilkerson v. Utah, 99 U.S. 130 (1878).

Taylor v. Crawford, U.S. 8th Cir. No. 06-13-97.

2

Death Penalty Opinion, Media Access to Executions, Consensual Executions, and the Relationship between Lynching and the Death Penalty

Assessing Scholarly Opinion of Capital Punishment: The Experts Speak[1]

6

MATTHEW B. ROBINSON

Contents

Introduction

The main arguments in favor of capital punishment are that it is a legal punishment, carried out under constitutional authority by the federal and state governments, and that it is deserved by those who receive it. In the simplest terms, advocates of capital punishment assert that death is a proper punishment for those who commit the most heinous crimes because offenders owe their lives to society as payment for the harms they inflicted on society (retribution). Furthermore, the death penalty makes us safer by causing fear in would-be murderers so that they do not commit their crimes (deterrence) and by taking away the lives of murderers who might murder again if not executed (incapacitation) (Cassell, 2004; Pojman, 2004; Pojman & Reiman, 1998; van den Haag, 1997).

The main arguments against capital punishment are that it is morally wrong, it is cruel and unusual, it constitutes a human rights violation, and that its practice is plagued by numerous problems (Bedau, 2004; Bright, 2004; Reiman, 1998; Zimring, 2003). Although some opponents of capital punishment reject it for moral reasons (Bedau, 1997), others reject the death penalty for the way it is applied (National Coalition to Abolish the Death Penalty, 2006). The main problems that allegedly plague the application of capital punishment in the United States are it is exploited for political reasons, it is excessively costly, it is applied in an arbitrary and discriminatory manner, it is occasionally used against the innocent, and capital juries are confused about their job and often make mistakes.

This chapter presents the findings from a survey of death penalty experts that assesses whether the experts think the justifications of capital punishment stated above are actually achieved. Also presented are findings with regard to whether the experts believe there are "fatal flaws" to the death penalty. The survey on which this study is based addressed the issues of bias (arbitrariness and/or discrimination) by race, class, and gender, and the innocence issue. The goal of the study was to capture the reality of the death penalty in the United States, according to the experts who study it for a living.

Justifications for Capital Punishment

Vengeance and Retribution

Vengeance is a strong human emotion for revenge when a person is harmed by another. Research shows that vengeance is one of the normal emotions felt by family members of murder victims, along with grief, loss, and so forth. The five stages of grief, according to the evidence, are denial and isolation, anger, bargaining, depression, and acceptance (Kubler-Ross & Kessler, 2005). Vengeance, which is most likely to accompany anger, is not the same as retribution. Essentially, vengeance is a private emotion sought by individuals rather than a collective response by society. Retribution is a state-sponsored, rational response to criminality that is justified given that the state is the victim when a crime occurs. It is punishment given to an offender aimed at rebalancing the scales of justice that were unfairly tipped in the favor of the offender when he or she committed a crime.

In sum, although retribution and vengeance are related, they are not synonymous. First, vengeance is private but retribution is public. Vengeance is a human emotion experienced by individual people. Retribution is a collective response to wrongdoing from society rather than individual family members. Also, it is not rooted in emotion but instead in logic and rationality.

Second, vengeance is not justified by law, as is retribution. Although it is natural to feel intense emotions when harmed and to want to get even with those who harm you, it is not appropriate in law to engage in vigilantism. Retribution is appropriate, legal, and justified.

Third, vengeance entails the offender being paid back by the victim, but retribution entails the offender paying back society. An example of vengeance would be a murder victim's family member taking the law into his or her own hands for the purpose of settling a personal vendetta in order to (temporarily) feel better. Retribution is a rational process and outcome that instead aims to have the offender pay back society for the harm inflicted by him or her; in the case of murder, one manifestation of retribution is the offender paying society with his or her life to make amends for the harms he or she committed.

Finally, vengeance is thought to be a natural emotion rooted in our biology, but retribution is believed to be the product of socialization. That is, whereas vengeance generally does not lead to any real (permanent) social benefit, retribution through punishment can help in the process of defining and reinforcing social norms. Capital punishment in earlier American history clearly had a better chance of achieving this function when thousands of citizens turned out to watch executions in order to state a strong moral objection to the crimes committed by offenders and to demand justice for those harmed (Banner, 2003).

One major issue of contention with regard to retribution is whether capital punishment actually achieves retribution. The findings of this study answer this question.

Deterrence

Deterrence is the notion that by administering punishment to offenders, the state can cause fear in both the offender (special deterrence or specific deterrence) and in others (general deterrence) so that they will not want to commit crimes in the future. Obviously, capital punishment cannot achieve special or specific deterrence because once the offender is dead, he or she cannot be afraid of future punishment. When people speak of the death penalty as a special deterrent or specific deterrent, they actually mean it prevents the murderer from killing again (which is actually a form of incapacitation rather than deterrence). Does capital punishment serve as a general deterrent by deterring would-be murderers, thereby saving lives? The findings of this study address that question.

Incapacitation

Incapacitation, as noted above, means taking away a person's freedom so that he or she cannot commit another crime. Although the typical form of incapacitation is incarceration (in a jail or prison), and the most common form is relatively mild (probation), the ultimate form of incapacitation is death. As with retribution, incapacitation is a legitimate justification for the administration of punishment because the primary responsibility of government is to protect its citizens from harm, and one of the goals of America's systems of criminal justice is to reduce criminality. The main issue of contention with regard to incapacitation is whether the death penalty is needed to achieve incapacitation. That is, could incapacitation be better achieved using another form of punishment, such as life imprisonment without the possibility of parole? The findings of this study address this question.

Problems with the Death Penalty

Arbitrariness and Discrimination

The death penalty in America is imposed arbitrarily because it is not mandatory upon conviction of certain crimes, and prosecutors and juries have much discretion in its use. Arbitrary means "determined by chance, whim, or impulse, and not by necessity, reason, or principle" (Dictionary.com, 2006). Arbitrariness occurs when capital punishment is based on extra-legal factors such as race, class, and gender that are not explained away by legal factors such as statutorily prescribed aggravating factors. The main issues of contention in terms of arbitrariness are whether death sentences and executions are arbitrary, and if so, does the presence of arbitrariness mean capital punishment is discriminatory. This chapter presents findings with regard to those questions.

Innocence

The most troubling allegation against the administration of capital punishment in the United States is that occasionally innocent people are wrongly convicted, sentenced to death, and executed. One might think that if this criticism could be proven empirically, every death penalty state would either halt using capital punishment or develop such severe restrictions on its use that innocent people could not be wrongly convicted and the punishment would virtually never be used. Conversely, it is possible that the execution of the innocent might be seen as a necessary evil in the pursuit of justice. The main issues of contention with regard to innocence are whether any innocent persons have been executed, how many, and does it matter? This chapter presents findings with regard to these questions.

Other Problems

Scholars have raised other alleged problems with capital punishment. They include the excessive cost of the punishment, problems with capital jurors, poor quality legal representation, a growing international isolation of the United States with regard to the practice, and many others. This chapter presents findings with regard to whether the administration of capital punishment is plagued by such other problems.

Methodology

A survey was created to address theoretical justifications and alleged problems with capital punishment. The survey was meant to assess whether capital punishment experts thought the death penalty met its goals and whether it was plagued by significant problems. The survey also assesses whether experts support capital punishment (or alternatives such as life imprisonment without the possibility of parole), and whether they favor a temporary halt on executions (moratorium) and/or abolition of capital punishment.

A sample of death penalty experts was selected to participate in the study. For purposes of this study, an expert was defined as a person with a high degree of knowledge of capital punishment, someone who is widely recognized as a reliable source of knowledge due to prolonged experience through practice and education related to the death penalty, and whose judgment is accorded authority and status by the public or their peers. Experts in this study consisted of capital punishment scholars, people who had recently published books and articles on the death penalty.

An earlier study of "expert opinion" of the deterrent effect of capital punishment was based on a survey of current and former presidents of the American Society of Criminology (ASC), the Academy of Criminal Justice Sciences (ACJS), and the Law and Society Association (LSA). In the article, which focused exclusively on the issue of deterrence, the authors wrote:

> [W]e must first answer the question of how to define "expert." One plausible definition is anyone who has published peer-reviewed research on the death penalty and deterrence. Surely those who have been active researchers in an area over many years are experts. However, such an approach has limited utility because 1) it is possible that only death penalty abolitionists, for whatever reasons, are motivated to conduct such research, 2) there would be a problem in differentially weighing the opinions of scholars who have published several acclaimed deterrence studies in major criminology journals from those whose research is less abundant or respected, and 3) surveying researchers in the field of deterrence would ask them to, in effect, evaluate their own work. (Radelet & Akers, 1996)

For these reasons, the authors of that study chose not to survey scholars who had published in the area of deterrence, but instead chose to survey presidents of major criminological organizations. In the current study published scholarly experts were chosen, meaning the three limitations identified above apply to this study.

The total sample of death penalty experts was 96 individual scholars who either had written books or articles on the death penalty between 2001 and 2005. After sending out surveys to each of the 96 experts, it was learned that two of them had recently passed away, reducing the sample size to 94 experts. Others had moved to new jobs and may have never received the surveys. Completed surveys were received from 45 respondents. Thus, 47.9 percent of the 94 experts chosen for the sample participated in the study. Ideally, a higher number of responses might have been more useful, but a response rate of 47.9 percent is considered adequate for studies conducted via the mail (Babbie, 2003).

Some possible reasons why the response rate was not higher are the length of the survey (12 pages), the controversial nature of some of the questions, and because some individuals did not want to be identified. In retrospect, designing the survey to be entirely anonymous probably could have increased the response rate and sample size.

The data presented in this chapter are limited in several ways. First, there is some question about whether all scholarly capital punishment experts had a chance to be included in the sample. When attempting to locate death penalty experts, the focus was on books and articles using the search terms "capital punishment" and "death penalty" in the subject line of the databases. Conceivably, scholars who published works on capital punishment-related topics who supplied different subject terms or whose works were categorized for some reason under different terms would not show up in the searches. There is no way to know how many of these individuals were excluded.

Second, there is also some question about the representative nature of the experts. It is likely that most scholarly experts on capital punishment are opposed to the punishment. That is, it is probable that most people who write about the death penalty have not only an academic interest in the death penalty but also have recognized some problem(s) with it that motivates their writings. Similar to the suggestion of the authors of the study of presidents of major criminological organizations discussed earlier, the findings of the study might reflect the biased opinions of the sample of experts surveyed. This assumes that scholars who support the death penalty are less active in scholarship because they have no (or little) problem with the practice of capital punishment in the United States or because the sanction is legal and thus not likely to generate writings that seek to justify its use.

Third, no effort was made to distinguish between those experts who have published an enormous amount of work on the death penalty in top journals or with university presses, from those experts who have published less work in lower-tiered journals or with textbook publishers. Yet, as someone who teaches and reads a good bit about the death penalty, this author is very confident that the individuals who participated in this study do comprise a highly qualified and respected sample of experts as a group. Perhaps follow-up research will verify or refute this claim. In this study, no single expert's voice was given more amplification than the others.

As a result of these limitations, it is possible that the data presented are not representative of the opinions of all death penalty experts. There is no way to know if this is true. Yet, it appears that the sample is comprised of most of the top experts on the topic of capital punishment. The study is also superior to the earlier study of current and past presidents of major criminological societies because not all of the presidents surveyed were death penalty experts. In fact, few likely had studied the death penalty in any detail whatsoever. The authors of that study acknowledged this, writing, "although few of these scholars have done research on capital punishment in general or deterrence in particular, they are generally well versed in central criminological issues, such as crime causation, crime prevention, and criminal justice policy" (Radelet & Akers, 1996). Those who participated in the current study were all capital punishment experts who represent at least 625 years of research on capital punishment, 345 years of teaching about the death penalty, and 273 years of activism related to the death penalty.

Findings: The Experts' Views

Does Capital Punishment, as Actually Practiced in the United States, Achieve Retribution (i.e., Provide Justice for Murder Victims, Their Families, and Society at Large)?

As shown in Table 6.1, the largest proportion of capital punishment experts (36 percent) responded that they did not think the death penalty achieves retribution, but a sizable proportion of death penalty experts (31 percent) indicated that it did ("provide justice for murder victims, their families, and

Table 6.1 Expert Opinion on Whether Capital Punishment Achieves Retribution.

Yes	31%
No	36%
Unsure	33%
N = 42	

society at large"). Another third of the experts (33 percent) answered they were unsure.

The Death Penalty Does Not Achieve Retribution

Experts who responded that the death penalty did not achieve retribution claimed that the death penalty is not used frequently enough to achieve retribution. For example, one expert wrote that the death penalty "is imposed far too infrequently and illogically to serve as retribution." Another expert agreed, writing: "At the present time, capital punishment is utilized far too infrequently to provide justice for more than a few murder victims and their families."

One respondent wrote that capital punishment might provide retribution for families of murder victims, "but it can't for broader society. No social science evidence to suggest that it has any 'therapeutic' value for anyone." Similarly, an additional respondent reasoned: "There is no retribution possible after a murder because the scales of justice can never be balanced. No amount of punishment will redeem the value of the dead victim."

Other experts focused on what actually happens to victims' families after executions. For example, one expert explained: "Research indicates many families still feel sorrow and have no sense of closure. What is needed is counseling for the families and friends of murder victims. Additionally, retribution is not a good goal for society. The offender can be punished and society protected by using LWOP." Another answered this way:

> This is a difficult question to answer because it is to some degree a matter of opinion. I expect that there are families of murder victims who do feel that the execution of the perpetrator provided justice for them. Others feel the precise opposite. In a broader sense, the failings of the criminal justice system and the inequities of society at large make it unlikely that any punishment could be imposed in a way that provided retribution. In an ideal society in which burdens and benefits were distributed solely on the basis of merit, the situation might be different. Given the system we have and the propensity of humans to error, it is impossible that we can impose death sentences in a just way, making it impossible that we can achieve justice through this punishment.

One expert who answered that the death penalty does not achieve retribution focused on philosophical issues related to retribution and the issue of wrongful convictions and execution of the innocent, writing:

> Retributivism, at least as Kant and other deontological philosophers have postulated it, requires equal respect for the individual autonomy of all persons. Thus, the consistent retributivist must show equal concern for innocent people who are executed. Moreover . . . our present capital punishment system increases the probability of convicting and executing the innocent.

> While the retributivist might argue that in an ideal world there would be a one-to-one correlation between guilt and execution, in the real world and any we can hypothesize, it is inevitable that we will execute the innocent. And the true retributivist is not concerned with instrumental justifications—it should not matter whether the death penalty deters, is racist, or has excessive costs associated with it. The retributivist is not concerned with justifying moral outcomes by appealing to consequences; the only thing that matters is whether each individual gets his or her just deserts. So the true retributivist must be concerned by a system that systematically gets it wrong as much as ours does. Those who are innocent are plainly getting unjust punishment, not just deserts. The problem of innocence is the Achilles heel for retributive justifications of capital punishment. A mixed retributivist fares no better on this analysis. What is this claimed benefit of 'respect for the majesty of the law' that they gain as against the loss of innocent persons lives. These kinds of arguments strike me as bootstrapped and bordering on incoherence.

Another expert who also answered that the death penalty does not achieve retribution focused on not only philosophical issues related to retribution but also to harms caused by the death penalty process:

> I don't think retribution is an appropriate motivation for punishment. How can you make things right for someone who is dead? You cannot. That is nonsense. It is also highly variable as to how well the families are served. Many think that it will bring closure, but it usually does not. Others are more victimized by the death penalty than served. Many families of victims oppose capital punishment. None benefit from going through the repeated cycles of the appeals process and concurrent media attention. As for society, I think it feeds into a very negative part of our psyche, feeds our aggression. Furthermore, it creates a new class of victims—friends and families of the accused as well as those working within the system.

Similarly, one expert who indicated that the death penalty does not achieve retribution focused on his belief that the death penalty is destructive:

> Of course, I can't speak for any particular murder victims or their families, so this is a tough question to answer. In the broader sense, I don't think the death penalty serves these populations well at all. It may indeed achieve some sense of revenge or retribution for some co-victims or some members of society at large, but it certainly does not for others. The bigger question is: Is serving this form of revenge constructive or destructive for these individuals (or society at large)? My answer to this would be that it is destructive.

One capital punishment expert who answered that the death penalty does not achieve retribution addressed the wording of the question, suggested that capital punishment is destructive and also nontransparent:

> The wording of your question implies that retribution (i.e., "a paying of tribute," "something given or exacted in recompense," as my Webster's has it) is justice: a life for a life. I'm sure you're aware that this model of justice is only one of several proposed by criminologists and sociologists. I don't think the retributive model is the most constructive one. It throws away a human life and makes killers of every citizen of the polity—man, woman, and child. At the same time, the way execution is handled distances us from what our political and enforcement representatives are doing in our name. Last, retribution encourages us to believe that meting out punishment is a transparent process, potentially a simple one. Our retributive system hides the realities, including but not limited to the prevalence of plea bargaining, the inequalities of legal representation, and the numerical tokenism of the death penalty.
>
> "A life for a life" will always attract a following if only because it's a story—someone is killed, the killer is pursued while we look on in breathless suspense, then the killer is killed in turn. That's hard to beat for closure. And recent research into the human brain suggests that we're wired to look for closure with almost as much urgency as for food, shelter, and sex. Story trumps argument. That's why we need our justice system—so that argument, reason, and making the case can sometimes win.

The Death Penalty Achieves Retribution

Respondents who believe that the death penalty achieves retribution explained that at the least, capital punishment "provides justice for murder victims, their families, and society at large" in at least some cases. For example, one expert wrote that "in some cases it clearly does." Another respondent said: "Sporadically so, for some." And another expert wrote: "It does in some cases but fails to do so in many cases."

One respondent was adamant about the retributive effect of capital punishment, writing: "Of the various historical, economical, political, ideological, and practical arguments made by those who favor capital punishment, retribution is the ONLY issue supported by empirical evidence; that is, when analyzed by the totality of events, circumstances, and experiences of the offender, victim, legal system, and society." Another expert who answered that capital punishment achieves retribution wrote: "It is an emotional response to the horrific crime of murder."

One expert, who answered that the death penalty achieves retribution, explained:

> By "retribution," I mean taking from the criminal the advantage he has unfairly taken by committing the crime in question. Any penalty assigned according to the principles of a reasonably just legal system . . . will do that (the death penalty as much as any human penalty). Justice for the victims or families is a civil matter for which a tort claim is the appropriate remedy; it is a matter of compensation rather than retribution. Criminal justice is retribution (with or without clemency).

Although a large proportion of experts acknowledged that the death penalty achieves retribution, they did so reluctantly and with major caveats. For example, one expert wrote: "I would think the [death penalty] does provide for retribution, but the delay in actually carrying out the execution may serve to lessen any retributive effect." Another expert agreed, writing: "To a limited extent. Because of its uncertainties and delays, it is often uncertain as to if [and] when families of victims will receive the sense of completion that an execution sometimes brings."

Others pointed out that alternatives to capital punishment would also provide for retribution. For example, one expert wrote: "It can reasonably be argued that death for murder is a morally just punishment. It is not the only morally just punishment, but it is one." Another said: "Yes—it may achieve retribution for murder victims & some families but [life imprisonment without parole] (LWOP) would also severe [sic] retribution (I feel)."

One expert who indicated that capital punishment achieves retribution focused on the issue of fairness. He wrote: "It is administered in a manner that is as fair as humanly possible. The crime categories narrow the types of murder that are death-eligible and prosecutors further narrow the pool to those that are most culpable."

Unsure

Death penalty experts who were unsure whether the death penalty achieved retribution provided numerous justifications for their answers. One simply said: "Retribution is a philosophical notion with no unambiguous empirical referent." Another respondent who answered unsure wrote that it is "[h]ard to pinpoint what is 'deserved' and what punishment is 'equal in value' to any crime based largely on moral considerations. I would generally think this impossible to determine." Another who answered unsure wrote: "The definition of 'retribution' as encompassing 'justice' remains a contested concept. I would say it allows for 'an eye for an eye,' but whether that is just is difficult to say." Another answered: "Unsure . . . As a philosophical matter, one can be a retributivist while at the same time rejecting death as a legitimate form of punishment."

One respondent wrote that it:

> depends on whether you consider retribution to be a subjective experience or an objectively identifiable phenomenon. We know that many victims' families are not satisfied with [capital punishment] while others are satisfied by a life sentence. I am not sure what people (i.e., politicians) mean when they say a punishment must be consistent with the wishes of the community. Who is this "community"? How does a prosecutor or judge or politician know what the will of the people is other than a survey/poll that shows a majority opinion? I am not sure that making justice decisions upon the majority opinion is always the best policy.

Another pointed out: "You can argue this point both ways: in some cases it has brought 'closure.' Many people maintain that retribution requires the death penalty. I would argue that a life sentence achieves retribution without risking the execution of an innocent person. Besides, and to my point about victims' families, that most people 'feel' a sense of retribution does not justify the use of the death penalty." Another expert who answered unsure wrote: "I suppose it achieves retribution for some victims' families, but other victims' families don't necessarily want retribution—it won't bring their loved ones back and, once the offender is dead, closure may not necessarily follow. It is a desire to see someone pay for their actions, and all of us feel this way at one time or another. However, I am not sure the [death penalty] is the way to do it." Similarly, another respondent wrote: "Probably some murder victims' families and some members of society think so, but non-death penalty jurisdictions (both inside & outside the U.S.) are apparently able to achieve justice without capital punishment."

Some experts who answered unsure to the question of retribution also focused on harms produced by the death penalty process. For example, one expert said: "It seems that victims are re-victimized by having to re-live the nightmare—as the justice wheels slowly turn." Another expert said: "There are no studies that establish one way or the other what, if anything, the death penalty does for victims' families. It is my suspicion that the death penalty actually harms family members and victims' families would be better off without it. So even if victims' families were to say that the death penalty provided them with retribution, I think it may come at a high cost to them." And one expert pointed out that although the death penalty "may be expressive of moral condemnation (retribution) it may also be, instead, an expression of moral outrage (vengeance)."

Finally, two respondents who answered unsure to retribution questioned the way the definition of retribution was defined in the survey and whether retribution was even an appropriate goal of capital punishment. The first wrote: "Justice for murder victims is not an element of retribution. Retribution is about giving the offender what he deserves." The second said: "I'm not sure that retribution is or should be a goal of capital punishment."

Does Capital Punishment, as Actually Practiced in the United States, Achieve Deterrence (i.e., Prevent Future Murders by Causing Fear in Would-Be Murderers So That They Do Not Commit Murder)?

As shown in Table 6.2, only a small fraction of death penalty experts (9 percent) indicated that they thought capital punishment achieves deterrence ("prevents future murders by causing fear in would-be murderers so that they do not commit murder"). The largest proportion of capital

Table 6.2 Expert Opinion on Whether Capital Punishment Achieves Deterrence.

Yes	9%
No	79%
Unsure	12%
$N = 43$	

punishment experts (79 percent) responded that they did not think the death penalty achieves deterrence, and 12 percent answered they were unsure.

The Death Penalty Does Not Achieve Deterrence

Many experts were insistent that the death penalty does not deter. For example, one expert answered: "It clearly does not. I am in the midst of a meta-analysis of studies examining the deterrent effects of capital punishment. So far only poorly executed studies produce evidence of any deterrent effect. Upon correction the data used for many of these studies fails to support deterrence." Another said: "The empirical evidence I know does not convince me that death is any better a deterrent than life in prison."

Another expert, citing the empirical evidence, wrote: "The research strongly suggests that capital punishment has little deterrence value. Most murderers are not rational people who think out their actions. Moreover, many murderers give little care about living or dying. In fact, the research suggests that the death penalty may actually increase violent crime." Another expert agreed: "No debate here for me. Never has deterred; never will deter. [Cesare] Beccaria is on target here: life imprisonment carries as much, if not more, deterrent value (of course, Beccaria argues for life imprisonment at hard labor, which I cannot support)." And so did another: "Studies show that the death penalty is not a superior deterrent than [life imprisonment without the possibility of parole] (LWOP)—no I don't feel that [capital punishment] achieves deterrence."

One expert suggested that the "[e]vidence is clear: it doesn't deter [and] probably increases murder rates." Another respondent agreed, writing:

> A detailed, careful, and honest investigation of capital punishment in the United States does not support the deterrence thesis. Likewise, a sound examination of the existing empirical literature on capital punishments reveals that deterrence is minimally achieved, if at all. To the contrary, there is some evidence showing the *increase* of homicide, following an execution—better known as the "brutalization effect." Hence, the concept of "deterrence" has little to do with practicality . . . it's simply a powerful political weapon used by policymakers during elections . . . and to silence a feared society.

One expert answered that the "weight of evidence suggests little if any deterrent effect." And another wrote that capital punishment "does not deter others from committing similar crimes in the future." An additional expert answered no and wrote: "I assume you mean by comparison to a system of sentencing murderers to life in prison." Similarly, another respondent answered: "In this question . . . it is not a matter of how I feel; it's a matter of what the evidence shows. My study of the history of capital punishment and my reading of the research evidence leads me to conclude that the death penalty has no marginal deterrent effect greater than that of alternate punishments."

One respondent answered that the death penalty does not deter and referenced an example from England in the 16th through 18th centuries: "The research clearly demonstrates that it does not. I always tell my students about hangings at Tyburn, which were public outings, almost festivals. As the pickpockets swung from the gallows, guess who worked the crowds? Yep, you've got it—the pickpockets. Not much deterrence, was there?"

Other answers from experts who said the death penalty does not deter murder include:

- "Not the way it is currently carried out in the U.S."
- "No. I'm not persuaded by the recent studies finding a deterrent effect."
- "I know of no credible studies that suggest capital punishment is an effective deterrent."
- "Deterrence is a scientifically weak claim, no evidence to support it that meets social science standards for causal inference."
- Lots of evidence on this."
- "To the best of my knowledge, there is not meaningful evidence that [capital punishment] deters murder or any other crime. The earlier studies that reported deterrent effects have been seriously challenged on methodological & substantive grounds. It simply defies common sense, logic, and human experience to think that [capital punishment] will prevent a murder, but a life sentence will not. Individuals contemplating death eligible crimes are simply not evaluating potential punishment in a manner necessary of [capital punishment] to be a deterrent. On the other hand, I do not think that [capital punishment] has a significant 'brutalization' impact either. I do not think that we conduct enough executions to affect public/individual psyches in the manner suggested by such hypotheses."
- "If deterrence is achieved, then states that use the [death penalty] extensively—[Texas, Virginia], etc.—should have the lowest murder rates in the nation. Deterrence assumes that offenders are thinking about the consequences of their actions [and] the [death penalty] is largely the result of prosecutorial discretion—these cases are so selectively chosen to move forward, how could it possibly be a deterrent?"

- "Except for specific deterrence [incapacitation], the death penalty does not deter. States with the death penalty often have higher murder rates than neighboring states without the death penalty."

Perhaps the most forceful answer about the deterrence issue was this one: "No one, not even the most vehement prosecutor, makes this argument today. With only one in a hundred killers getting a death sentence, and only one in three or four of these eventually being executed, the odds are pretty slim—if murderers were calculating odds, which most are not at the time of the crime."

Another forceful answer addressed the issue of the irrational nature of murder:

> Please—I can't believe anyone is still wasting time on this one. Playing the game of finding that one 0.001th of a statistical advantage point and getting a journal article/consulting career out of it. What does actual observation say about how a killing takes place? "Let's see (mmm, this rock is some good sh*t, must put the dealer on my dialer!)—does this state have the death penalty, or should I go to Michigan to rob a convenience store/kill my ex-wife's boyfriend/cover up my other illegal activities with a little murder? Screw it, my beater of car won't take me that far. Anyway, they'll never catch me. . . ." Someone under a compulsion—be it addiction, rage, sexual desire, jealousy, or deviance, fear, greed—making up the scenario as s/he goes along, and dumb, egotistical, or unimaginative enough to believe in not getting caught.

Some respondents who said that the death penalty did not achieve deterrence were less adamant about their responses. For example, one expert wrote: "Probably not." Another responded:

> The empirical evidence is mixed. Sociologists say no. Economists say yes. My research . . . shows that what first appears to support the relationship is but an illusory correlation upon closer examination. Given that [Texas] actually accounts for the overall relationship found by economists examining U.S. data . . . it is unlikely that a properly specified model will find evidence of deterrence. However, this is not to say that it may not exist, but that it is simply impossible to measure empirically (you know, an event that does not occur).

Other experts who answered that capital punishment is not a deterrent speculated that it might actually deter some murderers but that the effect would be cancelled out by the opposite effects of executions on crime. For example, one expert wrote: "It may deter some individuals, but that effect is probably canceled out by its counter deterrent or brutalizing effect. It does not appear to have a marginal deterrent effect." Other respondents answered: "I do not believe that the death penalty provides any additional deterrent value beyond LWOP. I also think that some of the research indicating that the death penalty may actually increase crime is very persuasive;" and: "The evidence suggests that deterrence of any consequence does not occur due to the death penalty. Of course, this is still debated by many, but my own personal feeling on it is that any marginal amount of deterrent effect is overridden by a brutalization effect."

The Death Penalty Achieves Deterrence

The few experts who responded that the death penalty achieves deterrence cited some research. For example, one expert answered that the "[l]atest studies support this." Another answered: "At the present time, capital punishment is utilized far too infrequently to provide a strong deterrent to homicide. But on the basis of my own research on capital punishment, I believe there is a statistically perceivable deterrent effect, although it is a numerically quite weak effect owing to the infrequency of application."

Finally, one respondent answered this way:

> To say otherwise would be to admit that potential murderers are not rational (and thus admit that they should not be subject to criminal justice at all). I have no doubt that the death penalty, like most lesser penalties, has some deterrent effect. I also have no doubt that is the wrong question to ask. The right question is whether the death penalty has significantly more deterrent effect than lesser penalties (even, say, ten years imprisonment). After two centuries of trying to establish that it does, I think we are entitled to conclude that whatever added deterrent effect the death penalty has (and I believe it must have some), it is not large—not large enough to measure.

Unsure

Two experts responded they were unsure about the deterrent value of capital punishment. One said the death penalty "probably has a slight effect." Another answered: "There [are] data on both sides of the deterrence argument. I don't believe it has (or can be) adequately studied in order to assess—certainty and timeliness have never been part of the research equation." Finally, one respondent who did not provide a yes or no answer to the question nevertheless noted that the question I asked about deterrence was "poorly framed." He added: "I believe that [capital punishment] probably does deter some crimes but so does imprisonment. I think there is *no evidence* that [capital punishment] deters *better* than prison."

Does Capital Punishment, as Actually Practiced in the United States, Achieve Incapacitation (i.e., Prevent Future Murders By Killing Murderers Who Would Murder Again)?

As shown in Table 6.3, most death penalty experts (64 percent) indicated they thought capital punishment achieves incapacitation ("prevents future

Table 6.3 Expert Opinion on Whether Capital Punishment Achieves Incapacitation.

Yes	64%
No	24%
Unsure	12%
N = 41	

murders by killing murderers who would murder again"). Yet, about a quarter of capital punishment experts (24 percent) responded that they did not think the death penalty achieves incapacitation, and 12 percent were unsure.

The Death Penalty Achieves Incapacitation

Experts who responded that the death penalty achieves incapacitation explained that evidence of incapacitation was obvious with each execution. One expert, really speaking about incapacitation, wrote that the death penalty "has a specific deterrent effect—those who are executed are unable to commit more crimes. While death row and life sentence murderers do (very rarely) escape, generally, life sentences serve a similar function." Another replied similarly, saying only that capital punishment provided "specific deterrence." Another responded: "Presumably, once the delays in execution have passed and the defendant is put to death, he or she is incapacitated."

Yet, experts did offer caveats to their responses. For example, one expert wrote: "The incapacitative effect is self-evident, however, murderers do not have high rates of recidivism." Another expert answered: "No doubt there is some downward pressure on the homicide rate owing to an incapacitation effect, but owing to the infrequency of application, it would have to be a very minor effect, probably statistically unmeasurable." Similarly, another expert answered that the "incapacitation effect is probably very modest."

Another expert asked the following:

> . . . incapacitation compared to what? The logic of incapacitation is simple and convincing. Yet, the fact is that states or countries that let their murderers out of prison after twenty years do not have higher murder rates than those that keep them for life or execute them. Hence, whatever effect incapacitation has cannot be large. And, of course, incapacitation presupposes that each murder is an independent event, that executing (or imprisoning for life) one murder [sic] does not, for example, open a position for another to enter (as may well be the case with hired killers or gang members). Like deterrence, incapacitation is a utilitarian argument lacking actual evidence of utility.

Another expert agreed, writing:

> If the person is actually executed right after s/he commits the murder, capital punishment achieves incapacitation, by definition. Why? The defendant will

> not be released back into society, and his/her stay in prison will be short—reducing incarceration time and thus possibility of killing while incarcerated. However, reality differs. First, the typical murderer tends to be young—meaning that if s/he is going to kill again, it will be shortly after—indicating a quick execution. If the person is not executed right after committing the murder, the "aging" process begins—eventually diminishing incapacitation and the rationale behind the incapacitation. And indeed, it takes several years (about 11) before a person is actually executed in the United States. This means, then, that in regards to achieving incapacitation (i.e., preventing murderers from killing again), the death penalty in the United States has little utility. The other reality is even more important: the concept of incapacitation, as practiced in the US, hides the reality of death row. First, young or old, the possibility of killing while on death row is next to nothing. Hence, if a person commits an additional murder, it will be after s/he is removed from death row or released back into the community. However, in both situations, the chances are very low. Why? Because even if a person commits a homicide while s/he is fairly young, s/he will serve many years in prison before s/he is released back into society.

Other experts who responded that capital punishment produces incapacitation mentioned that alternative punishments also achieve the same goal. Many experts discussed how life imprisonment without parole (LWOP) would also provide incapacitation of offenders:

- "Yes, it does guarantee that an executed murderer will not kill again. LWOP does almost as good a job at incapacitation but it cannot guarantee it."
- "While capital punishment incapacitates a person, LWOP does the same at a lower cost and no risk of killing an innocent person."
- "Certainly, in some cases; cannot argue this point. . . . However, life imprisonment also achieves incapacitation (yes, some could kill in prison but policies can be implemented which limit that concern or threat)."
- "LWOP would also serve incapacitation."
- "In some cases. Some executed people are unlikely to murder again. For those that are life imprisonment without parole would be equally effective."
- "If LWOP is to work, it has to be utilized and enforced. The [death penalty] itself does not achieve incapacitation, but alternatives like LWOP can achieve it, if utilized properly."

Other experts who believed that capital punishment achieved incapacitation pointed out other issues need to be resolved. For example, one wrote: "Definitely—though the question should be whether it incapacitate [sic] an especially dangerous population." Another said: "The problem, of course, is that we cannot accurately predict which convicted murderers would kill again. Thus, we would have to execute all of them to prevent any one of them from killing again. We don't do that [and] I don't think we ever would. Only about 1–2% of convicted murderers are ever executed, and some of them will turn out to be innocent of the murder charge."

Other experts provided similar answers, including:

- "But with lots of false positives who would never kill again."
- "But only to the extent that those executed would murder again."
- "Murderers are unlikely to murder again."
- "Most murderers do not murder again. Most are not sentenced to death. This question is tied to a misperception by the public about murder and murderers. Most first-degree murders are actually robberies or other felonies that go awry—someone panics."

One expert was more definitive, saying: "Yes. If the question is do we eliminate any possibility that a person who is executed could cause future harm, then the answer is obvious." Another expert agreed, but also raised additional issues:

> I think that it obviously does . . . killing someone is the most effective way to incapacitate them. But, my response to this is a bit more complex. I think the death penalty system fails to incapacitate when it convicts innocent people of the crime. In this case, the murderer is allowed to remain in society due to the fact that the wrong person has been tried, convicted, incarcerated, and potentially killed in his or her place. Of course, this is not a problem unique to the death penalty system, but I do believe that the death penalty system contributes to a higher rate of wrongful convictions for numerous reasons. One final thought on this is that the question works on the assumption that the executed murderers would have murdered again had they not been killed. Although this may be true in some of the cases, I believe that most murderers would not murder again regardless of whether or not they received the death penalty (and we have plenty of evidence to support this).

The Death Penalty Does Not Achieve Incapacitation

Experts who responded that the death penalty did not achieve incapacitation justified their answers on the grounds that the death penalty is too rarely used to provide an incapacitative effect and that most murderers would not kill again. For example, one expert answered: "Obviously, for those executed, it serves an incapacitative function. However, my own research shows that the probability of a future homicide being committed by a first-degree murderer while incarcerated for a life term is less than 1%." Another said: "Evidence shows murderers almost never have a second victim." Another respondent raised an additional issue about the failure of capital punishment to incapacitate, saying: "The answer is no, simply because of replacement or substitution."

One expert provided a more detailed answer. He wrote:

> James Marquart and Jon Sorensen's classic study of post-Furman death row inmates whose sentences were commuted demonstrates that we would have to execute massive numbers of persons to prevent even a few murders. They followed 558 of these inmates (out of 613 total) for 15 years and found only seven killed again. They reported that four of the 558 had been exonerated and later figures by Radelet and Bedau upped that to five exonerated persons. While the recidivism number is no doubt quite solid, I view the number of persons exonerated as quite conservative. This is because murders tend to get reported and solved, while exoneration is a matter of luck. So we likely would execute more lives than we would save, thus making it a poor trade-off for society.

Another expert echoed this answer, writing: "Those condemned prisoners whose death sentences were commuted to life after Furman did not commit additional murders at a rate any higher than non-condemned convicted murderers."

Finally, another expert who answered no to the incapacitation question, wrote: "In the simplest sense, of course the death penalty incapacitates the offender. But in the modern US, offenders serve such long sentences before their executions that many of them have aged out of their dangerous years before they are executed. While it is possible that some convicted murderers may kill again in prison, with reasonably good supervision this is likely to be exceptionally rare."

Unsure

Those who were unsure about the incapacitative effects of capital punishment wrote:

- "Unsure how to answer this one. One might say that [capital punishment] is ineffective [regarding] incapacitation as so few are executed. On the other hand, having inmates under tight security effectively incapacitates them. Is this really LWOP or 'capital punishment as practiced in the US?'"
- "Undoubtedly those persons executed cannot harm society again—absolute incapacitation. This is true of even the innocents who have been executed. The question is 'does the death penalty provide a marginally superior incapacitation effect above that provided by alternative punishments?' While the research on this question is sparse, it appears that there is not [sic] marginal incapacitation effect of the death penalty relative to LWOP or life sentences."

- "I do not think there are studies on this one way or the other but my concern is that people who have been sentenced to death may actually be more dangerous to other people in the prison environment than those who were not sentenced to death. For example, if I hated my cell mate or a particular guard I might decide to murder him or her because I didn't have anything to lose since I was going to be executed anyway."
- "Can't answer. By comparison to what? Not by comparison to a system of sentencing murder defendants to prison for their natural lives."
- "We *know* that [capital punishment] incapacitates—but we do *not* know whether it prevents future murders."
- There are two questions. Obviously it incapacitates the murderer. Whether this person would kill again is another matter."

Is American Capital Punishment Plagued by a Racial Bias of Any Kind?

The experts were asked about possible race, class, and gender biases in capital punishment, and were given the opportunity to raise these issues in the open-ended questions about whether there were any problems with capital punishment and whether any of those problems were serious enough to make the punishment unacceptable as a government punishment.

As shown in Table 6.4, a very large majority of capital punishment experts (84 percent) believes that the death penalty is "plagued by a racial bias" of some kind. Some respondents (7 percent) do not think that the death penalty is "plagued by a racial bias" of some kind, and a few respondents (9 percent) were unsure.

Table 6.4 Expert Opinion on Whether Capital Punishment Is Racially Biased.

Yes	84%
No	7%
Unsure	9%
N = 43	

The Death Penalty Is Racially Biased

Experts who responded that the death penalty is racially biased cited empirical, anecdotal, and historical evidence in support of their answers. They also tended to mention the race-of-victim effect that seems to drive most death sentences. For example, respondents wrote:

- The death penalty "appears to discriminate on basis of race of victim."
- "Studies show that racial bias (especially race of victim) persists with the administration of [capital punishment] in this country."

- Empirical evidence "indicates that race of victim has strong effect of execution risk."

One respondent simply cited the "[r]ace-of-victim bias."

Other experts who discussed race of victim bias wrote:

- There is "[v]ery little evidence of race of [defendant] discrimination, but a lot of evidence of race of victim discrimination—killers of whites more likely to get [death sentences] even after adjudicated for case severity."
- "Race of victim still controls how bad the defendants' moral merit is seen to be. The killers of the most valuable victims receive the worst punishments."
- "Although race of [defendant] literature is waning, race of victim literature points to a reverence for white victims. Also, even though [Black on Black] homicides are perhaps the most common, they are the least likely to get a [death sentence]—even when controlling for legally relevant factors. Disparity exists, but whether it is due to racism/discrimination is hard to prove, especially given the high standard of proof required by courts."
- "There is not doubt. All one needs to do is look at the statistics on race of offender and race of victim across all executions which have occurred in the United States. I think that the primary racial bias comes in when we look at the race of the victim. An offender is much more likely to be executed for killing a white person than a racial minority."

One expert wrote: "A quarter century of research documents racial bias in the administration of the modern death penalty. The evidence on this point is overwhelming." One expert wrote: "Selection of cases eligible for [capital] punishment is racially skewed." And another expert blamed "[s]ystemic racism in the criminal justice system."

Another expert cited evidence indicating "both race of offender and race of victim bias." The opinion of another expert supported this view: "There are numerous studies from around the country establishing that race plays a role in the death penalty—either due to the race of the defendant or the victim. In my own experience, I believe race plays a role, too. One way that racism manifests itself that is often not discussed is that the police are less likely to solve crimes where black people are the victims."

An additional respondent answered:

> Yes. During the pre-*Furman* era, there was clear and convincing evidence of a race of defendant effect. In the post-*Gregg* or present era, there is now clear and convincing evidence of a strong race-of-victim effect and less clear evidence of a race-of-defendant effect. Also there is emergent evidence that

> legally relevant factors are *not* racially invariant. Aggravating circumstances are more aggravating for black defendants and mitigating circumstances are stronger mitigators for white defendants.

Another expert agreed, writing: "The evidence I am aware of convinces me that the race of the victim does play a role in the capital punishment process not of legally relevant factors."

One expert was more specific, pointing out that:

> [t]hose of color who kill a white female are the most likely to be put to death. In addition, those who are poor are more likely to receive the death penalty. In the U. S., race and SES (socioeconomic status) are highly correlated. The least likely to receive the death penalty are poor minorities who kill a poor minority person. This sends a message that some lives are worth more/more important than others.

Another respondent similarly answered:

> Generally. I think the post-Furman reforms have reduced the amount and changed the type of racial disparity in [capital punishment]. "Bias" implies intentional discrimination and I think it is more subtle than this. Great improvements have been made, especially in the South. Most of the research suggests that little race of defendant disparity is found, but race of victim disparity continues. Generally, those who kill whites are treated more severely than those who kill blacks. The research that I and my colleagues have conducted, however, suggests this may be a function of how severely the criminal justice system responds to the murder of white females, though this is only been recently examined.

One expert asserted that racial bias is a more significant problem than thought by most:

> Historically, capital punishment has been plagued by racial and ethnic bias, prejudice, and discrimination . . . For years, researchers have been documenting the differential treatment, particularly against African Americans. More recently, scholars are showing vis-à-vis empirical investigations that the situation of discrimination in capital punishment is worse that we thought . . . when we take two additional factors into consideration: (1) the inclusion of ethnic variation . . . and (2) the investigation of capital punishment by the totality of final outcomes.

One respondent compared the question to that of deterrence, writing: "Another dead horse we can go on beating, or not. As a [capital punishment] opponent, I do think racial bias might be a more worthwhile topic to keep pursuing than deterrence, simply because racial bias seems to carry some weight in courts."

Another expert argued that the real problem is not so much race but instead is social class:

> I think that justice serves those with more resources better than those with limited or no resources. This has more to do with social class than race. Race affects the [death penalty] because blacks are disproportionately poor. With ample resources, not only can we afford more justice, we have an advantage in all of society's institutions. We live in better and safer homes, attend better and safer schools, drive better and safer vehicles, and work in better and safer environments, etc.

Two experts discussed the issue of racial bias in all criminal justice operations. The first said: "I regard this question as irrelevant to capital punishment since it is true of the entire criminal justice system. Racial stereotypes change over time, but at any time a society will have some and the criminal justice system will show it." Another wrote: "Racial bias is deeply embedded in most aspects of the criminal justice system, including [the] death penalty."

Four experts noted studies by David Baldus in justifying their belief that capital punishment is racially biased:

- "Yes. See the Baldus studies."
- "See the Baldus research, for openers."
- "The Baldus studies, and others, are quite convincing on this point. The effect is too strong and too pervasive, both in the North and South, for this to be a statistical artifact. As others have pointed out, the correlation between race and capital punishment is stronger than the correlation between smoking and heart disease."
- "Obviously. The statistics tell the story. See the Baldus study and all other racial analyses since then."

The Death Penalty Is Not Racially Biased

A few respondents believed that the death penalty is not racially biased. One reasoned:

> No, the only recent evidence supporting this argues for a white victim effect at the prosecutorial stage of processing. Recent evidence from [Texas] does not support this relationship. Regardless, these studies do not adequately control for victim SES, enough circumstances of the crime, wishes of the victims' families, and failure of the defendants (in cases of [blacks killing whites] to accept a plea negotiation.

Another expert agreed that the "race-of-victim effect is not proven to be caused by race discrimination." Finally, one expert acknowledged the possibility of discrimination "... very rarely, mostly in smaller towns and I think most often in sex crimes."

Unsure

Three experts responded they were unsure about racial bias in capital punishment. One answered:

> Clearly in the past there was disproportionate application of capital punishment to blacks and other non-whites. I'm quite confident that this problem has been considerably reduced, but I would not go so far as to say it has been eliminated. The OJ [Simpson] case suggested strongly that under some circumstances, black-dominated juries will set impossibly high standards of proof where the accused is black and the victim white. But cases like this are exceptionally rare and are not necessarily indicative of a statistically meaningful phenomenon. Another factor in the OJ case was that the accused was sufficiently wealthy to afford an exceptionally competent defense. Conceivably in that case it was the high-powered defense even more than the racial aspect that resulted in the acquittal.

Another responded:

> This is a difficult question to answer. Studies are very divided on this point. There does seem to be some correlation between race and capital punishment, but other variables, especially class and wealth, also affect the imposition of a death sentence. I suspect that even if these variables are controlled for, racial bias exists; however, the nature and strength of the relationship remains muddled.

Finally, one respondent took issue with the wording of the question and provided what sounds like support for his belief that there are biases in the death penalty based on race: "I resent the use of the value-laden word 'plagued.' Is there a racial bias of any kind? There are several: more whites are executed than any other race (historically); more executions of those with white victims; etc."

Is American Capital Punishment Plagued by a Social Class Bias of Any Kind?

As shown in Table 6.5, a very large majority of capital punishment experts (80 percent) believes that the death penalty is "plagued by a social class bias" of some kind. A few respondents (4 percent) do not think that the death penalty is "plagued by a social class bias" of some kind, and a few more (16 percent) were unsure.

Table 6.5 Expert Opinion on Whether Capital Punishment Is Class Biased.

Yes	80%
No	4%
Unsure	16%
$N = 45$	

The Death Penalty Is Class Biased

Some respondents related class bias in the death penalty to class bias in the criminal justice system. For example:

- "Of course. The entire justice system is plagued by a social class bias."
- "It is unrealistic to think that a class bias which permeates the decision making of the criminal justice system, would not exist in [capital punishment]. However, it is likely that the class bias is least prominent in capital cases. There is significant research (and from my own experience) to indicate that there is some validity to the liberation hypothesis. Thus, in the most serious cases (i.e., death eligible homicides) we are likely to see the least amount of disparity, though the fact that some disparity remains, even in the most restricted & public decision areas, is disturbing."

Others pointed to data and studies. For example, one expert answered: "Absolutely. I think that this [sic] is a great source of bias in regard to the offenders who are likely to be charged with a capital crime and ultimately convicted and sentenced to death. Look at any death row and this becomes immediately apparent. Even when taking into account the class distribution of murder, the bias persists." Another answered: "Most of all death row inmates are from the lower class." And another expert said: "The studies . . . convincingly demonstrate class bias."

One respondent who concluded that capital punishment was class biased wrote: "There is much less research on this than on racial bias and it is likely to be harder to measure. The effects of social class permeate society, from prenatal care to schooling to access to mental health services to the ability to hire top notch legal representation. Many of the effects of social class occur before engagement with the criminal justice system." Another respondent answered: "Retribution is a class-based system. It promises justice by lowering another human; it is classist to assume that justice involves wielding coercive power to subjugate another."

Respondents who answered that the death penalty is biased by social class focused on the quality of defense attorneys of those accused and convicted of capital crimes. One expert, for example, characterized such defense attorneys as "incompetent." Others wrote:

- "The poor cannot afford good legal representation, and a good lawyer makes a great deal of difference."
- "The poor cannot afford defense attorneys that are competent [and] thus are more likely to be falsely convicted & executed."
- "With very few exceptions, only the poor are executed. One of the biggest problems are [sic] class differences in legal representation."
- ". . . Poor people, with or without bad lawyers, are the prime pool for the death penalty."
- "How many of those on death row would be considered middle-upper class? Also, how many were represented by appointed attorneys/public defenders?"
- "To state the obvious: A relevant aspect of social class, maybe the main one, is whether or not the individual has the money to mount an effective defense. It's also the case that people with more money profit more than the poor from long-range planning and can more often get what they want without resorting to murder."
- "With a few notable exceptions, middle class or upper class people do not end up on death row. The aphorism, 'Capital Punishment—them that don't have the capital, get the punishment,' is true.
- "Those without the capital get the punishment."
- "To paraphrase a wise observation: The criminal justice system knows who pays for it—and no place in the world are they the poor."

One expert who also focused on the quality of defense attorneys wrote:

> Unquestionably, capital punishment in the United States is plagued with social class bias, even more than race and ethnic bias. As point[ed] out in several recent investigations, "the American legal is divided into four distinct systems: one for the poor and defenseless, one for the rich and powerful, one for Euro-Americans, and one for African Americans and Latinas/os, particularly Mexicans." Here too, legal theory and reality clash, in that due process and justice are more a matter of money than a matter of guilt or innocence. Those who have money can buy "justice," but those who live from pay check to pay check (which constitutes a large segment of society) cannot afford justice . . . and so they are further victimized by the state—legally!

The issue for many experts clearly was access to resources. For example, one expert explained: "I believe that social class is more relevant than race when it comes to the [death penalty]. I believe that blacks with ample resources will be just as likely to avoid the [death penalty] as whites with similar resources." Another said that only the "poor and disadvantaged get the death penalty."

Other answers that involved the issue of resources included:

- "It mainly is a SES or victim effect—higher SES victims, risk of [death sentence] is higher."
- "Name one wealthy murderer on death row. See OJ Simpson: death not even sought for a wealthy man accused of a brutal double murder."

The Death Penalty Is Not Class Biased

Two experts who responded that the death penalty is not biased by social class explained that the poor are more likely to get death sentences and be executed simply because they commit more capital crimes. One claimed that the "death penalty is applied fairly, overall, to those sorts of crime statutorily determined to be capital. Wealthy persons do not (rarely) commit robbery, murders, or killings of police officers. Those that kill for insurance money appear to be as likely (in [Texas]) to receive a death sentence, regardless of their SES." Another expert agreed, writing "[u]pper class persons rarely engage in violent crime such as capital murder."

Unsure

At least two of the four experts who answered that they were unsure about class bias in the death penalty seemed to suggest through their answers that the death penalty is biased against the poor. For example, one expert claimed: "Systematic data on the SES of defendants and/or victims are not available. But proxy or surrogate data suggest such a bias, especially as reflected in attorney type & quality." Another expert who said he was unsure also wrote: "I can't recall what the studies find, but I think they do detect class bias."

One expert did challenge the wording of the question, and then offered his own interpretation of the issue:

> It would depend on how you define "plagued." Certainly wealthy defendants who can afford top quality lawyers are less likely to suffer capital punishment than defendants of more modest means. Wealthy people can afford more of everything, including legal defense when they commit murder or are accused of committing murder. But I would not go so far as to say this is a "plague" on the enforcement system. It is an imperfection, like the various adverse side effects of "wonder drugs." I can't imagine America becoming so egalitarian that all accused murderers would receive the same state-sponsored defense, no more and no less. The vast majority of people today believe that someone accused of a serious crime has a "natural right" to buy as competent a defense as he or she can afford.

Another respondent noted his trouble with the term "plagued," but then he wrote: "Obviously more lower class than upper class."

Finally, one respondent who answered unsure wrote: "Race & class are inextricably linked."

Is American Capital Punishment Plagued by a Gender/Sex Bias of Any Kind?

As shown in Table 6.6, half of capital punishment experts (50 percent) indicated that they thought the death penalty is "plagued by a gender/sex bias," and only 12 percent answered no. A sizable proportion of the experts responded they were not sure (38 percent).

Table 6.6 Expert Opinion on Whether Capital Punishment Is Gender or Sex Biased. Is American capital Punishment Plagued by a Gender or Sex Bias of Any Kind?

Yes	50%
No	12%
Unsure	38%
N = 42	

The Death Penalty Is Gender Biased

Experts who responded that the death penalty is biased by gender or sex explained that killers of females are most likely to get death sentences, while females who kill are not. For example, one expert wrote: "Defendants are more likely to be executed if they killed female victims. Females convicted of capital murder are less likely to be executed than males." Another wrote: "Killers of female victims are more likely to receive the death penalty; ceteris peribus, males are more likely to receive the death penalty than females." He added that this disparity, along with those dealing with race and social class are "the result of prosecutorial discretion."

Others suggested that:

- "American capital punishment is reserved, almost exclusively, for males."
- "Clearly females are less likely to receive the [death penalty] and are less likely to be executed."
- "Women escape death sentences under circumstances which would result in death for male defendants."
- "Women are disproportionately treated with mercy."
- "Females, though the gender discriminated against generally, generally are less likely to receive a capital sentence than males otherwise similar."

- "Men are disproportionately violentized [sic] & locked into using violence. Women still are not perceived as violent as men."

One expert even seemed to justify the gender disparity by rhetorically asking, "Who wants to kill a woman?" Similarly, one expert pointed out: "We seem to be remarkably squeamish when it comes to executing women." And another wrote: "We seem to have difficulty bringing ourselves to execute mothers. And I think that agency, or autonomy of intention and action, is in general attributed less to women than to men. But these remarks are completely impressionistic. I would love to see psychologists devote themselves to controlled experiments about 'executability.'"

One expert offered a different line of thought, writing: "Capital punishment in the United States is plagued with gender prejudice and discrimination. Even though women are not given the sentence of death at the same rate that men do, women are treated as second and third class citizens . . . suffering oppression, manipulation, exploitation, and brutality."

One expert wrote about his own research, in which he found a gender bias in capital punishment that often hurts women:

> I wrote a report about women on death row, which involved studying all of the cases of women on death row since 1976. Although I cannot establish conclusively that there is sexual bias, I observed much bias anecdotally. For example, most women who are on death row are there for killing family members or close intimates, whereas this does not appear to be the case with men who are more likely to be sentenced to death for killing a stranger. I observed that women received a more severe sentence for crimes than men did in cases with male co-defendants. Also, women on death row were frequently the victims of abuse from their spouses or their families of origin and many did not have this abuse adequately raised at trial in either the guilt or the punishment phases.

Perhaps the clearest evidence of a gender/sex bias offered by a death penalty expert was this response: "We just don't execute many women (they represent 1.5% of those on death row and about 1% of those executed since 1977), even though they account for a significant proportion of murderers." The underrepresentation of women, according to one expert, made it difficult for him to answer the question: "There are so few female defendants in death eligible homicides that it is difficult to confidently assess this aspect with any confidence. However, it appears (and certainly historically in the South especially) that those who kill female [sic], especially white females, may be treated more severely)." Another expert agreed with this last point, writing: "White and female victims are singled out, according to recent research that killers of females are considered more offensive points to bias. However, black females don't necessarily have the same status as white females, so the combo. Of the revered white female victim is where potential gender bias comes in."

The Death Penalty Is Not Gender Biased

Respondents who wrote that the death penalty is not biased by gender or sex explained that either they were unaware of any evidence showing a bias or that there were other explanations for disparities by sex. For example, one expert wrote: "There may be an exception, sort of a chivalry, given to mothers who kill their children. Under the law, however, there is typically a means of lessening their *mens rea*, so I am not sure about this. Similarly, fathers & live-in boyfriends are not likely to get death for killing their children." Another expert said, simply: "Women tend not to commit 1st degree murder; thus, they are not likely to be sentenced to death."

Unsure

Those who were unsure wrote that the death penalty "[p]robably discriminates against male defendants by affording more leniency to female killers" and: "Possibly women convicted of homicide are less likely to suffer capital punishment than equivalent males owing to the persistence of traditional sexual stereotypes . . . I would not describe this situation, even if it exists, as serious enough to be described as a 'plague.'" Another who questioned the use of the term "plague" wrote: "Certainly more males than females have been executed."

Another expert's answer was more complex, stating:

> This has many different answers. At first glance, one could argue that capital punishment is chivalrous, that it is directed towards men. However, that would tend to ignore the very different nature of homicides (on average) perpetrated by men and by women. There is certainly a bias in terms of the type of victims that we think should be avenged through death sentencing. If the victim is a young (or elderly) white female, the crime is seen as more horrendous than if the victim is a black male in his early 20s. This is about more than gender, though. It is about age, race, sex and social class.

Another respondent who indicated he was unsure about the issue of a gender bias in capital punishment wrote: "Not too many studies on gender bias to make an informed decision." Similarly, an additional expert answered: "Since so few women are convicted of crimes for which capital punishment might be imposed, at least compared to men, this is a difficult question to answer. Perhaps there is a bias in conviction rates in the first place. In any case, I am unaware of data showing gender bias, although there may be."

Another expert wrote that the evidence is ". . . mixed. Most female murder [is] less aggravated than male murder." And another expert who answered unsure wrote: "Women commit so few of the sorts of murders that usually are prosecuted as capital cases it is difficult to draw firm conclusions. There is some evidence that women may be condemned in cases involving prior abuse by the victim. These are cases that present strong mitigating circumstances and perhaps should not even have been charged as capital crimes." Finally, one expert who answered unsure wrote: "Murder rates for [women] are too low to detect bias."

Is American Capital Punishment Ever Used Against the Innocent?

The experts were asked about the issue of innocence in capital punishment, as well as given the opportunity to raise the issue in the open-ended questions about whether there were any problems with capital punishment and whether any of those problems were serious enough to make the punishment unacceptable as a government punishment.

As shown in Table 6.7, a clear majority of capital punishment experts (76 percent) indicated that they thought the death penalty has been "used against the innocent," but many were also unsure (22 percent). Only a small number of respondents (2 percent) indicated that they thought the death penalty has never been used against the innocent.

Table 6.7 Expert Opinion on Whether Capital Punishment Is Used Against the Innocent.

Yes	76%
No	2%
Unsure	22%
N = 42	

The Death Penalty Is Used Against the Innocent

Experts who responded that the death penalty has been used against the innocent often spoke confidently. For example, experts said:

- "For years, researchers have been documenting case after case of innocent people being executed by the state. More recently, comprehensive investigations have revealed that capital punishment in the United States is contaminated with gross error."
- "The evidence is quite clear on this count. Irrevocable errors of this type occur on a rate of about 5% annually. While most are not executed, some have been and some more likely will be."
- "The literature is replete with innocent persons released from death row. Over 100 innocent people have been set free from death row. Every year Project Innocence proves that many innocent people receive a death sentence."

- "Certainly regarding the *sentence* of death, facts to this effect are readily available. Studies of executions of the innocent are now in progress."
- "A number of studies attempt to illustrate this point. The Innocent Project is attempting to highlight this point."
- "Absolutely—there is irrefutable proof of this—It also is common sense that mistakes are made."
- "Absolutely."
- "The evidence indicates it has. Innocent people were certainly executed pre-*Furman*."
- "Sure, though I think we catch most of them before they are executed."
- "This has been documented with reasonable certainty."

One expert who indicated he thought innocent people were subjected to capital punishment wrote: "There is no doubt that innocent people are accused, prosecuted, and convicted in death penalty cases. While there is no absolutely proven case of an innocent person being executed post-Furman, the likelihood that this has happened is high." Yet, another expert noted a specific case—the "Griffin case out of Missouri"—that he said:

> seems the most likely candidate at present, but it is almost inevitable that we will discover that we have in fact executed innocent people. There have been 122 exonerations and most of those occurred not because the system worked but because a ragged band of volunteers persisted after prosecutors and police had given up. Indeed, career oriented police and prosecutors have little incentive to admit errors of this magnitude. That was certainly the case for my friend Gary Gauger—despite overwhelming evidence to the contrary, Gary's prosecutors continue to insist that they prosecuted the right person. We discover cases of innocence only through blind luck, and it would be amazing if there were no additional error rate over and beyond that which we can, under the current circumstances, discover. Even a small error rate calculated over the thousand plus executions (say 1%) yields a probability of less that 3 in 10,000 that we have only executed the guilty.

Another expert, citing information provided by the Death Penalty Information Center (DPIC), wrote: "A good proportion of the people on the DPIC's list of innocents releases [sic] from prison are factually innocent." Another referred to the Death Penalty Information Center's list, saying: "This has been shown over 122 times."

Others answered that they believe the death penalty is sometimes used against the innocent, but expanded with far less certainty. For example, one expert answered: "I would think so. I doubt that any system of justice is completely flawless." Another respondent wrote: "Yes. I have to believe that we've made at least one mistake somewhere along the line."

One expert who wrote he thought the death penalty is used against the innocent found it non-problematic, saying:

> I am pretty sure that there have been at least a few cases in which people who were executed were later absolutely proven to have been innocent. It happens in the movies. . . . It seems reasonable that it has also happened in reality, even excluding cases of lynching. Since I personally believe that capital punishment could be a strong deterrent to homicide, I don't have a major problem with erroneous application of capital punishment. That happens far too infrequently—although clearly if capital punishment were used more frequently than it is now, there would be more cases of erroneous application. I would describe this possibility as no more than an "imperfection." Excepting those who commit homicide, people would be safer against premature death if capital punishment were being applied frequently.

Another expert answered:

> I am sure that historically (pre-*Furman*) there were numerous cases of factually innocent persons having been executed—especially against minorities. Today, it is more likely that defendants who could have been legally adjudicated as either not guilty or guilty on less than capital charges would occur due to attorney error. Recently, there has [sic] been several cases . . . that appear to identify post-*Gregg* factually innocent executions. But, I am not sure this is generally accepted yet. I do believe it is just a matter of time before this happens or we find out about it."

Another expert spoke of a personal experience that indicates to him that innocent people do in fact end up on death row. He wrote:

> I have a close friend who spent several years on death row for a crime he did not commit. In his case, the prosecution ignored evidence pointing to someone else. In fact, 20 years after the murder, the police have only recently decided to reopen the case to see if they can find a match to a bloody fingerprint found at the scene. This is just one of many cases. Our criminal justice system is composed of humans, and humans make mistakes.

Similarly, another said that innocent people are subjected to capital punishment, "[a]ll too frequently, including my former client . . ."

Another expert expounded on ways in which the death penalty has been used against the innocent. He wrote:

> It's used against the innocent in a couple of ways. First, it is used against the innocent when an innocent person is apprehended, tried, convicted, and/or sentenced to death for a capital crime they did not commit. At every step along this path it is being "used" against an innocent person. Second, it is used against the innocent when the threat of the death penalty is used to coerce an innocent defendant to plea bargain for a lesser sentence by "admitting" to a

lesser offense (usually non-capital murder). We know of numerous examples of both of these situations. It is a little more difficult to determine if innocent people have been executed, although I think we have pretty good evidence that it has happened at least several times (see, for example, the case of Ruben Cantu in Texas). Capital punishment is "used" against the innocent in all of these cases and I say "used" because I believe that capital punishment makes the conviction of innocent people inherently more likely in the criminal justice system. Emotions, public outrage, pressure on public officials and law enforcement & prosecutorial zealousness run high in such cases of brutal and disturbing murder, death qualification biases juries toward conviction, and defense attorneys are ill-equipped to defend capital clients. These are just some of the documented problems contributing to capital punishment being used against the innocent.

Finally, at least two experts explicitly wrote about the use of DNA testing as it relates to the issue of innocence. These responses were:

- "Yes, of course, anyone who would deny that would in effect deny that humans administer criminal justice. But I think the question is more serious. Thanks to DNA tests, Illinois was able to check the accuracy of its process in . . . 22 capital cases. These were all cases where DNA bearing material happened to service [sic] as part of the evidence kit. Half of the 22 were exonerated. Philosophers will debate whether ten guilty men should go free rather than one innocent be convicted or whether it should be one hundred guilty men should go free to prevent one innocent conviction. But no one would argue that the standard of judicial safety should be so low as one to one. The evidence so far is that this low safety rate was a characteristic of death penalty cases in particular, not of criminal justice in general. Apparently, prosecutors tried harder than they should have to get convictions. Death penalty cases are 'sexy' in a way other cases are not. They are good for one's career, etc. Illinois has not abolished the death penalty, but it has now adopted procedures to protect the accused making it likely that very few will receive a death sentence in the years to come."
- "There seems to be mounting evidence that innocent defendants are given capital punishment sentences, as recent DNA analysis and other new evidentiary techniques have demonstrated. As to whether innocent defendants have been executed, I do not know [sic] of any modern examples—setting aside Ethel Rosenberg or Sacco and Venzetti, for example—but there probably are instances when these things have occurred."[1]

One expert seemed to question whether the issue of innocence even mattered. He answered: "At sentencing they are considered guilty."

The Death Penalty Is Not Used Against the Innocent

The one expert who responded that the death penalty is never used against the innocent answered: "There is no evidence that convinces me that during the modern period of capital punishment that an innocent was executed. Maybe . . . but not convincing proof."

Unsure

Those who were unsure about whether capital punishment was used against the innocent provided answers such as: "Perhaps? I'm not sure if it has happened since *Gregg*, but we have come close—too close." Another answered: "Probably not. No evidence that any innocent was executed since 1976." Similarly, another expert wrote that "[i]nnocent people are surely sentenced to die; whether an innocent has been executed post-*Gregg* is yet unproven." Still another expert said: "It probably has, but we'll never know for a vast majority of those executed (because tests can't be done, etc.). It is best to hope that the system can catch those individuals before execution, but with legislation in place to curb appeals, etc. it is going to be harder to prove. I guess we'll have to rely on groups such as The Innocence Project to do the job of the government."

Finally, one respondent questioned the wording of the question and wrote:

> This question should result in 100% responding yes [and] as written is unfair.[2] So, I will pick unsure. I can tell you that the likelihood of this happening is extremely small. The List of Innocent published by DPIC confuses legal with factual innocence. In [my book] I found that the seven [Texas] cases included on the list were almost certainly guilty, but were released due to problems with particular evidence, or witnesses (co-offenders) who now were unhappy with their "deal," refusing to cooperate. DNA evidence applies to only a few commuted offenders [and] none completely excludes the offenders' involvement.

A similar answer was: "Ever is a big word. Obviously there have been innocent men and women executed. The question is 'How many innocent executions are acceptable in a system that is not perfect and [is] run by human beings subject to their own imperfections?'"

In Your Opinion, Are There Any Other Problems (Not Addressed in the Questions Above) with the Way Capital Punishment Is Practiced in the United States?

In response to the open-ended question as to whether there were any other problems with the way capital punishment was administered, most death penalty experts (80 percent) said yes. In fact, only 10 percent responded no. An additional 10 percent responded with unsure. Table 6.8 shows this distribution.

Table 6.8 Expert Opinion on Whether Capital Punishment Has Other Problems.

Yes	80%
No	10%
Unsure	10%
N = 39	

The Death Penalty Has Other Problems

Respondents who answered yes, discussed many other problems with capital punishment, including its excessive costs; the length of time it takes to complete the appeals process; problems with jury selection, jury instructions, and interpreting how to weigh aggravating and mitigating circumstances; the problematic nature of victim impact statements; ineffectiveness of counsel; politics; geographic disparities; its arbitrary nature; a lack of proportionality, judicial, and appeals review; inadequate resources and representation for the poor; the unwillingness of parole boards or governors to grant clemency in deserving cases; improperly being applied when the victim is culpable; conditions of death row and the length of confinement; the effects of the death penalty on families of defendants; the potential for a brutalizing effect; and executing the mentally ill. Others reiterated that they felt the punishment is immoral, that methods of execution are inhumane (e.g., with botched executions), and that the reputation of the United States is suffering as a result of its continued use of capital punishment. Another expert wrote that the death penalty "is expensive and polarizes communities." Finally, one expert noted that "[t]he Illinois Commission that was created by Gov. Ryan identified many other issues of unfairness & unreliability in the way [capital punishment] is administered."

Following are responses about legal and judicial aspects of capital punishment that are viewed as problematic:

- "I feel that it is applied too often in cases where the victim is clearly culpable. I don't think that it should be involved when someone robs & kills a drug dealer or kills a rival gang member."
- "Jury selection is highly problematic, especially the death-qualification process. Also problematic are jury understanding of penalty phase instructions, effectiveness of counsel, opportunity for judicial override of a jury recommendation of life."
- "A) [I]nstructions to juries remain vague or problematic. B) [H]ow are aggravating and mitigating circumstances (factors) to be weighed?

C) [P]roblematic nature of victim impact statements. D) [C]onfusion between mental retardation and mental illness."

- "The variable nature of the selection process resulting from prosecutorial discretion in local jurisdictions."
- "Lack of proportionality review. Lack of judicial review—procedures limit courts. Lack of clemency review."
- ". . . There is a general complaint about the complexities of legal procedures in death penalty cases. This complexity is itself a product of using the death penalty when so many people are uncomfortable with it. Legal systems that have the death penalty tend to carry over these complex procedures into cases involving less serious crimes, making the who [sic] system more cumbersome than necessary."
- "Lots. 1) [Death] qualified juries predispose a jury to be pro death penalty, pro victim, and more punitive. 2) [Quality] of representation—although there is some evidence this is improving, for much of post-*Gregg*, there were few requirements for defense [attorneys] to represent capital defendants—Texas in particular had a bad reputation for capital defense. 3) [L]ack of willingness among parole boards or governors to exercise clemency in deserving cases. Politically, it is suicide to commute a death sentence—that is why nearly all death sentence commutations occur at the end of a governor's last term in office."
- "Inadequate legal representation at and before trial. Inordinately complex rules for collateral challenges."
- ". . . [P]rosecutorial discretion is largely ignored in [death penalty] cases—how many homicides that are truly death-eligible get downgraded to 2nd degree, etc. by prosecutors? Also, how many 'iffy' cases get upgraded to 1st degree by prosecutors? What factors play a role in prosecutorial discretion? We consider juries and judges, but why not prosecutors? Also, use of victim impact statements at sentencing—research has show [sic] that some victims are more 'worthy' than others."
- "Arbitrary—depends unduly on the local prosecutor's agenda and budget as well as non-relevant characteristics of the accused and of the crime. Numerically insufficient in application to be treated as a legitimate punishment."
- ". . . [A]ppeals take too long."
- "The methods of execution are inhumane (botched executions), proportionality issue (2 Co-d[efendant]s)."
- "There are enormous problems with representation at trial and on appeal. . . . The doctrine of procedural default limits access to appellate courts . . . Capriciousness of decisions by prosecutors, jurors, trial and appellate judges, and governors . . . The cruelty of methods of execution."

Comments related to costs included:

- "It is expensive and polarizes communities."
- "It costs far more to execute a person than to keep her/him behind bars."
- The penalty is "[t]oo costly."
- "Cost is disproportionately high relative to any of its putative benefits."

Two experts discussed issues related to the political nature of capital punishment and failures of law enforcement and prosecutors to adequately investigate cases. For example, one expert noted that the death penalty is "too political at the local level." He also described the death penalty as "[d]isproportionate" and noted the "[g]eographic disparity within a state," implying differential use of capital punishment across counties. Another expert wrote:

> There are so many, I would not know where to begin. It bothers me when police and prosecutors get a theory of the crime and fail to explore other avenues. It bothers me even more when they do underhanded things to promote that theory or suppress alternate ones. In Oklahoma City, the prosecution used a police chemist who was woefully inadequate for the job, had her testify in ways that they knew were not defensible. People have been executed as a result, countless cases overturned and retried, at a huge expense to the state.

Other experts responded:

- "I don't think there can ever be fair way of administering the [death penalty] when those with ample resources will almost always be able to avoid this punishment, while those who are poor will be the most likely candidates for execution."
- ". . . The only other one that springs to mind is the concern about the lapse of time between conviction and execution. Critics of capital punishment say the time is cruel because it makes defendants wait with a death sentence hanging over his head. Proponents of capital punishment say the time lapse hurts deterrence because defendants know they have a long time to wait and it may make them secure in the possibility that they will die naturally before they can be executed."
- "The ideology or story that supports it plagues the way we approach all wrongdoers & undermines just retaliation based on need, not merit."

Three experts specifically mentioned how the "use of [capital punishment is diminishing [the] reputation of the U.S." One expert gave an expansive explanation of this idea:

Our international isolation on this issue is presenting problems with extradition, the Vienna Convention on Consular Relations, and the International Criminal Court. I am amazed at how isolated we are. There are 122 abolitionist nations, many of which will not extradite without assurances that the death penalty will not be imposed. Of the 74 retentionist nations, 4 provide 97% of all executions and even if the outlier China were to be excluded, the 5 remaining "leader" nations would still conduct the vast majority of all executions. We are truly isolated on this, and the costs to the U.S. legal system are immense. Capital punishment imposes significant diplomatic costs and the consequences reach beyond time-consuming diplomatic protests. It adversely affects substantive cooperation as well. As recently as January 26, 2006, Felix G. Rohatyn, former ambassador to France, wrote in the *New York Times*: [N]o single issue was viewed with as much hostility as our support for the death penalty. Outlawed by every member of the European Union, the death penalty was, and is, viewed in Europe as a throwback to the Middle Ages. When we require European support on security issues—Iran's nuclear program; the war in Iraq; North Korea's bomb; relations with China and Russia; the Middle East peace process—our job is made more difficult by the intensity of popular opposition in Europe to our policy. Moreover, sentiment against the death penalty is getting stronger in those nations that have abolished capital punishment. I have recently acquired the data from the Gallup Millennium Survey and have looked at several other recent surveys and have found that: 1. Public opinion in abolitionist countries is resoundingly hostile to the U.S. position. According to the Gallup Millennium Survey from 2000 . . . only 34% of European respondents supported capital punishment while 60% opposed. In some parts of Europe, such as Scandinavia, support approaches single digits (13% support in Iceland with the greatest support coming from Denmark at 20% for and 74% against), while in Spain only 19% support the death penalty. Even in the former communist countries of Eastern Europe, support for capital punishment is noticeably weak, with majorities or pluralities opposing it in six of the Eastern European countries surveyed. Similarly, in Latin America 55% oppose capital punishment and in Africa death penalty only a majority of 56% support the death penalty and opposition runs strongly in some regions. 2. Support has dropped even among our closest allies with similar criminal justice systems. The United Kingdom provides a prime example. In 1960, 70% of all British supported capital punishment. According to Roger Hood, by 1965 the possible capital conviction of a possibly innocent (and later exonerated) man, "produced a healthy majority for abolishing the death penalty for murder" leading to suspension in 1965 and outright abolition in 1969. Support for capital punishment has waxed and waned since then and currently (January 2006) support has again dropped below 50% even for the murder of police officers. 3. Similarly, by 2001 Canadian support for capital punishment had dropped to 52%. Support dropped even further to 37.6% when respondents are given the option of life imprisonment without the possibility of parole. A more recent poll in 2004 showed a plurality of 49% opposed to the death penalty.

Another expert offered two reasons related to mental illness and two related to human rights and international law:

> There are many other problems facing the capital punishment process in the United States. The list is too long to even begin dialogue, but here are a few: the U.S. has a tradition of executing mentally ill criminals; it is common to execute in violation of human rights; it is common to execute foreign nationals in violation of international treaties; and it is common to execute criminals suffering from severe illness, like depression.

And another expert pointed out the deleterious effects of capital punishment when it comes to America's "consistent violations of the Geneva Convention on Consular Relations when prosecuting foreign nationals" and cooperation from foreign allies ". . . on extradition and evidence gathering on terrorism suspects."

Finally, two experts specifically pointed out that it "is morally wrong to take a life . . ." and: "There is a moral issue of asking jurors to decide death. There are problems turning prison staff into executioners."

The Death Penalty Does Not Have Other Problems

Of the four respondents who answered that the death penalty does not have other problems, only one wrote anything to explain his answer. He wrote: "No other problems that come readily to my mind."

Unsure

One expert who responded he was unsure about other problems with capital punishment wrote: "The criminal justice system, in general, has extensive inherent problems. The reality is that these cannot and will not be remedied. Capital punishment (or any other punishment) is surely a reflection of these inherent problems."

Conclusion

From the comments of the respondents who participated in this study, it is safe to conclude that capital punishment experts generally believe the death penalty, as actually practiced in the United States, does not meet its goals. First, most experts do not think the death penalty achieves retribution, defined as providing justice for murder victims, their families, and society at large. Second, a very large majority of experts do not believe the death penalty achieves deterrence of murder or other crimes. Third, although most capital punishment experts think capital punishment achieves incapacitation, many conclude that the size of the effect is small (due to the infrequency with which executions actually occur in America), that the incapacitative effect is not without significant costs, and that incapacitation can be achieved through other means, such as life imprisonment without the possibility of parole. Empirical evidence supports each of these conclusions. Thus, from the perspective of whether the death penalty meets its goals, a review of the empirical evidence leads to the conclusion that it does not, and by this standard, capital punishment is a failed policy.

Additionally, it is safe to conclude that capital punishment experts believe the application of the death penalty is plagued by significant problems. That is, the experts think that the death penalty is racially biased, class biased, and to a lesser degree, biased based on gender or sex. A clear majority of capital punishment experts also think the death penalty has been used against the innocent. Furthermore, a large majority of capital punishment experts listed other problems with capital punishment in America, including excessive costs; the length of time it takes to complete the appeals process; problems with jury selection, jury instructions, and interpreting how to weigh aggravating and mitigating circumstances; the problematic nature of victim impact statements; ineffectiveness of counsel; politics; geographic disparities; a lack of proportionality, judicial, and appeals review; inadequate resources and representation for the poor; the unwillingness of parole boards or governors to grant clemency in deserving cases; improperly being applied when the victim is culpable; the immoral nature of the punishment; inhumane methods of execution; that the reputation of the United States is suffering as a result of continuing to utilize capital punishment; and the polarizing nature of the punishment.

If these capital punishment experts are correct, the lesson is that not only does the death penalty generally fail to meet its goals and thus provide little benefit to society, it is also characterized by significant costs such as biases based on race, class, and gender or sex and a significant risk of convicting and/or executing innocent people, among many other problems. Empirical evidence supports the conclusion of the death penalty experts whose opinions are provided in this study.

Given this, one might wonder what options are available? Two possibilities come to mind. First, capital punishment could be used more. This would increase the likelihood of achieving the goals of retribution, deterrence, and incapacitation. It would also probably lessen the likelihood of arbitrary and discriminatory application, especially if all capital murderers were executed. It would, however, increase the chances of convicting and executing innocent people. A second possibility is the abolition of the death penalty.

In *Woodson v. North Carolina* (1976) and subsequent cases such *Harry Roberts v. Louisiana* (1977) and *Sumner v. Shuman* (1987), the U.S. Supreme Court has made clear that mandatory death sentences are not permissible. Furthermore, given the unwillingness of prosecutors to seek the death penalty, of juries to impose it, and of counties to pay for it, it is unlikely that a significantly greater number of capital murderers could be executed to achieve the goals of retribution, deterrence, and incapacitation. In fact, over the past several years, the number of death sentences and executions has been decreasing not increasing. If criminal justice policies such as capital punishment should be influenced by empirical evidence, and if the opinions of the experts in this study reflect this empirical evidence, the only justifiable policy is to abolish capital punishment.

Notes

1. This chapter presents summary findings from my book, *Death Nation: The Experts Explain American Capital Punishment*. Upper Saddle River, NJ: Prentice Hall.

References

Babbie, E. (2003). *The Practice of Social Research* (10th ed.). Belmont, CA: Wadsworth.

Banner, S. (2003). *The Death Penalty: An American History*. Cambridge, MA: Harvard University Press.

Bedau, H. (2004). An abolitionist's survey of the death penalty in America today. In H. Bedau & P. Cassell (Eds.), *Debating the Death Penalty: Should America Have Capital Punishment? The Experts from Both Sides Make Their Case*. New York: Oxford University Press.

Bedau, H. (1997). *The Death Penalty in America: Current Controversies*. New York: Oxford University Press.

Bright, S. (2004). Why the United States will join the rest of the world in abandoning capital punishment. In H. Bedau & P. Cassell (Eds.), *Debating the Death Penalty: Should America Have Capital Punishment? The Experts from Both Sides Make Their Case*. New York: Oxford University Press.

Cassell, P. (2004). In defense of the death penalty. In H. Bedau & P. Cassell (Eds.), *Debating the Death Penalty: Should America Have Capital Punishment? The Experts from Both Sides Make Their Case*. New York: Oxford University Press.

Dictionary.com. (2006). Entry for "arbitrary" available at http://dictionary.reference.com/search?q=arbitrary. Website consulted June 3, 2006.

Kubler-Ross, E. & Kessler, C. (2005). *On Grief and Grieving: Finding the Meaning of Grief Through the Five Stages of Loss*. UK: Scribner.

Marquart, J. & Sorensen, J. (1989). National study of the Furman-commuted inmates: Assessing the threat to society from capital offenders. *Loyola University of Los Angeles Law Review* 23(1): 5–28.

National Coalition to Abolish the Death Penalty. [Online]. Available: http://www.ncadp.org/. Website consulted June 14, 2006.

Pojman, L. (2004). Why the death penalty is morally permissible, In H. Bedau & P. Cassell (Eds.), *Debating the Death Penalty: Should America Have Capital Punishment? The Experts from Both Sides Make Their Case*. New York: Oxford University Press.

Pojman, L. & Reiman, J. (1998). *The Death Penalty: For and Against*. New York: Rowman & Littlefield.

Radelet, M. & Akers, R. (1996). Deterrence and the death penalty: The views of the experts. *Journal of Criminal Law & Criminology* 81(1): 1–16. Quoted from [Online]. Available at http://sun.soci.niu.edu/~critcrim/dp/dppapers/mike.deterence. Website consulted February 21, 2006.

Reiman, J. (1998). *The Death Penalty: For and Against*. New York: Rowman & Littlefield.

van den Haag, E. (1997). The death penalty once more. In H. Bedau (Ed.), *The Death Penalty in America: Current Controversies*. New York: Oxford University Press.

Zimring, F. (2003). *The Contradictions of American Capital Punishment*. New York: Oxford University Press).

7 Police Managers' Attitudes toward Capital Punishment

GENNARO F. VITO, GEETHA SURESH, AND WILLIAM F. WALSH

Contents

Introduction

Public opinion polls have been a recognized barometer of death penalty support in the United States. Bohm (2003, p. 254) reminds us that public opinion polls on capital punishment could be used by justices of both state supreme courts and the U.S. Supreme Court to measure "evolving standards of decency" regarding what constitutes cruel and unusual punishment under the Eighth Amendment to the U.S. Constitution. In fact, this argument was promoted by Justices Brennan and Marshall in the *Furman v. Georgia* (1972) decision that temporarily suspended executions in this country. Public opinion polls were considered a method to determine the national consensus as to what constitutes cruel and unusual punishment (del Carmen et al., 2005, p. 279).

Recent results of national death penalty opinion polls reveal that support for the ultimate punishment is declining, especially when sentences of life without parole as an alternative sanction are given as an option. Although death penalty support has remained fairly constant at 65 percent over the past three years, this level of support drops to about 46 percent when citizens consider the punishment of life without parole (Death Penalty Information Center, 2006).

Expert Opinion

Prosecutors, Public Defenders, and State Legislators

Another population whose death penalty opinion has been surveyed is "experts," persons who due to their status and experience have specialized knowledge or influence over the operation of capital punishment in the United States. For example, Whitehead (1998, pp. 247–248) surveyed chief prosecutors ($N = 25$), public defenders ($N = 22$), and state legislators ($N = 40$) in Tennessee. In this sample, 76 percent of the respondents supported capital punishment, but this level of support dropped to 50 percent when the respondents were offered the alternative of a sentence of life without parole, either with or without restitution to the victim's family. In addition, death penalty support declined to 55 percent for juvenile offenders and 37 percent for mentally ill offenders.

In an extension of this study, Whitehead et al. (1999) surveyed the death penalty opinions of Tennessee legislators, prosecutors, and public defenders and compared them to those of citizens. They found that nine out of ten legislators and prosecutors and 75 percent of Tennessee citizens favored capital punishment, whereas 80 percent of the public defenders opposed it. However, the level of support changed dramatically when life with no possibility of release on parole was considered as a sentencing option to the death penalty. Under this proposal, 65 percent of the legislators, 67 percent of the prosecutors, 11 percent of the public defenders and 37 percent of Tennessee citizens would still support the death penalty (Whitehead et al., 1999, p. 252). Seventy percent of the legislators feared that they would not be re-elected if they opposed capital punishment (Whitehead et al., 1999, p. 253).

In terms of racial bias, one third of the legislators, 90 percent of the public defenders, but only eight percent of the prosecutors agreed that a death sentence is most likely in cases featuring black offenders and white victims. Accordingly, 90 percent of the legislators, all of the public defenders, but only 65 percent of the prosecutors felt that laws should guarantee no racial bias in the administration of capital sentencing (Whitehead et al., 1999, p. 253).

Hamm (1989) surveyed Indiana legislators' attitudes toward the execution of juveniles. He found that half of the legislators surveyed supported the death penalty for juveniles. Another survey of Indiana legislators revealed a 73 percent level of death penalty support that declined substantially to 47 percent when life without parole (with work and restitution to the victim's family) was offered as a sentencing alternative (Sandys and

McGarrell, 1994, p. 660). The Indiana legislators did not fear that opposition to the death penalty would harm their chances for re-election (Sandys and McGarrell, 1994, p. 662). They also expressed distaste for the execution of mentally ill offenders.

Regarding these groups, it appears the role these experts play in the capital sentencing process determines their attitudes toward the punishment. In Tennessee but not Indiana, legislators were influenced by fears of how their opinions could affect their political future. Prosecutors expressed faith in the capital sentencing system whereas public defenders questioned it. Among the public and defense attorneys, life without parole was preferred over the death penalty as an ultimate sanction. However, among legislators and prosecutors, death penalty support was lowered by the consideration of life without parole but not preferred.

Prisoners and Criminologists

Other specific groups have also been questioned about the death penalty. In their survey of 309 close security inmates from a southwest Ohio prison, Wilcox and Steele (2003, p. 472) found that only 43 percent supported the death penalty, whereas more than 52 percent opposed it. Only about 25 percent of the inmates felt that the death penalty was an effective deterrent (Wilcox and Steele, 2003, p. 475). As with other respondents on this subject, inmate attitudes toward the death penalty changed when a sentence of life without parole was offered as an alternative. Only 27 percent of the inmates who initially supported the death penalty continued to do so when a punishment of life without parole was an option (Wilcox and Steele, 2003, p. 474).

Leaders of academic criminology and criminal justice also believe that capital punishment is unnecessary to deter crime. Responding to a survey about death penalty attitudes, 80 percent of past presidents of the Academy of Criminal Justice Sciences, American Society of Criminology, and the Law and Society Association expressed the belief that capital punishment did not reduce rates of criminal violence more than long imprisonment (Radelet and Akers, 1996, pp. 8 and 10).

Police Officers and Chiefs

Police officers have also been queried about the death penalty. For example, Fagan (1986) surveyed 78 Washington state police officers to determine their attitudes toward capital punishment. Almost all of the officers (94 percent) expressed support for the death penalty. Seventy-one percent of the officers believed that executions deterred "terrible crimes" (Fagan, 1986, p. 195). Eighty-four percent of the officers disagreed with the statement: "The death penalty does not solve the crime problem." Fifty-one percent of the officers disagreed with the statement: "There is no evidence that the death penalty reduces crime" (Fagan, 1986, p. 195). In general, police attitudes were much more supportive of the death penalty and its utility than the attitudes of a sample of Washington residents.

Another survey found that a sample of police chiefs (*N* = 386) did not share the Washington state police officers' belief in the utility of capital punishment. Deiter (1995, p. 3) reported that the police chiefs ranked "expanded use of the death penalty" dead last as a primary focus for reducing violent crime. Only one percent of the police chiefs named expanding the death penalty as a primary focus for reducing violent crime. Less than five percent of the chiefs ranked insufficient use of the death penalty as a major problem area. In terms of "cost-effective priorities," the chiefs ranked "imposing the death penalty more" last. Only 29 percent of the chiefs chose the death penalty as a cost-effective priority (Deiter, 1995, p. 4). The chiefs also felt that the death penalty was a failure as a deterrent to crime. Only 26 percent of them felt that the death penalty significantly reduces the number of homicides (Deiter, 1995, p. 6). The chiefs believed that the predominant reason for this failure was that youths were exposed to a culture of violence and, thus, the threat of capital punishment did not concern them. When the chiefs were offered the alternative sentence of life without parole, their general death penalty support fell to 50 percent (Deiter, 1995, p. 11).

The aforementioned two studies show that the police officers and the chiefs surveyed differed in their beliefs about the deterrent impact of the death penalty. Although the surveys were conducted almost 20 years apart and the officer sample was limited to one state, police officers expressed a firm belief in the ability of the death penalty to combat crime, whereas the police chiefs clearly questioned it. The chiefs also agreed with other specific groups that life without parole was a preferable sanction to the death penalty.

The Present Study

The present study adds to the analysis of death penalty opinion through a survey of police managers attending the Administrative Officer's Course of the Southern Police Institute at the University of Louisville. In comparison to the police respondents in the previous studies, they represent a group of officers in middle-management positions. The basic research questions are: (1) How do their attitudes on capital punishment compare to those of other specific groups that have been studied so far? (2) What factors justify their belief in capital punishment? (3) What factors aggravate and mitigate their death penalty positions?

The Sample

The officers in this study were surveyed during the years 2005 to 2007. In this convenience sample, 104 persons responded to the survey (a 98 percent response rate). The sample was predominantly male (86.5 percent) and white (86.5 percent). The majority of officers (69.2 percent) were college graduates or above in their educational level. Their average age was 40.5 years, and their average time of police service was 16.5 years.

A majority of the respondents worked for municipal law enforcement agencies (75.0 percent), 11.5 percent were employed in sheriff's offices, 10.6 percent worked in state police agencies, and 2.9 percent were from other types of departments. The majority of officers were lieutenants (39.4 percent) and sergeants (38.5 percent). At the time the survey was administered, the majority of these officers were assigned to patrol duties (59.2 percent). Most of the officers were from states that had death penalty legislation in force (90.3 percent). About 20 percent of those states had conducted an execution in the past three years.

Findings

Support for capital punishment was very high in this sample with 88.5 percent of the respondents in favor of the death penalty for persons convicted of first-degree murder; 65.4 percent were strongly in favor and 23.1 percent were somewhat in favor. Unlike the previous study of police officers, these respondents cited retribution rather than deterrence as the key justification for executions: 77.9 percent chose retribution, whereas "only" 55.6 percent chose deterrence. As was the case in some of the other studies of specific groups, support for the death penalty among these officers fell, but not as much, to about 68 percent with 10 percent not sure when life without possibility of parole was offered as an alternative punishment for homicide.

Research shows that death penalty positions typically change when survey respondents are given more detailed information about the offense and the attributes of the offender (Durham et al., 1996). In the present study, death penalty support rose to even higher levels when certain aggravating factors were present. For example, execution-style killings (92.2 percent) as well as murders of police officers and murders involving multiple victims (both 91.3 percent) drew more support than did unspecified murders, but murders featuring female victims (88.3 percent) garnered a bit less support.

Some mitigating factors lowered general support for the death penalty. Capital punishment support was lowest in cases involving mentally retarded offenders (20.2 percent), mentally ill offenders (56.4 percent), and juvenile offenders (58.6 percent). Support declined less in cases in which the convicted offender was not the "triggerman" in the homicide (62.4 percent), was sexually abused as a child (77.9 percent), or was under the influence of either alcohol (85.3 percent) or drugs (86.4 percent).

The only empirical evidence that significantly lowered the death penalty support of these officers was evidence that innocent persons had been executed (43.3 percent), the death penalty was more costly than life in prison (69.9 percent), the death penalty was racially biased in its application (75.0 percent), the death penalty was more likely to be imposed on poor defendants (76.0 percent), or the death penalty failed to deter homicides (82.7 percent). Only evidence that innocent persons had been executed reduced these officers' support for the death penalty below 50 percent.

Multivariate analyses with two models using death penalty and life without parole positions as the dependent variables were also conducted. The independent variables consisted of aggravating and mitigating factors that are typically used in capital sentencing, demographic variables, and rationales for the death penalty (e.g., deterrence) and are listed in Table 7.1.

In the death penalty support model, ordinary least squares (OLS) regression was used to analyze the influence of the independent variables on death penalty position. The analysis (r^2) revealed that 82 percent of the variation in officers' death penalty opinion was explained by five independent variables (see Figure 7.1 and Table 7.2). Death penalty support was significantly related to murders featuring a female victim (beta = .262), an execution style killing (beta = .227), a drug-abusing offender (beta = .185), the belief that an execution would serve as a deterrent to others (beta = .12), and the payback to society justification (beta = .12). Thus, the support for the death penalty expressed by these officers is primarily a function of these five independent variables.

In the support for life without parole model (see Figure 7.1 and Table 7.2), logistic regression was used to analyze the life without parole dependent variable. Results of this analysis revealed that white officers were 112 times more likely than nonwhite officers to favor the death penalty over life without parole. Officers also favored the death penalty over life without parole if the offender deliberately executed the victim (344 times more likely), even if the offender was under the influence of drugs (5.6 times more likely), or if the offender was physically or sexually abused as a child (7 times more likely). Officers who favored deterrence as a justification for the death penalty were 4 times more likely to oppose life without parole as an alternative sentence.

When we compare both models, three variables (execution-style killing, drug-abusing offender, and deterrence) emerged as significant predictors in both. Therefore, it appears that these officers believe that these punishments should focus upon a heinous type of killing, offenders who abuse drugs, and a belief in the deterrent power of these sanctions.

Table 7.1 Police Managers' Attitudes toward the Death Penalty: Frequency Distribution

Opinion	% in Favor of Death Penalty
Death penalty position	88.4
Life without parole	22.1
Aggravating Factors	
Execution-style killing	92.2
Police victim	91.3
Multiple victims	91.3
Female victim	88.3
Mitigating Factors	
Mentally retarded offender	20.2
Mentally ill offender	56.4
Juvenile offender	58.6
Offender not the "triggerman"	62.4
Abused offender	77.9
Drug-abusing offender	86.4
Alcohol-abusing offender	85.3
Death Penalty Justification	**% in Favor of Death Penalty**
Retribution	77.9
Deterrence	55.6
Empirical Evidence	**% in Favor of Death Penalty**
Innocents are executed	43.3
Death penalty more expensive than life imprisonment	69.9
Minority groups more likely to receive death penalty	75.0
Poor more likely to receive death penalty	76.0
Death penalty fails to deter homicides	82.7

Discussion

One explanation of the punitive nature of the respondent's attitudes toward capital punishment may be found in the literature on police personality. Bittner (1970, p. 8) posited that policing is a "tainted occupation" because it deals with the problems society does not want to address. As a result, the officers feel they are performing "dirty work," are cut off from society, and are unfairly stigmatized. For more than 40 years, it has been hypothesized

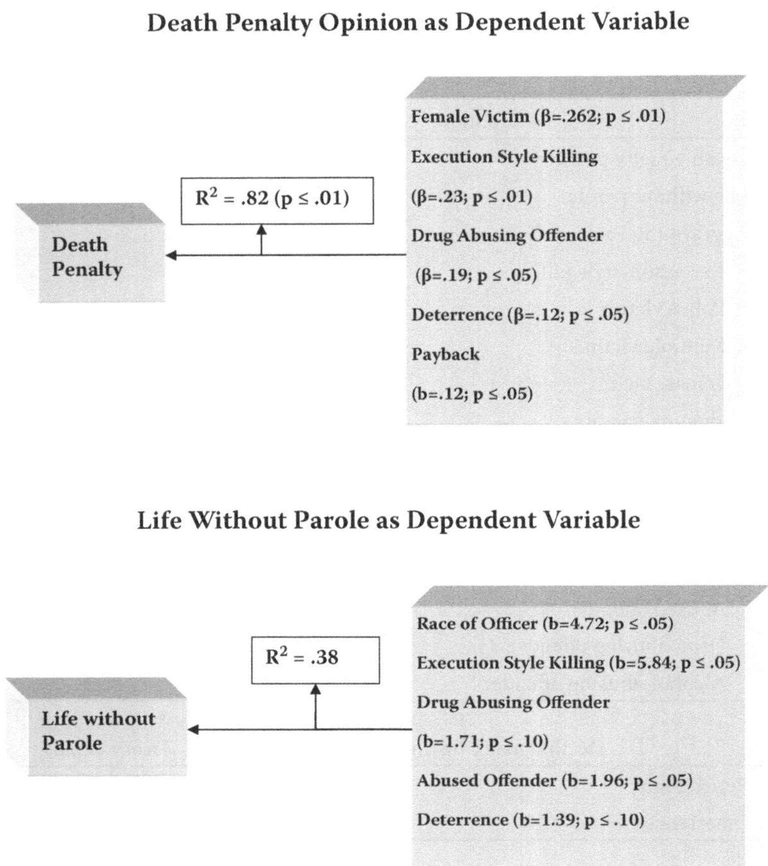

Figure 7.1 Multivariate analyses.

that police officers' occupational experience produces a distinct set of values, attitudes, and behavior (Clark, 1965; Toch, 1965; Dodd, 1967).

This discussion has centered on whether people who possess certain characteristics are more likely to be attracted to police work, or whether people who become police officers are socialized into a distinct attitudinal construct because of a complex process of recruitment, selection, training, and experiential learning (Gray, 1975, Broderick, 1987, Van Maanen, 2002, Alpert et al., 2006). The majority of this research suggests that police officers are not psychologically different from the general population to begin with but are socialized into a culture of values dominated by authoritarianism (Niederhoffer, 1967, Reiner, 1985, Brogden et al., 1988).

Skolnick (1966) was the first to posit a distinct police "working personality" that is composed of three main elements: danger, authority, and efficiency. Danger creates suspicion, which leads to isolation and alienation from those

Table 7.2 Death Penalty and Life Without Parole Positions with All Independent Variables Considered Simultaneously

Variables	R^2	*F*	*P* value	*b*	beta	*t*	*p* value
Death Penalty Position	.82	33.189	.000				
Female victim				.243	.262	3.009	.003
Execution-style killing				.252	.227	2.785	.007
Drug-abusing offender				.172	.185	2.345	.021
Retribution				.099	.123	2.120	.037
Deterrence				.103	.124	2.476	.015
	−2LL?	Chi-Square	*p* value	*b*	*SE*	Exp (*B*)	*p* value
Life Without Parole Position	23.264	77.950	.000				
Race of officer				4.720	1.945	112.213	.015
Execution-style killing				5.842	4.591	344.328	.032
Drug-abusing offender				1.719	1.026	5.580	.094
Offender abused as a child				1.958	5.340	7.084	.021
Deterrence				1.392	2.991	4.024	.084

other than fellow officers. Characteristics such as bravery, authoritarianism, cynicism, conservatism, solidarity, alienation, and aggression have been associated with the police working personality (Banton, 1964, Skolnick, 1966, Niederhoffer, 1967; Balch, 1977, Manning, 2006). Niederhoffer (1967) identified cynicism as a distinct characteristic of the police personality. He posited that uniqueness of the police role continually has them confronting people at their worst. This eventually destroys their idealism and ability to empathize. It leads to personal and organizational isolation and cynicism. Cynicism is the contemptuous distrust of human nature and motives (Behrend, 1980; Regoli, 1976). All of these would explain why these respondents favor retribution, in addition to deterrence, as justifications for the use of the death penalty. Clearly they are concerned with punitive payback as well as deterrence.

Conclusion

Overall, the findings of this study reveal that these police managers were unabashedly punitive in their support for the death penalty. Their level of support for capital punishment was comparable to that expressed by prosecutors but was higher than that registered by legislators, public defenders, prison inmates, and criminologists. In comparison to the other groups covered in the death penalty attitudinal literature, they expressed much greater belief in the deterrent value of capital punishment, especially in comparison to criminologists, police chiefs, and prison inmates. Death penalty support remained firm even in light of empirical evidence demonstrating that the death penalty fails to deter homicides. Perhaps, this staunch support is related to either skepticism about the validity of deterrence research or confusion about the deterrent and incapacitative effects of the death penalty. Another possible source of this support is the nature of the police officers' working personality and the cynicism that it engenders.

With regard to evidence of racial bias in death penalty cases, the attitude expressed by these police managers (75 percent would still support executions) was closer to that registered previously by prosecutors (arguably their closest allies in the criminal justice system) than the denunciation given by both legislators and public defenders.

The police managers in this study were also relatively unmoved by the availability of a sentence of life without parole as an alternative to execution in comparison to the other groups. Although death penalty support fell, along with the other groups, when life without parole was offered as substitute penalty, about 68 percent of these police managers still favored the death penalty when this alternative was available. Only juveniles and the mentally ill would be spared the ultimate punishment by these police managers.

In sum, the attitudes of these police managers were much closer to those expressed by police officers in the Fagan (1986) study than those of the police chiefs in the Deiter (1995) study. Evidently, these police managers do not share the police chiefs' view of capital punishment's limits. The organizational world view of police chiefs may be the source of this difference. As the head of the agency, a police chief must be attuned to and deal with the forces in the external environment of the organization. The impact of the death penalty on the entire criminal justice system may be more apparent to them. The occupational views of the police managers, on the other hand, are probably more narrowly focused on the day-to-day job of preventing and controlling crime.

The multivariate analyses help to reveal the sources of the police managers' death penalty support. They felt that the death penalty was justified for those offenders who murdered females or committed execution-style killings. Drug-abusing offenders were singled out for capital punishment and deterrence served as the overall justification for executions. These variables were the strongest predictors of death penalty support.

The major limitation of this study is the sample employed was not randomly selected. Therefore, results of the study may not be representative of the views of other police managers, especially in other regions of the country. Future research should attempt to survey representative samples of police officers, managers, and chiefs in different regions and jurisdictions.

References

Alpert, G.P., Dunham, R.G., and Stroshine, M.S. (2006). *Policing: Continuity and Change*. Long Grove, IL: Waveland.

Balch, R. (1977). The police personality: Fact or fiction. In D.B. Kennedy (Ed.) *The Dysfunctional Alliance: Emotion and Reason in Justice Administration*. Cincinnati: Anderson, pp. 10–25.

Banton, M., (1964). *The Policeman in the Community*. New York: Basic Books.

Behrend, K.R. (1980). Police cynicism: A cancer in law enforcement? *FBI Law Enforcement Bulletin*, August 8–11.

Bittner, E. (1970). *The functions of police in modern society*. Washington DC: Government printing office.

Bohm, R.M. (2003). *Deathquest II: An Introduction to the Theory and Practice of Capital Punishment*. Cincinnati: Anderson.

Broderick, J. (1987). *Police in a time of change* (2nd ed.) Prospect Heights, IL: Waveland Press.

Brogden, M.F., Jefferson, T., and Walklate, S. (1988). *Introducing Policework*. London: Allen & Unwin.

Clark, J. (1965). Isolation of the police: A comparison of the British and American situations, *Journal of Criminal Law, Corrections and Police Science* 56: 307–319.

Death Penalty Information Center. (2006). National Polls and Studies. Retrieved February 15, 2007 from the Death Penalty Information Center Website at http://www.deathpenaltyinfo.org/article.php?did=2163#gdp.

Deiter, R.C. (1995, February). On the front line: Law enforcement views on the death penalty. Retrieved January 29, 2007, from http://www.deathpenaltyinfo.org.

del Carmen, R.V., Vollum, S., Cheeseman, K., Frantzen, D., & San Miguel, C. (2005). *The Death Penalty: Constitutional Issues, Commentaries and Case Briefs*. Cincinnati: Anderson.

Dodd, D.J. (1967). Police mentality and behavior, *Issues in Criminology* 3,47–67.

Durham, A.M., Elrod, H.P., & Kinkade, P.T. (1996). Public support for the death penalty: beyond Gallup. *Justice Quarterly 13*, 705–736.

Fagan, R.W. (1986). Police attitudes toward capital punishment. *Journal of Police Science and Administration. 14*, 193–201.

Gray, T.C. (1975). Selecting for a police subculture, in J.H. Skolnick & T.C. Gray (Eds.), *Police in America*, Boston: Educational Associates, p. 46.

Hamm, M.S. (1989). Legislator ideology and capital punishment: The special case for Indiana juveniles. *Justice Quarterly. 1989*, 219–232.

Manning, P.K. (2006). The police: Mandate, strategies, and appearances. In V.E. Kappler (Ed.), *The Police and Society: Touchstone Readings*, Long Grove, IL: Waveland, p. 99.

Niederhoffer, A. (1967). *Behind the Shield: The Police in Urban Society*. Garden City, NY: Anchor.

Radelet, M.L. & Akers, R.L. (2001). Deterrence and the death penalty: The views of the experts. *Journal of Criminal Law and Criminology. 87*, 1–16.

Regoli, R. M. (1976). An empirical assessment of Niederhoffer's police cynicism scale, *Journal of Criminal Justice*, 4 (3) 231–242.

Reiner, R. (1985). *The Politics and Police*. Brighton: Wheatsheaf.

Reuss-Ianni, E. (1983). *Two-Cultures of Policing: Street Cops and Management Cops.* New Brunswick, NJ: Transaction.

Sandys, M. & McGarrell, E.F. (1994). Attitudes toward capital punishment among Indiana legislators: Diminished support in light of alternative sentencing options. *Justice Quarterly. 11*, 651–677.

Sandys, M. & McGarrell, E.F. (1995). Attitudes toward capital punishment: Preference for the penalty or mere acceptance? *Journal of Research in Crime and Delinquency. 32*, 191–213.

Skolnick, J. (1966). *Justice Without Trial: Law Enforcement in a Democratic Society.* New York: John Wiley and Sons.

Toch, H. (1965). Psychological consequences of the police role. *Police* 10, 22–25.

Van Maanen, J. (2002). Observations on the making of policemen. In R.G. Culbertson & R.A. Weisheit (eds.) *Order Under the Law, Readings in Criminal Justice* (6th ed.) Prospect Heights, IL: Waveland, pp.63–83.

Whitehead, J.T. (1998).'Good ol' boys and the chair: Death penalty attitudes of policy makers in Tennessee. *Crime and Delinquency. 44*, 245–256.

Whitehead, J.T., Blankenship, M.B., & Wright, J.P. (1999). Elite versus citizen attitudes on capital punishment: Incongruity between the public and policymakers. *Journal of Criminal Justice. 27*, 249–258.

Wilcox, N. & Steele, T. (2003). Just the facts: A descriptive analysis of inmate attitudes toward capital punishment. *The Prison Journal*, *83*, 464–482.

8 The United States Can't Televise an Execution Because It Will Make Condemned Men Feel Bad about the Death Penalty: Issues Raised by the Suit to Make McVeigh's Execution Public

PAUL LEIGHTON

Contents

Introduction

Throughout much of European history, executions were not just public, but they were conducted in public squares with pageantry and spectacle. At times, tens of thousands of people would attend an execution, and the atmosphere was so festive that one of the terms for celebration—gala—comes from the word gallows (Johnson 1998). The tradition of public executions was brought to the Unted States and persisted into the 20th century. Extra-legal executions (lynchings) attracted crowds and families even as states curtailed legal executions conducted with portable electric chairs set up so the local community could watch offenders be punished (Johnson, 1998).

States started the slow process of restricting public access to executions in the 1830s through "private execution" statutes, which Bessler (1993, p. 335) claims were aimed at reducing unsightly public spectacles and preserving the death penalty. Courts accepted paternalistic justifications about the detrimental effects on the public of witnessing executions and upheld laws limiting public access to them. One court, in upholding a fine for publishing details of a hanging that took almost 15 minutes to complete, stated that the execution needed to be surrounded "with as much secrecy as possible, in order to avoid exciting an unwholesome effect on the public mind. For that reason it must take place before dawn, while the masses are at rest, and within an enclosure, so as to debar the morbidly curious" (Bessler, 1993, p. 365). Even though they were denied direct access to the execution, people in states such as Mississippi during the 1940s gathered "late at night on the courthouse square with chairs, crackers and children, waiting for the current to be turned on and the street lights to dim" (Oshinsky 1996, p. 207).

Media representatives are no longer prohibited from publishing detailed accounts of executions, although lawsuits and other attempts to photograph or videotape an execution have not been successful. The press has filed several lawsuits, all after 1976 when the Supreme Court lifted its moratorium on executions and the death penalty again became the subject of widespread intense debate. The cases usually pit various arguments about the First Amendment against an array of concerns about prison security and the privacy of individuals involved in the process. So far, the courts have given deference to wardens and prison officials, based not only on a string of cases involving suits to televise executions, but also on suits where courts have upheld restrictions about media access to prisons in general.

The most recent case, which is the focus of this chapter, is McVeigh's execution for the bombing of the federal building in Oklahoma City. The execution was carried by closed circuit television to an auditorium of survivors and victim family members in Oklahoma City, but a judge denied a request to make it widely available through the Internet. McVeigh waived his privacy rights and endorsed making his execution more publicly available because he favored scrutiny of government actions. The gleefully pro-death penalty President Bush declined the chance to show the public how the government gets tough with terrorism. He had an opportunity to show European skeptics of the "barbaric" American death penalty the execution of a mass murderer with a pinprick in a case that involved no substantial lingering questions of factual innocence or embarrassing questions about racism in the criminal justice system. In short, McVeigh's execution was as legitimate as they get, and it was already being televised to a limited audience. But the Bush administration decided to prevent it becoming available on the Internet by defending the federal law—28 C.F.R. § 26.4—that criminalizes making a photographic recording of an execution. (Presumably, no one recorded the closed circuit broadcast, and the law would not be violated if it were shown but there was no photographic recording.)

Although this situation raises many questions, one of the main issues examined by this chapter concerns why a photographer at an execution is a criminal? In McVeigh's case, why is it a crime to make a videotape of a mass murderer being put to sleep? Given the number of unsuccessful lawsuits filed by media to televise an execution, a second aspect of analysis concerns not just the First Amendment but the larger issue of an open democratic society which nevertheless uses the coercion of the criminal law to prevent photographic recordings of executions. In McVeigh's case, it is particularly striking that the terrorist who blew up a day care center in the Oklahoma City federal building is the one in favor of public scrutiny of government actions, and the government putting him to sleep objects to public accountability.

These perplexing questions exist within the framework of the death penalty as a controversial legal, moral, and political and public policy issue, and the idea of televising executions—or making them more available to the public through streaming video on the Internet ("Webcasting")—creates additional legal, moral, and political and public policy controversies. To help examine these issues, this chapter starts by reviewing the lawsuits that have challenged the limitations on the media. Although courts have rejected a number of legal theories arguing in favor of televising an execution, the idea has gained advocates who are both for and against the death penalty. The odd alignments have the potential to create important coalitions for future episodes of potentially televised executions, so this section also provides a brief review and critique of the arguments about deterrence, the undermining of public support, and the desensitizing or brutalizing effect on the public.

The next section provides an overview of McVeigh's crime and the antigovernment ideology behind it. Before being sentenced to death, he speaks only a few sentences, quoting a dissent from a Supreme Court case (*Olmstead v. U.S.*, 1928) about how, "Our government is the potent, the omnipresent teacher. For good or ill, it teaches the whole people by its example." Although President Bush amassed an impressive record for a large number of executions without any moral qualms, he declined to make this execution public to teach the world by this example, so the legal case played out between the Internet Entertainment Group suing for access and Warden Harley Lappin defending the federal law. This section examines the lawsuit, as well as the Bureau of Prison's contention that televising an execution would cause inmates to see executions as "sport" that dehumanizes them, and that they are likely to cause disturbances when they feel devalued. The court accepts this reasoning, which is critiqued in the conclusion.

Televised Execution Lawsuits and Democratic Values

The first lawsuit over a televised execution was *Garrett v. Estelle* in 1977, when a station wanted to televise the first execution in Texas since 1964. Although official witnesses to an execution include media representatives, the media policies prohibited cameras, so the First Amendment concern about prior restraints on the free press was limited to visual media. Thus, the suit argued for access in terms of equal protection based on "reporting tools": if a print reporter with a notebook is allowed, then a photojournalist with a camera should also be allowed. Although Texas was willing to set up a closed circuit broadcast of the execution to accommodate reporters beyond the two official media representatives, the state defended its prohibition on all forms of recording.

The lower court in this case struck down the Texas law and ordered prison officials to allow the taping:

> If government officials can prevent the public from witnessing films of governmental proceedings solely because the government subjectively decides that it is not fit for public viewing, then news cameras might be barred from other public facilities where public officials are involved in illegal, immoral, or other improper activities that may be "offensive," "shocking," "distasteful" or otherwise disturbing to viewers of television news. (Quoted in Bessler 1993, p. 375)

But the Appeals Court disagreed, arguing "the press has no greater right of access to information than does the public at large." (Indeed, "As the late Chief Justice Warren wrote for the Supreme Court, 'The right to speak and publish does not carry with it the unrestrained right to gather information'.") Much of the court's opinion rested on general precedents restricting media from access to prison and inmates, however, it also included a striking comment suggesting that actual footage of the event carried no more information than a re-enactment in terms of informing the public about executions:

> In order to sustain Garrett's argument we would have to find that the moving picture of the actual execution possessed some quality giving it "content" beyond, for example, that possessed by a simulation of the execution. We discern no such quality from the record or from our inferences therein. Despite the unavailability of film of the actual execution the public can be fully informed; the free flow of ideas and information need not be inhibited. (Garrett, 1977)

KQED v. Vasquez is a 1992 case that arose when a public television station sued San Quentin's warden to tape the execution of Robert Alton Harris, California's first execution since 1967. Although the warden had prohibited the press from bringing pencils, notepads, and sketchbooks, part of KQED's suit was based on the "reporting tools" argument in *Garrett*. Warden Vasquez then expanded the ban to include all media representatives, with KQED responding that the role of the media is a watchdog, the eyes and ears of the public, so they should be allowed to attend. The television station based its claim on a series of Supreme Court rulings that allowed cameras into courtrooms. These rulings specifically allowed camera access to Harris' trial, and "were being used to argue that such coverage should be extended, albeit for the first time in history, to the execution itself" (Lesser, 1993, p. 29).

The state argued the prohibitions were grounded in various concerns about security, especially because the case had already inflamed public opinion: inmates may riot if they saw the execution, guards may be identified and be in jeopardy, and bulky camera equipment could break the glass on the gas chamber causing the release of poisonous gas (Lesser, 1993, p. 29). Apparently, "Prison Warden Daniel Vasquez even expressed concern that a television camera operator might become upset during an execution and throw the equipment against the glass to stop the execution" (Shipman 1995, p. 100).

Ultimately, the judge decided that the media should be able to witness the execution and report on it, but without cameras. In an ironic twist, Harris' "execution *was* videotaped by the state of California by order of a Federal District Court judge for use in any future cases involving the constitutionality of a gas chamber execution" (Yanich, 1996, p. 306). So, after a court denied KQED the right to tape the execution, another court, over the objection of the prison, ordered the execution to be taped because of its relevance to a debate about whether the gas chamber is cruel and unusual punishment. The court order was quite specific in requiring the camera to focus only on Harris and not show guards or witnesses. The tape was never used because the state of California did not challenge the statements of witnesses about the twitching and spasms that followed inhalation of lethal gas. Instead, the state called toxicologists and challenged the value of the lay witnesses who "did not have the scientific training to distinguish conscious pain from unconscious reflexes" (*New York Times*, 1994, p. 35). When the case was resolved, the tape was no longer relevant to the legal case, so the judge ordered the tape destroyed.

The 1994 case of *Lawson v. Dixon* involved a death row inmate suing the prison to allow then talk show host Phil Donahue to tape his execution. The footage was to air in a documentary about Dixon's life, which the inmate said he hoped could:

> [S]erve as an example to others of the effects of child abuse, anxiety disorder, depression and the pitfalls of a life of crime; and that it be used as an educational medium to aid in the prevention of and hopefully as a deterrent to others who might fall into the same lifestyles and patterns of conduct which I followed. I also feel and am equally committed to do all within my power to inform the public of the true significance of the death penalty and thereby to make a meaningful contribution to the significant public debate over the use of the death penalty (quoted in *Lawson v. Dixon*).

The courts ultimately found that Dixon did not have a right to have Donahue as a witness with a camera, and that Donahue could attend as a witness, but did not have a right to attend with a camera. Nothing prevented him from talking about what he witnessed, but access to the event with a camera was not part of the First Amendment right, or one that was outweighed by security concerns and the weight of precedent restricting media access to prison.

Based on this small number of cases, it is evident that prisons are generally opposed to taping an execution, although the Texas prison in *Garrett* seemed open to the closed circuit broadcast that was ultimately used in McVeigh's case. The one time an execution was taped, the tape was quickly destroyed. That prisons are willing to have cameras but not recordings of executions suggests the concern is not a security issue with cameras and photographers, but a reluctance to have images of executions be disseminated to the public because of an assumed power the images might have.

Suits by media and others have not focused on the likely results of showing the images to the public, but have been based on a right of access. The exception is *Lawson*, where Donahue became involved out of a belief that showing an execution would undermine public support for capital punishment (Goodman, 1994, p. C15). Although others who are anti-death penalty share this opinion, many who are pro-death penalty believe that public dissemination of an execution would be beneficial as part of a tough on crime campaign that would help achieve deterrence. Those who oppose televising executions are also on both sides of the death penalty debate and argue that the spectacle would brutalize people or desensitize them to violence. Thus, many people assume that an image of an execution would be quite powerful and have an effect on the public, but they disagree about what it would be.

Although the literature contains an extensive analysis and critique of these beliefs (Leighton, 2001a), it is worth noting that the possible effect of a televised execution could include all options: some people may be deterred by the reality of executions, some people may become less supportive of the death penalty when confronted by the reality of executions, some people may become more comfortable engaging in violence if they feel the message conveyed by state killing is that "a man's life ceases to be sacred when it is thought useful to kill him" (Camus 1960, p. 229), or if they think that killing will make them a criminal folk-hero (Kooistra, 1989).

Furthermore, the idea that the image of an execution would be powerful is an assumption rather than a taken-for-granted conclusion. For example, the argument for greater deterrence from more public executions rests on a rational choice model that does not apply to many homicides done by perpetrators who are drunk, on drugs, with brain damage or impulse control problems, and so on. Images of lethal injections may create complacency with executions, especially because they focus on the moment of execution rather than on a decade or more of confinement enduring conditions on death row. New evidence suggests that lethal injection may amount to "chemical asphyxiation" and "the conventional view of lethal injection leading to an invariably peaceful and painless death is questionable" (Zimmers et al., 2007), but images would not convey that information. More generally, some believe that by the time execution footage has

> been dissected and analyzed and shown again and again on news programs, and by the time it makes its way to MTV and some sort of music video that's supposed to make us think deeply about ourselves as a society, so what, it won't—it will lose its power to scare us and stop us and make us think about, hey, we're killing a guy today. (in Lesser 1993, p. 95)

Understanding the possible effect of a televised execution is important (especially if it might cause additional violence through a brutalization dynamic), however, the fundamental issue is whether a democratic society that conducts executions should allow cameras at the event. Capital punishment is an ultimate act of state power, so people should have maximum information in order to decide whether they want the state to kill in their name. Certainly the public has access to information other than pictures and video, but in the age of C-SPAN, COPS, and Court-TV, executions and Supreme Court oral arguments remain two areas of government noticeably resistant to video coverage. Even those who do not want to watch a video of an execution should scrutinize justifications for government minimizing openness and transparency, especially when protecting morally questionable activities.

McVeigh and Government Teaching by Example

Timothy McVeigh was convicted and executed for the 1995 bombing of the Alfred P. Murrah federal building in Oklahoma City. The "deadliest terrorist attack in United States history" (Kittrie and Wedlock, 1998, p. 776) to that time killed 168, including children in the day care center directly above the blast. McVeigh's motivations appear to be rooted in an anti-government ideology fueled by the government's killing of Randy Weavers' wife and child at Ruby Ridge, and 76 Branch Davidians (including children) at Waco, an event occurring exactly two years prior to Oklahoma City. He believed government actions were growing "increasingly militaristic and violent, to the point where at Waco, our government—like the Chinese—was deploying tanks against its own citizens" (Vidal, 2001, p. 410).

McVeigh is described as having a high IQ and a relatively normal childhood that included playing war with the children he babysat, including variations such as Star Wars: "What seemed to attract him was the battle of good and evil," in which McVeigh "always took the side of the good guys" (Michel and Herbeck, 2001, p. 26). His growing fascination with guns and survivalism led to his enlisting in the Army in 1998. While in the military, McVeigh first read *The Turner Diaries*, a fictional racist account of Earl Turner's resistance to the "Zionist Occupied Government" that overtakes the United States and disarms white citizens. McVeigh did not share the book's racism, but identified with "the *Diaries*' obsession with guns and explosives and a final all-out war against the 'System'" (Vidal 2001, p. 409).

During Operation Desert Storm, McVeigh killed for the first time, although he took no pride in killing Iraqi citizens who had been coerced into fighting (Michel and Herbeck, 2001, p. 75). The military awarded him a Bronze Star for valor, among other commendations (Hamm, 1997, p. 149). After the Persian Gulf War, he washed out of Special Forces training, an event filling him with bitterness that began a period of time when he became a drifter. With a "postwar hangover," post-traumatic stress, and possibly Gulf War Syndrome, McVeigh spent the next years leading up to the bombing traveling the gun show circuit, making contacts in the survivalist right, discussing *The Turner Diaries* and possibly taking methamphetamine (Hamm, 1997; Michel and Herbeck, 2001). When police arrested McVeigh near Oklahoma City, he was wearing a shirt with a quote attributed to Thomas Jefferson: "The Tree of Liberty must be refreshed from time to time with the blood of patriots and tyrants."

McVeigh's trial was shown via closed circuit TV to an overflow crowd of survivors of the bombing and victims' relatives. The jury convicted him on all 11 counts after four days of deliberations, and after the hearings in the penalty phase the jury deliberated two more days before handing down the death sentence (Michel and Herbeck, 2001). McVeigh believed the media would edit his comments before sentencing to distort his point and make him look crazy, so he uttered only four sentences, including a quote from former Supreme Court Justice Louis D. Brandeis: "Our government is the potent, the omnipresent teacher. For good or ill, it teaches the whole people by its example" (*Olmstead v. U.S.*, 1928). The case involved government wiretaps, and Brandeis dissented from the majority opinion because he found that the government had gone too far. Brandeis wrote about the importance of the "right of personal security, personal liberty and private property" and penned his classic phrase about how the Bill of Rights conferred "the right to be let alone." McVeigh thought his execution would be an example of government overstepping its bounds, which Brandeis said: "breeds contempt for the law; it invites every man to become a law unto himself; it invites anarchy—[and] would bring terrible retribution" (*Olmstead v. U.S.*, 1928).

The Bureau of Prisons made arrangements to show his lethal injection via closed circuit TV to victims back in Oklahoma, in the same way as his trial. McVeigh requested that his execution be broadcast more publicly and the Internet Entertainment Group (IEG), best known for titillating Webcam footage of dorm rooms, sued the Bureau of Prisons (BOP) for access to the video feed of McVeigh's execution so they could provide streaming video (Webcast) to the public (Leighton, 2001b). The IEG proposed using video provided by the BOP from cameras controlled by the federal government, and making it accessible through the Internet. The plan for the execution already called for cameras to provide footage to the audience in Oklahoma City, and using the footage taken by BOP officials should have helped with questions about media access, security, and privacy. To help ensure minors did not access the footage, The IEG proposed charging a small fee to be paid by credit card, which they would donate to a charity to help victims of McVeigh's bombing. McVeigh supported the arrangement, noting that he favored public scrutiny of government actions.

The stridently pro-execution President Bush made no comments on the option of making the execution available to the public, so an interesting unanswered question is why the administration defended the law that prevented the IEG from broadcasting the execution. McVeigh's confidence that his execution would teach the public by being an example of unjust government action would certainly meet its match in President Bush's confidence about the example of justice set by using lethal injection on a terrorist who killed 168 people. After all, as governor of Texas, Bush presided over the executions of 152 inmates, more than any other governor and more in five years, "than in any other state in all of the past 24 years since the death penalty was reinstated" (Deiter, 2002). Even as other states had experience with exonerations of those wrongfully convicted and considered halting executions, Governor Bush indicated he would not follow their lead. He seems to have had no moral qualms about the executions and, "when Bush left the governor's office, he had denied clemency in all cases and refused to commute from death to life imprisonment a single death sentence but one—that of Henry Lee Lucas—and that because knowledge of Lucas's innocence of the murder for which he was about to be killed had become the subject of such national scrutiny that Bush could not afford politically to ignore it" during the 2000 election (Prejean, 2005). When a journalist asked Alberto Gonzales (then state attorney general) "directly whether Bush ever read the clemency petitions, he replied that he did so 'from time to time'" (Prejean, 2005).

Bush even denied the clemency petition of Karla Faye Tucker, whose abusive childhood and drug addiction led to a double murder with a pick-ax before she found God and became born again. Normally pro-death penalty evangelists such as Pat Robertson and Jerry Falwell urged commutation, as did Pope John Paul II. Bush let the execution proceed and according to Tucker Carlson, a journalist who had admired Bush, the Governor even mocked the condemned woman's pleas for mercy: "I must look shocked—ridiculing the pleas of a condemned prisoner who has since been executed seems odd and cruel, even for someone as militantly anticrime as Bush—because he immediately stops smirking" (Carlson, 1999).

Bush's run for the presidency raised many questions about executions because his time as Governor of Texas included "executions of juvenile offenders, the mentally retarded, foreign nationals not informed of their rights under international treaties, defendants with sleeping lawyers, and others with serious doubts about their guilt" (Deiter, 2002). But what better way to silence critics, both domestic and the more vocal Europeans, than by showing McVeigh's execution? Here was a terrorist, a mass murderer who blew up a day care center being put to sleep by lethal injection (the executioners even swabbed his arm with alcohol to prevent infection!). Here was an execution with no questions of guilt, no problematic race issues, no sleeping lawyers, no retardation or mental illness questions, and no religious conversion issues to raise the mercy question.

In short, McVeigh's execution was as legitimate as they get in the United States. The execution was already being filmed by the Bureau of Prisons for the people in Oklahoma City, and the lawsuit could provide cover to turn the upstart new media Internet companies into a vehicle for state-created, state-controlled, and state-supplied footage of a controversial social issue. One can even imagine a speech, invoking the sanctity of victims' rights, to argue that a nation victimized by domestic terrorism should be able to partake in the (alleged) therapeutic benefits of watching the perpetrator be executed. (One can acknowledge the primary victimization of those in Oklahoma City while arguing for a more widespread indirect victimization, although because this argument is based on 168 deaths it may be difficult to appreciate with a post-September 11 mindset.)

Despite the confident swagger and willingness to unflinchingly defend an expansive death penalty, it is Bush who seemed to feel uncomfortable with the broader public scrutiny of this execution. President Bush stayed removed from the situation, so the case played out between the Internet Entertainment Group and Warden Lappin, who became responsible for arguing the reasonableness of the federal law prohibiting the photographic recording of an execution. The affidavit submitted by the warden is the longest contemporary legal argument for not televising executions. Judge Tinder summarizes the Bureau of Prisons' position as being based on:

> (i) the prevention of the sensationalizing of executions, (ii) the preservation of the solemnity of executions, (iii) the maintenance of security and good order in the Federal Prison System, and (iv) protection of the privacy rights of a condemned individual, the victims, their families and those who participate in carrying out the execution. (*Entertainment Network v. Lappin*, 2001)

The judge then characterizes and quotes from the warden's affidavit:

> Drawing from his experience in corrections, Warden Lappin makes the following points: *first*, that to maintain security and good order in a prison setting, it is important that inmates understand and believe that they will be treated like human beings and not dehumanized; *second*, that the government's interests in not sensationalizing and preserving the solemnity of executions is based upon the danger that if prison inmates were to see the execution on television or receive word of the televised event through other means, the inmates may well see the execution as "sport" which dehumanizes them; *third*, that when inmates feel that they are dehumanized or devalued as persons, agitation amongst the inmates is frequently fomented, which in turn can lead to prison disturbances; *fourth*, that a broadcast would violate the privacy of condemned persons, and would also 'strip[ ] away' the privacy and dignity of victims and their families; and *fifth*, that "a public broadcast of the execution would violate the privacy and seriously put at risk the safety of those charged with implementing the sentence of death." (*Entertainment Network v. Lappin*, 2001, pp. 24–25)

Although there is much to analyze and critique here (Leighton, 2001b), the government's interest in "preserving the solemnity of executions" is a novel argument in the case law about televising executions. The BOP has a great deal of power to define conditions of incarceration and protocols of execution, however, this rationale takes a dangerous step when the BOP claims control of news and images because they might undermine perceptions of justice. In essence, the argument is that government-preferred interpretations of justice have primacy when threatened by possible accurate, but negative, understandings about the administration of "justice."

The argument is also curious because it is not the presence of the camera and act of broadcasting the solemn execution to a theater in Oklahoma City that turns it into a dehumanized sport, but rather something about the release of the program to the wider audience that radically transforms executions. Apparently, even when the cameras are controlled by the BOP, the opportunity basically to make a government propaganda video about the lethal injection of a terrorist still results in the perception of executions as dehumanized sport precisely because the video is widely disseminated.

The court's decision in favor of the BOP and the Bush administration did not go into privacy rights, which makes sense because the cameras would be controlled by BOP employees who could be issued guidelines about privacy. For example, it would be easy to specify that the faces of executioners not be shown and that the camera should not be turned on the audience, the same rules that governed taping of the Harris execution. The court's decision does not mention the protection of those who participate in executions, but more generally finds "it appropriate, and indeed virtually imperative, to defer to the BOP" in the area of security concerns. According to Judge Tinder:

> Warden Lappin's explanations depict an environment which has been characterized as one of unremitting tension between guards and inmates, who are forced to co-exist "in a closed, tightly controlled environment peopled by those who have chosen to violate the criminal law and who have been lawfully incarcerated for doing so." *Wolff v. McDonnell*. When a measure is taken or a measure is limited by recognition of this fact, and in so doing promotes the security of the prison, see *Hewitt v. Helms*, ("[t]he safety of the institution's guards and inmates is perhaps the fundamental responsibility of the prison administration"); *Pell*, (security is "central to all other corrections goals"), it is difficult to gainsay the judgment of prison administrators. (*Entertainment Network v. Lappin*, 2001, pp. 25–26, internal citations omitted)

The judge found that matters of execution procedures are especially within the province of prison administrators, and courts should defer to their judgment unless there is substantial evidence indicating an exaggerated response.

The court did have before it a declaration from Raymond K. Procunier, who had 50 years of experience in corrections, had been chief correctional officer in five states, had previously consulted with the Federal Bureau of Prisons, and was the named party in several cases upholding the right of prison administrators to control press access. Procunier, who had presided over executions, disagreed with the warden about a televised execution causing the inmates to see the death penalty as sport: "To the contrary, inmates have the same reactions to heinous crimes and injustices as the general public. Inmates frown upon terrorist acts the same as do persons in general society" (Procunier declaration, 2001). He took pains to indicate that he is in favor of the death penalty, and made the same point he did as a witness for the television station in the KQED case: "Any prison properly administered is aware of possible prison disturbances and has the ability to prevent them or to control them quickly" (Procunier declaration, 2001). Procunier concluded that: "Understanding the prison system, as well as security and privacy concerns, the only conclusion I can come to as to why the government would not permit the broadcast of an execution is that the government wishes to interfere with the free flow of information relating to an execution" (Procunier declaration, 2001).

The judge characterized this affidavit in general terms but dismissed it quickly because Warden Lappin was more familiar with both the Federal BOP and the specific facility in Terre Haute where the execution was to occur. In this context, Procunier's views did not provide substantial evidence of an exaggerated response. Indeed, the judge concluded in very sweeping terms that the "setting in which this case arises, and in which any foreseeable challenge to § 26.4(c) would arise, controls the outcome" (*Entertainment*

Network v. Lappin, 2001). In other words, as long as executions happen in prisons, the regulation on prohibiting the broadcast of executions makes sense if prison administrators say it does. The law is "reasonably related to legitimate penological interests," so "no other conclusion is warranted—nor indeed would another conclusion be possible—in the circumstances here" (*Entertainment Network v. Lappin*, 2001).

Photographer-Free Executions and Democratic Values

This chapter started by asking the question, Why is a photographer at an execution a criminal? The answer in *Entertainment Network v. Lappin* was that televising McVeigh's lethal injection beyond the auditorium in Oklahoma City might cause 20 inmates on the maximum security federal death row to riot because televising the execution of a terrorist makes the death penalty seem like dehumanized sport. The United States cannot show an execution, even of a mass murderer, because it will make inmates feel bad about executions. State control of the camera does not matter and, apparently, there are no readily available alternatives in the way of death row reforms that can be tried instead of banning the photographer.

Even if it were true that televising executions would lead to disturbances in prison, the court should have investigated whether it is the act of televising the execution that causes the problem, or if inmates will feel as if executions are sport that dehumanizes them because television shows the reality of a process that involves the planned killing of a helpless individual by a group. A policy banning cameras is better supported if the bad effects are related to the act of making the images of execution available to the public as opposed to the content of those images, but that conclusion should not be automatically assumed. The credible alternative argument is that cameras show an ugly reality of executions which conflicts with the officially held position that executions are solemn spectacles of justice. Prohibiting cameras because they show the ugly reality of government actions is an affront to democratic notions of openness and transparency. The government should not decide which of its activities are acceptable for public viewing, which was exactly the concern expressed in the district court's opinion in *Garrett v. Estelle*. By not examining this question, the court overlooked the possibility that television coverage, even when the camera is controlled by the state, would show the death penalty for the dehumanized sport it is. Rather than dealing with that potential truth, the court sought to avoid prison disturbances by suppressing images that could lead to accurate negative evaluations of government actions.

The judge also abdicated responsibility for critical thought by not exploring why the closed circuit broadcast of an execution does not lead to the perception of the death penalty as dehumanized sport, but the creation of a photographic image does. A credible argument can be made that the presence of a video camera and theater full of people watching on a big screen would undermine the solemnity of the act. Certainly wider distribution creates the possibility for execution tailgate parties, Happy Hours, and other questionable forms of entertainment that would undermine the solemnity of the event and mirror crowd behavior of a century earlier. But prohibiting information and images because of potential unseemly public reaction is once again questionable in terms of democratic values, especially when that image could be relevant to a serious ongoing public policy debate as well. Once again, the judge's uncritical acceptance of the government's position foreclosed discussion of meaningful distinctions that are crucial in a democratic society.

Furthermore, men living under sentence of death develop some intense feelings about the justice of executions, and it is difficult to see how a televised execution would make them more cynical. Indeed, if the death penalty is seen as sport, it might have something to do with George Bush mocking Carla Fay Tucker after the Pope asked for clemency; calls for executing juveniles and mentally ill people, tailgate parties to celebrate others being "fried", continued errors in imposing death sentences, an egregiously poor system for providing effective defense counsel that the United States refuses to remedy, and a long history of racial and class discrimination. Part of what makes the death penalty seem like dehumanized sport is how people trained to "think like a lawyer" follow politically infused rules to reach bizarre and disastrous conclusions (e.g., in *Herrera v. Collins* (1993), the Supreme Court ruled that a claim of actual innocence based on newly discovered evidence is not grounds for granting a further hearing in federal court, even if the failure to grant such a hearing could lead to the execution of an innocent person).

The judge in *Entertainment Network v. Lappin* took no notice of the larger "tough on crime" political environment, where the "execution card" is played more frequently and more cynically than the "race card." The actions of (Governor, then President) Bush and (Texas, then U.S., Attorney General) Gonzales have both reflected and substantially contributed to the political environment in which the death penalty can legitimately be seen as dehumanized (political) sport. But they now have become defenders of all that is solemn and dignified about executions. Executing people who had sleeping lawyers, or who are retarded, crazy, young, born again, or potentially innocent, and not reading clemency petitions; all that is fine, but televising an execution is going too far. Apparently, the photographer at an execution is the problem, so it is their duty to defend the law making it a crime to photograph an execution.

That is not a great day for democracy. Camus noted, "One must kill publicly or confess that one does not feel authorized to kill" (1960, p. 187). So perhaps it is an unacknowledged great day for those who believe state killing lacks moral legitimacy.

References

Bessler, J.D. (1993). Televised executions and the Constitution: Recognizing a First Amendment right of access to state executions. *Federal Communications Law Journal* 45:355.

Camus, Albert (Justin O'Brien, trans). (1960). *Resistance, Rebellion, and Death.* New York: Alfred A. Knopf.

Carlson, Tucker. (1999). Devil May Care. *Talk* (September).

Deiter, Richard. (2002). 2002 Presidential Candidates "Views on the Death Penalty." Available at http://www.deathpenaltyinfo.org/article.php?scid=18&=235. Website consulted August 3, 2007.

Goodman, Walter. (1994). Viewing an execution from the sofa. *The New York Times* 13 June, C15.

Hamm, Mark. (1997). *Apocalypse in Oklahoma.* Boston: Northeastern University Press.

Johnson, Robert. (1998). *Death Work: A Study of the Modern Execution Process,* 2nd ed. Pacific Grove, CA: Brooks/Cole.

Kittrie, Nicholas and Wedlock, Eldon (Eds). (1998). *The Tree of Liberty: A Documentary History of Rebellion and Political Crime in America,* Vol. 2 (revised ed.). Baltimore: Johns Hopkins University Press.

Kooistra, Paul. (1989). *Criminals as Heroes: Structure, Power and Identity.* Bowling Green: Bowling Green State University Popular Press.

Leighton, Paul. (2001a). Fear and loathing in an age of show business. In P. Leighton and J. Reiman (Eds.) *Criminal Justice Ethics.* Upper Saddle River, NJ: Prentice Hall. Available at http://paulsjusticepage.com > CJ Ethics > Televised Executions. Website consulted August 3, 2007.

Leighton, Paul. (2001b). Why is a photographer at an execution a criminal? *The Critical Criminologist,* Vol. 11, 3. Available at http://paulsjusticepage.com > CJ Ethics. Televised Executions. Website consulted August 3, 2007.

Lesser, Wendy. (1993). *Pictures at an Execution.* Cambridge: Harvard University Press.

Michel, Lou and Herbeck, Dan. (2001). *American Terrorist.* New York: HarperCollins.

New York Times. (1994). Videotape of a California execution is destroyed, February 13, p 35.

Oshinsky, David. (1996). *"Worse Than Slavery": Parchman Farm and the Ordeal of Jim Crow Justice.* New York: Simon and Shuster.

Prejean, Sister Helen. (2005). Death in Texas. *New York Review of Books,* Vol. 52, 1. January 13.

Rimer, Sara and Bonner, Raymond. (2000). Bush candidacy puts focus on executions. *New York Times on the Web,* May 14. Available at http://partners.nytimes.com/library/politics/camp/051400wh-gop-bush.html. Website consulted August 3, 2007.

Shipman, Marlin. (1995). Ethical guidelines for televising or photographing executions. *Journal of Mass Media Ethics,* Vol. 10, 2.

Vidal, Gore. (2001). The meaning of Timothy McVeigh, *Vanity Fair,* September, pp. 347–415.

Yanich, Danielo. (1996). Making the movies real: The death penalty & local TV news. *Crime, Law and Social Change,* Vol. 26, 4.

Zimmers, T.A., Sheldon, J., Lubarsky, D.A., López-Muñoz, F., Waterman, L., Weisma, R., and Koniariset, L. (2007). Lethal injection for execution: Chemical asphyxiation? *PLoS Med* 4(4): e156 doi:10.1371/journal.pmed.0040156. Available at http://medicine.plosjournals.org/perlserv/?request=get-document&doi=10.1371/journal.pmed.0040156. Website accessed August 3, 2007.

Cases Cited

Entertainment Network v, Lappin NO. TH01-0076-C-T/H. Decided 4/18/2001. Available at http://www.insd.uscorts.gov/opinions/BK0760O1.PDF p 24-5.

Entertainment Network v. Lappin. Declaration of Raymond Procunier. Available at http://www.findlaw.com.

Garrett v. Estelle, 556 F2d 1274 (1977).

Herrera v. Collins, 506 U.S. 390 (1993).

Lawson v. Dixon, 25 F.3d 1040 (C.A.4(N.C.), 1994).

Olmstead v. U.S., 277 US 438 (1928).

"Let's Do It!": An Analysis of Consensual Executions

9

MARGARET VANDIVER,
DAVID J. GIACOPASSI, AND K.B. TURNER

Contents

Introduction

Between January 1977, when Gary Gilmore faced a Utah firing squad with the words, "Let's do it," and the execution of Angel Diaz in Florida in December of 2006, 123 condemned prisoners have been executed after refusing to pursue their appeals. This is not an insignificant proportion of modern executions; the inmates who have dropped their appeals are nearly 12 percent of the 1057 inmates put to death in the last 30 years. Executions have occurred in 28 of the last 30 years; in all but three of those 28 years, at least one inmate has been executed after dropping his or her appeals (Death Penalty Information Center, 2006a).

Condemned prisoners who refuse to pursue all appeals available to them are generally referred to as "volunteers" and the executions as "consensual." Both terms are problematic, as they imply a level of rational free choice that may not be present. The use of these terms also obscures the wide variety of motivations and behaviors involved. Opponents of capital punishment have referred to such cases as "state assisted suicides" or as "prisoner assisted homicides" (Amnesty International, 2007). Recognizing the difficulties with all these terms, as well as the accurate but cumbersome "prisoners who have dropped their appeals and have been executed," we use the terms volunteer and consensual in this chapter.

The phenomenon of consensual executions raises a host of issues, only some of which are considered in this chapter. For attorneys, a client's desire to drop his or her appeals and be executed creates enormously difficult legal and ethical challenges (Deiter, 1990; Chandler, 1998; Oleson, 2006). Defense attorneys faced with a client's expressed desire to be executed generally raise a challenge to his or her competency to make that decision. A complex body of case law exists concerning the proper standard of competency (Strafer, 1983; Norman, 1998; Blume, 2005). The apparent preference for death over a long prison term among a significant minority of condemned prisoners challenges assumptions underlying the use of executions as the most severe permissible form of punishment. Some victims' family members are distressed by the appearance that the process is under the control of the inmate; the stepfather of one of Michael Ross's victims said, "It just makes me sick that he's still calling the shots" (Thornburgh, 2005).

These legal and moral issues are beyond the scope of this chapter, which focuses instead on three aspects of consensual executions. In the first section of the chapter, we provide a statistical profile of prisoners who have dropped their appeals, contrasting them to those who have been executed only after all appeals were exhausted. Drawing on Durkheim's theory of suicide, we explore whether his categories of suicide are applicable to the phenomenon of consensual executions. Finally, we examine individual cases to attempt to discover the various motives condemned prisoners have for dropping their appeals. We use these motives to create an exploratory typology of prisoners who volunteer for execution.

Consensual Executions Pre-*Furman*

We know very little about the phenomenon of consensual executions before 1972, when the Supreme Court's ruling in *Furman v. Georgia* resulted in the reduction of all existing death sentences and the invalidation of all death penalty statutes. The modern era of the death penalty began as statutes were rewritten and affirmed in the courts in the mid-1970s. In the era before the *Furman* decision, many condemned prisoners were executed without appeals; William J. Bowers's analysis of pre-*Furman* executions found that 41 percent of nonwhite inmates and 30.7 percent of white inmates were put to death without having any appeal (Bowers, 1984, p. 74, Table 301). When appeals were filed, they moved through the courts much more quickly than is the case under current laws.

Some historic executions occurred with amazing swiftness. Henry Wilson's 1902 execution in Sumter County, Florida, occurred the day after his trial; John Graham was executed in Florida in 1931 a mere eight days after he was sentenced to death. Henry Johnson was tried and sentenced to death in Memphis, Tennessee, only 11 days after his alleged crime. Johnson did have an appeal to the Tennessee Supreme Court, but the court ruled against him and he was executed in 1908, ten months after his trial (Vandiver, 2006, pp. 77–80, 99–101, 65–67). Thus, the administration of the death penalty during most of American history left little room for inmates to hasten or to delay the execution of their sentences, although occasionally inmates would express a desire for execution. In Florida, for instance, after T. Southworth was sentenced to death in 1929, he wrote the governor and other officials requesting "the 'favor' of his early execution." When Southworth learned from a reporter for the *Palm Beach Post* that the governor had signed his death warrant, he said, "That's swell," leading the paper to refer to him as "the champion of his own electrocution" (*Palm Beach Post*, January 24, 1931).

The pace of executions slowed significantly in the 1950s and early 1960s. More cases were appealed, both in state and federal courts, and death row stays began to extend from months to years. Some inmates actively sought to end their time on death row by expediting their executions. Emmett Clark Blake, convicted of murder in the course of armed robbery in 1962, wrote letters to Governor Farris Bryant of Florida demanding the immediate execution of his death sentence. Governor Bryant's insistence on having the pardon board consider the case resulted in renewed demands by Blake that he be executed. Blake eventually received his wish and in 1964 became one of the last two men executed in Florida pre-*Furman* (*The Florida Times-Union*, May 13, 1964; Miller, 1975, pp. 175–176).

The U.S. Supreme Court first addressed an inmate's right to drop his appeals and be executed in the 1966 case of *Rees v. Peyton*. The question the Court considered was whether the prisoner was competent to understand his situation and to rationally choose to end his appeals. The Court first ordered the Federal District Court to determine Rees's competence, then stayed its order, and then, bizarrely, allowed the case to remain in limbo for 30 years, finally dismissing it only after Rees's death in 1995 (Crocker, 2004).

The pre-*Furman* era of the death penalty ended and the post-*Furman* era began with consensual executions. Luis Jose Monge, the last person to be executed pre-*Furman*, killed his wife and three of their children. He turned himself in, cooperated with the authorities, and after allowing his lawyers to file a few appeals, decided to proceed with the execution. He was reconciled with his remaining children and appeared calm and happy before his execution, saying, "This is my time. I'm ready to die" (Gettinger, 1979, p. 14). After Monge was put to death in 1967, nearly ten years passed with no executions until Gary Gilmore refused all interventions on his behalf and was put to death by firing squad in Utah, thus beginning the modern era of capital punishment in America.

Consensual Executions Post-*Furman*

This chapter analyzes executions occurring in the 30 years between Gary Gilmore's execution in January of 1977 and Angel Diaz's execution in December of 2006. In that time, 1057 people were put to death in the United States. Nearly one in eight of those prisoners dropped their appeals. In a number of ways discussed below, inmates who have foregone the full appellate process differ from the prisoners who fought their executions.

The following analysis relies on data from the Death Penalty Information Center's database on modern executions (Death Penalty Information Center, 2006a).[1] DPIC's data include the following variables: prisoner's name; date of the execution; age of the inmate at the time of execution; number of homicide victims for whom the executed death sentence was imposed; race or ethnicity of the defendant and victim(s), with the ethnic category of Latino overriding the racial categories; gender of executed person; state and region where the execution took place (region following federal categories); method of the execution; whether the prisoner volunteered for execution; and whether the prisoner was a juvenile at the time of the crime, a foreign national, or mentally retarded.

The complexity of categorizing some cases as consensual or nonconsensual executions is demonstrated by DPIC's coding rules. DPIC codes a prisoner as a volunteer only if he or she has appeals available and waives them without picking them up again before execution. A person who drops his or her appeals and then resumes them is not a volunteer, even if the courts rule that the resumed appeals are too late and cannot be considered. A person who completes his or her appeals but waives consideration for clemency is not considered a volunteer. Likewise, a person who has completed the regular course of appeals but who waives a successor appeal is not considered a volunteer. This conservative definition of volunteer ensures that DPIC is not overcounting the occurrence of consensual executions.

Table 9.1 Consensual and Nonconsensual Executions by Race/Ethnicity of Offender

	Black	Latino	White	Other	Total
Nonconsensual	354 (98.3%)	61 (87.1%)	497 (82.4%)	22 (91.7%)	934 (88.4%)
Consensual	6 (1.7)%	9 (12.9%)	106 (17.6%)	2 (8.3%)	123 (11.6%)
Total	360	70	603	24	1057
Chi-Square Tests	Value	Df	Asymp. Sig. (2-Sided)		
Pearson chi-square	55.863[a]	3	.000		
N of valid cases	1057				

[a] One cell has expected count less than 5.

Table 9.2 Consensual and Nonconsensual Executions by Age of Offender

	20s	30s	40s	50s	60 & Above	Total
Nonconsensual	87 (82.1%)	396 (89%)	305 (90%)	114 (85.1%)	32 (97%)	934 (88.4%)
Consensual	19 (17.9%)	49 (11%)	34 (10%)	20 (14.9%)	1 (3%)	123 (11.6%)
Total	106	445	339	134	33	1057
Chi-Square Tests	Value	Df	Asymp. Sig. (2-Sided)			
Pearson chi-square	8.883[a]	4	.064			
N of valid cases	1057					

[a] One cell has expected count less than 5.

Demographics

Racial and ethnic groups present striking differences in the likelihood that individuals will drop their appeals (see Table 9.1). Of the six groups identified in the DPIC data, the numbers of African Americans, Latinos, and whites executed are large enough to make meaningful comparisons (only 6 Asians, 15 Native Americans, and 3 "others" have been executed). African Americans are exceptionally unlikely to drop their appeals: 98.3 percent of the African Americans executed have pursued their appeals to the end, compared with 87.1 percent of the Latinos, and 82.4 percent of whites. Whites are ten times as likely to drop their appeals as are blacks (17.6 percent versus 1.7 percent). These differences are statistically significant.

Although not statistically significant, the data suggest that younger inmates are the most likely to drop their appeals, while the oldest inmates are least likely to do so (see Table 9.2). (Age is the inmate's age at time of execution, not time of offense.) Among the 106 prisoners who were executed while in their 20s, 17.9 percent were volunteers. For those in their 30s, 40s, and 50s, the numbers are 11 percent, 10 percent, and 14.9 percent, respectively.

Only one prisoner out of the 33 aged 60 and older (3 percent) has volunteered for execution.

Perhaps surprisingly, a greater percentage of women have dropped their appeals than have men. This finding is unstable, however, because so few women have been executed. Of the 11 women executed, three (27.3 percent) dropped their appeals; of the 1046 executed men, 120 (11.5 percent) did not pursue their appeals. This difference is not statistically significant.

The Influence of Time and Place

With the exception of the first six years of post-*Furman* executions, when four of the six people executed dropped their appeals, the proportion of executions that are consensual has held fairly steady over time. Breaking the 30 years of the modern death penalty era into three 10-year time periods (1977–1986, 1987–1996, and 1997–2006) reveals no significant differences. In the first decade, 9 of 68 (13.2 percent) executions were consensual; in the second, 40 of 290 (13.8 percent) were consensual. During the final decade, there is a slight decrease in the proportion, with 74 of 699 (10.6 percent) of inmates dropping their appeals.

Seven states that enforce the death penalty have had no consensual executions between 1977 and the end of 2006: Colorado (1 execution), Georgia (39), Louisiana (27), Mississippi (8), Nebraska (3), Tennessee (2), and Wyoming (1). In five states, all executions have been consensual: Connecticut (1 execution), Idaho (1), New Mexico (1), Oregon (2), and Pennsylvania (3). In addition to these five states, ten other jurisdictions initiated the resumption of executions post-*Furman* with consensual executions.

The first inmates executed were volunteers in Delaware, the federal system, Illinois, Indiana, Maryland, Nevada, Ohio, Utah, Virginia, and Washington. Thus, although consensual executions account for slightly less than 12 percent of total post-*Furman* executions, they comprise 44 percent (15 of 34) of total first-in-jurisdiction executions. The proportion of consensual executions also varies between jurisdictions with high, medium, and low numbers of total executions. In the 21 states with the fewest executions (17 or fewer), the percentage of volunteers is 36.8; in the 8 states having between 22 and 43 executions, the percent of volunteers is 11.1; in the 5 states that have executed 64 or more inmates, volunteers comprise only 7.7 percent of the total.

A significant relationship exists between region of the country and the likelihood that an executed inmate dropped his or her appeals (see Table 9.3). Only four inmates have been executed in northern states and all four dropped their appeals. A surprising 40.9 percent of western executions have been consensual. The number for the Midwest is 13.9 percent; the South is the lowest, with only 8.7 percent of its executions being consensual. There is

Table 9.3 Consensual and Nonconsensual Executions by Region of Country

	Midwest	North	South	West	Total
Nonconsensual	105 (86.1%)		790 (91.3%)	39 (59.1%)	934 (88.4%)
Consensual	17 (13.9)%	4 (100%)	75 (8.7%)	27 (40.9%)	123 (11.6%)
Total	122	4	865	66	1057
Chi-Square Tests	Value	Df	Asymp. Sig. (2-Sided)		
Pearson chi-square	93.401[a]	3	.000		
N of valid cases	1057				

[a] Two cells have expected count less than 5.

Table 9.4 Consensual and Nonconsensual Executions by Number of Victims

	One Victim	Two Victims	Three or More Victims	Total
Nonconsensual	738 (90.4%)	167 (82.3%)	29 (76.3%)	934 (88.4%)
Consensual	78 (9.6)%	36 (17.7%)	9 (23.7%)	123 (11.6%)
Total	816	203	38	1057
Chi-Square Tests	Value	Df	Asymp. Sig. (2-Sided)	
Pearson chi-square	16.13[a]	2	.000	
N of valid cases	1057			

[a] One cell has expected count less than 5.

wide variation by state, even within regions. Fifteen percent of California's executions were consensual compared to 83 percent of Nevada's. Consensual executions in Virginia and Delaware represent 8 percent and 29 percent of those states' total executions, respectively.

Number of Victims

An intriguing correlation exists between the number of victims for whom the death sentence was imposed and the likelihood of dropping appeals (see Table 9.4). Among inmates who were executed for the killing of one victim, 9.6 percent dropped their appeals. For those executed for two victims, 17.7 percent dropped appeals, and for those executed for three and more victims, 23.7 percent dropped their appeals. This relationship is statistically significant.[2]

Method of Execution

The numbers of inmates executed by methods other than electrocution and lethal injection is so small as to make interpretation difficult. Two inmates

Table 9.5 Consensual and Nonconsensual Executions by Method of Execution

	Electrocution	Lethal Injection	Other	Total
Nonconsensual	146 (95.4%)	778 (87.6%)	10 (62.5%)	934 (88.4%)
Consensual	7 (4.6%)	110 (12.4%)	6 (37.5%)	123 (11.6%)
Total	153	888	16	1057

Chi-Square Tests	Value	Df	Asymp. Sig. (2-Sided)
Pearson chi-square	18.315[a]	2	.000
N of valid cases	1057		

[a] One cell has expected count less than 5.

have died by firing squad (both volunteered); eleven have been executed in the gas chamber (three volunteered); three have been executed by hanging (one volunteered). Thus, of prisoners put to death by methods other than electrocution and lethal injection, six of 16 (37.5 percent) volunteered for execution. As for electrocution and lethal injection, there is a significant difference between the rate at which inmates facing these methods have volunteered for execution (see Table 9.5). Only 4.6 percent of the 153 electrocutions have been consensual, compared to 12.4 percent of the 888 lethal injections.

It is possible that the violence and disfigurement of electrocution made it less likely that inmates sentenced to that form of execution would volunteer to give up their appeals. On the other hand, this finding may be related to the regional differences noted above: the West, which has had the highest rate of consensual executions, has not used the electric chair, whereas the South, with the lowest rate, made more use of electrocution than other regions. Numbers are sufficient to make comparisons only in the South; 3.4 percent of inmates in the South who were electrocuted were volunteers, whereas 9.7 percent of inmates in the South who were executed by lethal injection volunteered. This difference is statistically significant.

Theory of Suicide

The empirical analysis of characteristics of those who volunteer for execution reveals significant patterns that can help us understand who and, perhaps, why some death row inmates seek execution. Emile Durkheim was the first social scientist to study suicide by relating the individual and the individual's motivation to various social characteristics (Durkheim, 1951). Although Durkheim's work on suicide was first published more than 100 years ago, it still remains as the foundation for much of our understanding about suicide.

Durkheim observed that suicide is "any death which is the direct or indirect result of a positive or negative act accomplished by the victim himself" (Durkheim, 1951, p. 42). Drawing conclusions from his study of large numbers of suicides, Durkheim argued that collective and social forces are the most important determinants of suicide (Simpson, 1951, pp. 14–17). He found, for example, that suicide was more common among Protestants, the newly wealthy, males, and the unmarried than among Catholics, the poor, females, and the married (Simpson, 1951, pp. 14–16). Durkheim concluded that two major forces, degree of social integration and degree of moral regulation experienced by the individual, were important factors in determining who within a given population was more likely to commit suicide (Simpson, 1951, pp. 14–16). From this theoretical perspective, he identified four types of suicide.

Egoistic suicide occurs as a result of the lack of social integration (Durkheim, 1951, p. 214–215). The individual lacks social support and the result is isolation from society and its norms. Altruistic suicide is the polar opposite of egoistic suicide; that is, the individual has experienced too much social integration and the group and its welfare become primary, even to the point of sacrificing self for the greater good (Durkheim, 1951, p. 217). Anomic suicide occurs when an individual experiences a sudden change in society or in his or her life situation and this leads to a sense of "normlessness" where old rules no longer seem to apply (Durkheim, 1951, p. 258). Fatalistic suicide stands in contrast to anomic suicide (Durkheim, 1951, p. 276, n. 25). In fatalistic suicide, the social and moral regulation is strict, all-encompassing, and oppressive. The individual finds himself or herself in an intolerable situation, but with no means to modify the conditions. Although Durkheim saw little relevance in modern society, he viewed suicide by those in conditions of slavery as illustrative of fatalistic suicide.

Using Durkheim's theory as a guide, we develop an exploratory typology of volunteers. In some cases, Durkheim's theoretical perspective appears to fit well with what we observe occurring in death penalty volunteers. In other instances, the macro perspective does not appear to capture adequately the life experiences and motivations of condemned prisoners who seek to speed the end of their lives.

Volunteering for Execution: An Examination of Motives

From reviews of academic studies, newspaper interviews of volunteers, published accounts of volunteers' backgrounds and crimes, final statements given by volunteers before their executions, discussions with defense lawyers and mitigation specialists, and the experience of one of the authors in several cases, we have developed a tentative typology based on the apparent motivations of volunteers to speed the end of their lives. A variety of motivations combine, in a variety of permutations, to lead individuals to drop legal appeals that might delay and possibly even prevent their executions. Although many forces and motivations are influential, it is often possible to identify a primary or dominant motive or characteristic. The following is a discussion of the primary factors leading death row inmates to volunteer for execution.

Tough Guy

The tough guy volunteer is an individual who often had a long criminal career that culminated in murder. These individuals rarely express remorse for their anti-social activities but rather seem to relish the outlaw image. When faced with the prospect of execution at the end of a long and drawn-out process of appeal, they choose death, perhaps to maintain some control over their fate. They often express disdain for weakness and individuals afraid to die.

The first post-*Furman* execution was of Gary Gilmore in 1977 in Utah. Gilmore dropped his appeals and chose to be executed by a firing squad. Perhaps because his execution was the first after a hiatus of nearly ten years, Gilmore often stands out as an archetype of the tough guy volunteer. This image was fostered by an all-night "party" that Gilmore attended with family and friends the night before his execution in the prison mess hall where he apparently was in good spirits and had a good time. Gilmore told an interviewer that, as a child, all he wanted to be was "a gangster" when he grew up (Mailer, 1979, p. 659). When asked how he felt in court when given the death sentence, he replied, "I probably felt less than anyone in the courtroom" (p. 693). When the prison warden asked if Gilmore had anything to say before proceeding with the execution, Gilmore simply said, "Let's do it" (Mailer, 1979, p. 984). These words came to symbolize both Gary Gilmore's disdain for life and his willingness to die.

Aaron Foust, executed in Texas in 1999 for a strangulation murder, also presented himself as a tough guy who felt neither fear nor remorse. Dropping his appeals as soon as he found out he could, he was executed at age 26, having spent less than one year on death row. Foust was nicknamed "Conan" for his muscular build and physical toughness. He stated, "The bottom line is, if I was the type to feel remorseful, I wouldn't have done this in the first place. It takes a good deal of determination to put a man in a chokehold and choke the life out of him" (Graczyk, April 29, 1999). Foust described himself as a cold-blooded killer who did not want to spend the rest of his life in prison without a woman. He said the only reason someone would want to "stick around in a place like this is if they were afraid to die. I'm not" (Graczyk, April 28, 1999). His last words were "I'm ready, ready when ya'll are" (Graczyk, April 29, 1999).

Martyr

Although these individuals are few in number on death row, they are probably the most unambiguous type. They typically do not have a criminal record apart from their activities associated with some cause they perceive as noble. They kill for what they believe is some greater good, but society generally perceives them as dangerous extremists.

Timothy McVeigh is, perhaps, the best known of this category. McVeigh was executed under federal jurisdiction in 2001 for causing the explosion that destroyed the Murrah Federal Building in Oklahoma City, resulting in 168 deaths, including those of 19 children. McVeigh saw himself as a patriot at war with the federal government for what he believed were outrageous government actions at Ruby Ridge, Idaho, and Waco, Texas. In both instances, actions of federal agents led to the death of American citizens who refused to surrender to federal agents. Their resistance led to the deaths of more than 80 people, including 20 children at Waco (Stickney, 1996). McVeigh presented himself as a soldier fighting a war against government tyranny. McVeigh, although never publicly denying the bombing charge, pleaded not guilty at trial to have the opportunity to convince Americans that his actions were justified in the fight against government tyranny (Michel & Herbeck, 2001). He characterized the deaths of the 19 children at the federal building as "collateral damage." At his execution, he showed "a soldier's cool demeanor . . . offering no apology for killing 168 people in cold blood . . . in the end, there was only his steely stare" (Fagan & Squatriglia, June 12, 2001). McVeigh was seen as a hero by members of various paramilitary groups in the United States (Carey, June 11, 2001).

A second volunteer who viewed himself as a martyr was Paul Hill, executed in Florida in 2003 for the murder of a doctor who performed abortions; Hill also killed a man who was attempting to protect the doctor. Hill admitted to the killings, stated he had no regrets, and, "felt honored to receive the death penalty" (*Church & State*, 2003). Hill had written that he hoped to be a martyr and, "expected God to welcome him into heaven." Hill's final statement consisted of a call to resist abortion. After his execution, several of Hill's supporters praised his actions (LaPeter & Rondeaux, September 4, 2003).

Mentally Ill

The law makes a crucial distinction between mental illness, insanity, and incompetence. Insanity and incompetence have specific legal definitions. For example, to be eligible for trial and execution, an individual must be judged competent, that is, must understand the nature of the proceedings and have sufficient ability to consult with his or her attorney (Schmalleger,

2006). Mental illness, on the other hand, is a psychiatric or medical term that is nonspecific and may or may not conform to a legal judgment of insanity or incompetence (Samaha, 1999). John Blume found that 77 percent of the volunteers whose cases he studied were suffering some form of mental illness[3] (Blume, 2005, p. 962). These individuals often have long-term documented mental problems, and are judged competent, but it is impossible to know how their mental illnesses affect their decision to volunteer for death.

An example of a mentally ill individual who was executed after dropping his appeals is Harry Moore. Moore was executed in Oregon in 1997 for the murder of his in-laws, a crime that he had planned for a month. Moore's mother-in-law was also his half-sister. Moore was known as odd his whole life. He was an admirer of Adolf Hitler and suffered from paranoia and fits of rage. He was attracted to young girls, particularly in his own family. He married two of his young nieces. He stated that God ordered him to kill his in-laws because they were going to take his wife to Las Vegas, addict her to drugs, and then prostitute her. After his conviction, Moore waived all appeals and said he wanted to be executed as soon as possible. In media interviews, Moore would be affable one minute and threatening the next. His written final statement was rambling and nonsensical; after saying his daughter's name, his last words were, "Thank you" (Foster & Anderson, May 16, 1997).

Wilford Berry Jr., executed in Ohio in 1999, is a second example of a mentally ill person who volunteered to be executed after being convicted of a brutal murder. As a child, Berry suffered from epilepsy, a speech impediment, and a lung condition that often left him gasping for breath. By age nine, he had already attempted suicide and had been repeatedly raped and sexually abused by his babysitter's family, had been molested by a man in the Big Brother program, had been physically abused by his mentally ill mother, and had been abandoned by his father, who died in an institution for the criminally insane. At age 11, he walked home 77 blocks, naked, after being sexually abused. At 14, an institution for severely troubled youth almost rejected him because his pathology was so great. As an adult, he stole a car and served time in the psychiatric ward of a Texas prison, where he was raped and where he tried to commit suicide several times. He stopped taking the prescribed psychotropic drugs because they left him vulnerable to attack and instead opted for several years of solitary confinement. As an adult, he continued to experience visual and auditory hallucinations and stated that a "lady in black" had appeared to him in his prison cell on several occasions. In 1997, when a riot occurred in the Ohio prison where he was on death row, he was badly beaten and suffered a shattered face. When his mother requested clemency for her son, Berry threatened to kill his mother if the clemency were granted (Fisher, February 19, 1999; Johnson, February 21, 1999).

With a lifetime of diagnoses and treatment, there was no disagreement that Berry was mentally ill, but the legal arguments were over the degree of impairment and whether he was competent. He was found competent by the courts and was denied clemency by the governor who said he could find no compelling reason to grant clemency in this case (*New York Times*, February 20, 1999). By volunteering, Berry became the first person executed in Ohio in 36 years. Berry issued no final statement before his execution. (For further examples of severely mentally ill prisoners who were executed after being found competent to drop their appeals, see Amnesty International, 2007, pp. 12–19).

Remorseful

The remorseful volunteer is one who admits to the murder and accepts the punishment of death as justified. Often, there is a strong religious component in this willingness to accept the punishment, frequently based on a fundamentalist Christian belief in "blood atonement." Blood atonement is the belief that, as Jesus had to die on the cross to atone for the sins of mankind, God demands the blood (life) of sinners (Vandiver et al., 2002). A common element of the remorseful volunteer is an apology to the victim's family. Blume (2005, p. 967), who conducted a survey of the lawyers of individuals who dropped their appeals and were executed, found that in 36 percent of volunteer cases the lawyers believed that the decision to forego appeals was based in some degree on remorse and willing acceptance of death as atonement.

Arthur Bishop, a former Eagle Scout and Mormon missionary, exemplifies many aspects of the remorseful volunteer. Bishop was executed in Utah in 1988 for the sex-related murder of five boys. Bishop viewed the dropping of his appeals as an act of contrition that would bring peace to his victims' families. His last words were, "Give my apologies to the families of the victims." A prison chaplain stated that Bishop was "the most sorrowful and repentent [sic] and remorseful man" that he had seen in his 33 years as a prison chaplain (*New York Times*, June 11, 1988).

Arthur Wise, executed in 2005 in South Carolina, is similarly representative of the remorseful volunteer. Wise was convicted of murdering four former co-workers. At his trial, Wise refused to allow his lawyers to present mitigating evidence that might have resulted in a life sentence. Psychiatrists testified that he was competent and religious and that Wise believed that he should be executed for the murders he committed. Even though Wise had requested that the attorney general help speed his execution, a psychiatrist stated that Wise was not suicidal but rather like a patient with cancer who chooses to end chemotherapy. When asked at a competency hearing whether he was certain he wanted to waive his appeals, Wise replied, "I wish to proceed with my execution" (Collins, December 17, 2004).

Suicidal

Our examination of consensual executions has led us to identify three separate types of suicidal volunteering. The first and probably the rarest type is what may be termed intended suicide by execution, the equivalent of "suicide by cop" (see Pinozzotto, 2005, for a description of this phenomenon). The second type is the completion through execution of a previously attempted suicide. The "death row phenomenon" or "death row syndrome," discussed below, forms the third type.

Suicide by execution is illustrated by the case of Jeremy Sagastegui who was put to death in the state of Washington in 1998. From the time he murdered two women and a child, Sagastegui stated that he committed the murders because he knew he would be given the death penalty. Sagastegui acted as his own trial lawyer, never called any witnesses, and never introduced any evidence of the sexual and physical abuse he suffered as a child that might have led a jury to spare his life. He waived all right of appeal. The courts found him competent and the execution occurred two years after he was sentenced to death (Davila & Postman, October 13, 1998). In this case, it appears that the motive for the crime was to force the state to execute him and the tactic proved successful. Amnesty International notes that for such persons, the death penalty, rather than potentially serving as a deterrent, instead can be an inducement to homicide, serving as a "form of escape, whether from the torments of their lives, their crimes, or their minds" (Amnesty International, 2007, p. 5. See Solomon, 1975; West, 1975; and Van Wormer & Odiah, 1999, for discussion of similar cases.)

The second type of suicidal motivation is illustrated by Christina Riggs who was executed in Arkansas in 2000. Riggs worked as a nurse at a hospital and brought home potassium chloride (one of the chemicals used in lethal injections). She attempted to kill her son with an injection of potassium chloride, but was unsuccessful and killed him with morphine and by smothering him. She then killed her two-year-old daughter by smothering her. After the children were dead, Riggs injected herself with the potassium chloride in an unsuccessful suicide attempt (Amnesty International, 2001, pp. 38–39). She left a suicide note stating that she couldn't bear to live any longer and wanted to kill herself and her children. Riggs was tried and found guilty of killing her children and was sentenced to death. Riggs waived her appeals, saying she wanted to be reunited with her children in heaven, and was executed (Borger, May 4, 2000). In this case, it appears that although Riggs was unsuccessful in killing herself at the time of the murders, she succeeded in having the state complete the unfinished task. Riggs' lawyer commented, "It started out as a suicide and ended as a suicide" (Borger, May 4, 2000).

The third type of suicide is rooted in the death row syndrome (*Soering v. The United Kingdom*). The syndrome is a theoretical construct referring to the response prisoners may have to the exceptionally severe conditions of death row imprisonment and the resulting psychological stresses to which they are subjected. Although the data are not available, it appears that many inmates who ultimately volunteer for execution have attempted suicide at some point during their confinement. These stresses may be so intense that inmates drop their appeals, preferring death over the conditions of confinement. Some death rows have undertaken reforms, but conditions remain harsh and reforms have not been successful in alleviating the stress attending a sentence of death (Johnson, 2003). Although American courts have never recognized the legitimacy of death row syndrome, many people familiar with death row conditions believe that the death row syndrome is an important factor in the decision of many volunteers to drop their appeals. The case of Robert South illustrates aspects of the death row syndrome.

Robert South was executed in South Carolina in 1996 for the murder of a police officer in 1983. John Blume (2005) served as South's attorney and sought, against South's wishes, to continue the appeal process which he believed would lead to a life sentence. The courts found South competent, the appeals were terminated, and South was executed.

Blume's description of the conditions that led South to drop his appeals is typical of many on death row. South suffered terrible childhood physical and sexual abuse. One consequence of this abuse was post-traumatic stress disorder that resulted in daily flashbacks to the abuse. South also suffered from an inoperable but nonterminal brain tumor that disrupted his sleep cycle and resulted in severe headaches daily. South's ten years on death row had been a physical and psychological living hell. "In his own words, he was 'tired' and he no longer wanted to go on" (Blume, 2005, p. 939). South stated, "I have no desire to die, but I have even less desire to spend the rest of my life incarcerated" (*The [Charleston S.C.] Post and Courier*, May 31, 1996). Blume concludes that although South was legally competent, his decision was suicidal. The combination of South's personal history, physical disabilities, and the unrelenting harshness of the death-row confinement led South to end his life by dropping his appeals.

The conditions inherent in the death row syndrome apparently lead many volunteers to drop their appeals; Blume notes, however, that this presents an insurmountable problem for the courts. The law generally prohibits assisting individuals in committing suicide, no matter how rational the choice might be (Blume, 2005, p. 941). The courts, however, cannot distinguish suicidal motivation, which should not be complied with by the court, from "acceptance of responsibility in other civil and criminal contexts" (Blume, 2005, p. 955). The difficulty in distinguishing the basis for a volunteer's compliance with a death sentence is illustrated in the following case.

Michael Ross was the first person executed in Connecticut in 45 years. Ross was a Cornell University graduate who admitted murdering eight women. For many years, Ross attempted to waive all appeals to expedite his execution. Ross insisted that he wanted to drop his appeals and be executed to spare the victims' families further pain. Ross was intelligent and articulate and convinced the courts that he was competent. Consequently, he was allowed to forgo his appeals and was executed (Apuzzo, April 8, 2005).

Although Michael Ross's stated reason for dropping his appeals was an altruistic concern for the families of his victims, he also appears to exemplify many aspects of the death row syndrome (Blank, 2006). Ross described feeling intense isolation resulting from being confined in his cell for all but one hour each day. He attempted suicide three times while on death row. He stated that he wished to be executed to "end my own pain" (Death Penalty Information Center, 2006b, quoting Associated Press). He is quoted as saying in 2003 court papers, "I've been doing this for 19 years now—16 on death row—and it gets harder every year. . . . I honestly don't think I can do much more of this. I now understand why 12 percent of the men executed in this country were men who gave up their appeals and 'volunteered' for execution" (Christoffersen, February 1, 2005). Although the courts accepted Ross's statement that he wished to be executed to spare his victims' families further pain, his own father said that Michael Ross was incapable of compassion and that the real reason for his son dropping his appeals had nothing to do with concern for the victims' families (Apuzzo, April 8, 2005).

Conclusion

Cases such as those of Robert South, Michael Ross, and the others discussed illustrate the difficulty of determining the true motivations of many volunteers for execution. If the inmate is found to be competent, the courts often accept that the termination of appeals is a sign not of suicidal behavior but of the prisoner's compliance with lawful authority and of acceptance of responsibility for his actions (Blume, 2005, p. 955). Volunteering for execution is, in this view, laudable. The alternate view is that the state is assisting suicide by putting to death desperate individuals suffering from a variety of physical and psychological conditions that are little understood without extending to them all the protections of the legal system. It should be recognized, however, that distinguishing the true motivation of volunteers may be beyond the ability of the courts and the experts upon whom they rely.

Clearly, some of the apparent motivations of volunteers fit well with Durkheim's theory of suicide. Those who are truly remorseful and request execution to "pay their debt to society" are tightly integrated into the social and moral fabric and represent a form of altruistic suicide. The tough guys, on the other hand, have rejected the conventional social mores and lived a life of crime. They represent an egoistic form of suicide, where the lack of attachments to conventional society frees them to die without concern for social relationships or moral constraints.

Durkheim's anomic suicide, given great prominence in his explanation for suicides in the wider society, is poorly suited to explain death row volunteers. Although the condition of anomie initially appears common for most sent to death row, the condition is transitory. Almost all inmates on death row experience a jarring degree of normative change from what was experienced in free society; however, new norms are substituted that result in strict regulation of every aspect of the death row inmate's existence. The strictness of the norms contributes to death row syndrome, and is characteristic of fatalistic suicide, where the individual finds the social conditions unbearable but has no ability to change his life situation. Interestingly, the fatalistic suicide is often overlooked because of its rareness in modern society, but it may be viewed as one of the dominant types of suicides for death row inmates.

The greatest limitation of Durkeim's theory as applied to death penalty volunteers is that Durkheim focuses on social characteristics as a predictor of suicide, minimizing individual factors. Death row, however, is an extreme environment, far different from the free world, and the individuals on death row, because of their life experiences, often are dramatically atypical of their wider social groupings. Suffering childhood physical or sexual abuse, being born into a drastically dysfunctional family, or suffering mental illness are all prominent individual-level factors that contribute to the decision to volunteer for execution, but are not easily distinguished at the macro-level of Durkheim's theory.

The cases and theories reviewed here demonstrate the complexity of the issues. The refusal of American courts to recognize the validity of such concepts as "death row syndrome" should not limit the attempt to study and understand the complexity of motivations leading individuals to volunteer for execution. However, as our discussion of both Durkheim's typology of suicide and the discussion of the types of volunteers illustrates, multiple and disparate motivations are often apparent within and between the categories discussed. This discussion attempting to identify and explain the motivation for volunteering for execution should be seen as a first tentative attempt to advance our understanding of this complex phenomenon.

Notes

1. The authors wish to express our gratitude to Richard C. Deiter, executive director of DPIC, for the use of these data and for his assistance in clarifying DPIC's coding of variables.
2. It should be noted, however, that DPIC's data provides the number of victims for whose murders the death sentence was carried out, which

can vary from the number of victims killed. Gary Gilmore, for example, killed two victims on two subsequent nights; he was tried and executed for only one of those killings, however, and therefore the DPIC data show him with one victim.

3. Unfortunately, the prevalence of mental illness among executed inmates who did not drop their appeals is unknown, so comparison of the two groups on this variable is not possible.

References

Amnesty International. (2001). The illusion of control: "Consensual" executions, the impending death of Timothy McVeigh, and the brutalizing futility of capital punishment. AI Index: AMR 51/053/2001. Available at http://web.amnesty.org/library/index/engamr510532001. Website consulted September 4, 2007.

Amnesty International. (2007). Prisoner-assisted homicide – more "volunteer" executions loom. AI Index: AMR 51/087/2007. Available at http://web.amnesty.org/library/index/engamr510872007. Website consulted September 4, 2007.

Apuzzo, M. (2005, April 8). Serial killer's father says son lacks compassion. Associated Press. Retrieved December 27, 2006, from LexisNexis database.

Blank, S. (2006). Killing time: The process of waiving appeal: The Michael Ross death penalty cases. *Journal of Law and Policy* 14: 735–777.

Blume, J.H. (2005). Killing the willing: "Volunteers," suicide and competency. *Michigan Law Review* 103: 939–1009.

Borger, J. (2000, May 4). Mother executed for killing her children; guilt-ridden, Christina Riggs wanted to die. *Guardian* (London) Foreign Pages. Retrieved December 21, 2006 from LexisNexis database.

Bowers, W.J., with G.L. Pierce and J.F. McDevitt. (1984). *Legal Homicide: Death as Punishment in America.* Boston: Northeastern University Press.

Carey, Michael. (2001, June 11). McVeigh supporters gather outside prison. Retrieved January 19, 2007, www.abc.net.au/pm/stories/s311180.htm.

Chandler, C. (1998). Voluntary executions. *Stanford Law Review* 50: 1897–1927.

Christoffersen, J. (2005, February 1). Connecticut execution puts the spotlight on 'death row syndrome.' Associated Press. Retrieved December 27, 2006 from LexisNexis database.

Collins, J. (2004, December 17). Death row inmate allowed to give up appeals. Associated Press. Retrieved December 27, 2006, from LexisNexis database.

Crocker, P.L. (2004). Not to decide is to decide: The U.S. Supreme Court's thirty-year struggle with one case about competency to waive death penalty appeals. *The Wayne Law Review* 49: 885–938.

Davila, F. & Postman, D. (1998, October 13). Sagastegui put to death—State's first execution by lethal injection. *The Seattle Times*, p. A1.

Death Penalty Information Center. (2006a). Execution database. Available at http://www.deathpenaltyinfo.org/executions.php. Website consulted September 4, 2007.

Death Penalty Information Center. (2006b). Time on death row: The Michael Ross case. Available at http://www.deathpenaltyinfo.org/article.php?&did=1397. Website consulted September 4, 2007.

Deiter, R.C. (1990). Ethical choices for attorneys whose clients elect execution. *The Georgetown Journal of Legal Ethics* 3: 799–820.

Durkheim, E. (1951). *Suicide, a Study in Sociology* (translated by John A. Spaulding and George Simpson). Glencoe, IL: Free Press.

Execution in Ohio is first in 36 years. (1999, February 20). *New York Times*, p. A9.

Fagan, K. & Squatriglia, C. (2001, June 12). Death of a terrorist. *San Francisco Chronicle*, p. A1.

Fisher, A. (1999, February 19). A lifetime of pain nears its end. *The Columbus Dispatch*, p. 1A.

Foster, J.T. & Anderson, D.R. (1997, May 16). A murderer's last words: "Thank you." *The Oregonian*, p. A1.

Gettinger, S.H. (1979). *Sentenced to Die: The People, the Crimes, and the Controversy.* New York: McMillan.

Graczyk, M. (1999, April 28). Killer shows no remorse for crime. *Austin American-Statesman*, p. B1.

Graczyk, M. (1999, April 29). Remorseless killer executed for murdering man in 1997. *Austin American-Statesman*, p. B2.

Johnson, A. (1999, February 21). Quiet death ends years of debate. *The Columbus Dispatch*, p. 6D.

Johnson, R. (2003). Life under sentence of death: Historical and contemporary perspectives. In J.R. Acker, R.M. Bohm, and C.S. Lanier (Eds.), *America's Experiment with Capital Punishment: Reflections on the Past, Present and Future of the Ultimate Penal Sanction*, 2nd ed. (pp. 647–671). Durham, NC: Carolina Academic Press.

LaPeter, L. & Rondeaux, C. (2003, September 4). Hill's last words preach violence. *St. Petersburg Times*, p. 1A.

Mailer, N. (1979). *The Executioner's Song.* Boston: Little, Brown.

Michel, L. & Herbeck, D. (2001). *American Terrorist.* New York: HarperCollins.

Miller, G. (1975). *Invitation to a Lynching.* Garden City, NY: Doubleday.

Murderer of abortion doctor expects 'great reward' in heaven. (2003, Oct.). *Church & State*, 56 (9), p. 8.

Norman, M.T. (1998). Standards and procedures for determining whether a defendant is competent to make the ultimate choice – death; Ohio's new precedent for death row "volunteers" standard. *Journal of Law and Health* 13: 103–140.

"Not mad," slayer says just before death chair. (1964, May 13). *The Florida Times-Union*, p. 25.

Oleson, J.C. (2006). Swilling hemlock: The legal ethics of defending a client who wishes to volunteer for execution. *Washington and Lee Law Review* 63: 147–230.

Pinozzotto, A.J. (2005). Suicide by cop: Defining a devastating dilemma. *FBI Law Enforcement Bulletin* 74: 8–20.

Samaha, J. (1999). *Criminal Law* (6th ed.). Belmont, CA: West/Wadsworth Press.

Schmalleger, F. (2006). *Criminal Law Today* (3rd ed.). Upper Saddle River, NJ: Pearson/Prentice Hall.

Simpson, G. (1951). Editor's introduction: The aetiology of suicide. In E. Durkheim, *Suicide, a Study in Sociology* (translated by John A. Spaulding and George Simpson)(pp. 13–53). Glencoe, IL: Free Press.

Slayer of five boys is executed in Utah by injection of drugs. (1988, June 11). *New York Times*, p. 1–8.

Solomon, G.F. (1975). Capital punishment as suicide and murder. *American Journal of Orthopsychiatry* 45: 701–711.

State executes cop killer after South ends appeals. (1996, May 31). *The [Charleston, S.C.] Post and Courier.* Retrieved January 20, 2007, from http://venus.soci.niu.edu/~archives/ABOLISH/spring96/0091.html.

Stickney, B. (1996). *All-American Monster.* Amherst, NY: Prometheus.

Strafer, G.R. (1983). Volunteering for execution: Competency, voluntariness and the propriety of third party intervention. *The Journal of Criminal Law and Criminology* 74: 860–912.

"That's swell" says Southworth. (1931, January 24). *Palm Beach Post*, p. 1.

Thornburgh, N. (2005, April 18). When a killer wants to die. *Time*. Available at http://www.time.com/time/magazine/article/0,9171,1050322,00.html.

Vandiver, M. (2006). *Lethal Punishment: Lynchings and Legal Executions in the South*. New Brunswick, NJ: Rutgers University Press.

Vandiver, M., Giacopassi, D., & Gathje, P. (2002). "I hope someone murders your mother!": An exploration of extreme support for the death penalty. *Deviant Behavior* 23: 385–415.

Van Wormer, K. & Odiah, C. (1999). The psychology of suicide-murder and the death penalty. *Journal of Criminal Justice* 27: 361–370.

West, L.J. (1975). Psychiatric reflections on the death penalty. *American Journal of Orthopsychiatry* 45: 689–700.

Cases Cited

Furman v. Georgia (1972) 408 U.S. 238.

Rees v. Peyton (1966) 384 U.S. 312.

Soering v. The United Kingdom, 11 European Human Rights Review 439 (1989).

Some Hypotheses about Capital Punishment and Lynching

10

HUGO ADAM BEDAU

Contents

Introduction

In the September–October 2002 issue of the journal *Judicature*, I suggested seven ways in which a kinship could be discerned linking historic mob lynching and the death penalty as currently administered. By way of refreshing memory, here is my list of seven (slightly revised):

- The mentality that supported lynching a century ago is found today in support of legal executions.
- The states in which lynching was most frequent are for the most part the states where the death penalty was and still is most frequent.
- Both lynching and the death penalty manifestly disregard due process of law.
- Paradigm cases of lynching are racist and involve white-on-black victimization; paradigm cases of legal execution today involve black-on-white crimes.
- Opponents of lynching in the South relied on the argument that by using the death penalty society could achieve under color of law what lynching did lawlessly.
- In cases where a posse was formed to lynch an accused murderer (or rapist) and did so without further ado, it is virtually impossible to tell whether the killing should be classified as murder by a mob or as a quasi-legal summary execution.
- Lynching a century ago was defended by appeal to states' rights and involved resistance to federal interference; the same is true today in death penalty states in the South.

The only other or subsequent attempt to list such parallels, overlaps, and equivalences known to me is to be found in Margaret Vandiver's 2006 volume, *Lethal Punishment* (p. 10); there she cites four such features, two of which are on my *Judicature* list. Later in her book she cites all seven of the items on my list (p.183), but she does so without comment. From the context, however, it appears that she tacitly agrees with me and endorses all seven.

In the pages below I have set out for discussion not quite three dozen hypotheses of varying interest connecting lynching and the death penalty with comments on them. The truth of some of these hypotheses and of the comments on them is difficult (given current information) if not impossible to determine. For that very reason they deserve at least a tentative inclusion on the agenda of social science.

Hypotheses About Capital Punishment and Lynching

Hypothesis 1: Lynching is a form of capital punishment.

Comment: This is true, insofar as lynching itself is regarded as a form of punishment that always results in the death of the victim (does it?), as the death penalty does. It is not true insofar as lynching is illegal and capital punishment is lawful.

Hypothesis 2: Capital punishment is a form of lynching, "legal lynching."

Comment: Proponents and opponents of the death penalty will divide over the truth of this assertion. The point of the assertion is clear: it is to link the two practices in the boldest possible way, implying that the savagery, brutality, and lawlessness of mob lynching can also be found—at best in a quasi-regulated form—in the death penalty as administered today. Of course the concept of "legal lynching" is an oxymoron, because a lynching is by any definition a lawless act that, according to Randall Kennedy in his book, *Race, Crime, and the Law* (1997), represents what he called the "metaphorization" of the term "lynching" (p. 41); it is to be contrasted with what he called "*real* lynching." George Wright defined "legal lynching" as "manipulating the legal system to ensure that blacks accused of rape or murder receive the death penalty, the same punishment that would have been meted out by the lynch mob . . . the most brutal form of racial violence" in the 1997 volume edited by W. Fitzhugh Brundage, *Under Sentence of Death* (pp. 251–252). The Jesse Jacksons, father and son, with journalist Bruce Shapiro, titled their book *Legal Lynching* (2001) but never defined the term. They do say at the very end "We have inherited a death penalty that is a relic, in so many ways the worst of the American past" (p. 129). They argue in effect that the difference between classic mob lynching and modern capital punishment is vanishingly small. Whether the concept of legal lynching is a needless, essential, or harmful exaggeration remains to be seen. L. V. Gaither in his recent book, *Loss of Empire: Legal Lynching, Vigilantism, and African American Intellectualism in the 21st Century* (2006), describes a Texas case as one in which the victim was "legally lynched by the state. . . ." How so? Because the execution "was sanctioned for the most part by the entire . . . [white] community" (p. 12).

Hypothesis 3: The best definition of lynching is "capital punishment without the authority to punish."

Comment: A volume could be written on nothing more than the best way to define lynching. Brundage defines it as "a form of collective violence characterized by informal organization and a logic of individual liability" (p. 51). Raymond Bye, in his classic book, *Capital Punishment in the United States* (1919), defined it as "a species of capital punishment administered illegally by the laymen" (p. 62). James E. Cutler in his 1905 book, *Lynch-Law*, defined lynching as "now practically synonymous with summary and illegal capital punishment at the hands of a mob" (pp. 11–12). At the end of his book, he redefines the term in this manner: "A [mob] lynching may be defined as an illegal and summary execution at the hands of a mob or a number of persons who have in some degree the public opinion of the community behind them" (p. 276). L. V. Gaither starts down a different path when he suggests that "antiblack racism, lynching, and capital punishment [are] aspects of a totality," a totality of violence against innocent African Americans. This leads him to observe further that "Part of what needs to be done is to revisit, reconceptualize and redefine the meaning of lynching in such a way that it is historically connected to the present uses of the death penalty . . . (p. 27).

Hypothesis 4: Lynching and capital punishment are two versions of the same thing.

Comment: This is a bold, albeit vague, claim. It is trivially true to the extent that both practices involve deliberately killing people as a mode of punishing them. It could be argued that this common feature is of such paramount importance that it forces all contrasting features of the two practices into the background because of their lesser significance. But it could also be argued that this hypothesis is false because it fails to acknowledge the difference between flouting due process of law, as mob lynching always does, with at least giving lip service to due process of law, as capital punishment always does. Is the glass half full or half empty—or is it both?

Hypothesis 5: Mob lynching is the crime of murder; capital punishment is the law.

Comment: Taken at face value, this is true and importantly so. Any reasonable person must be distressed over the failings of the American death penalty system. Nevertheless, that system has to be judged an improvement over a different system that allows, indeed encourages, the lawlessness of mob lynching. Professing support for the rule of law, as supporters of our death penalty system do, must be seen as a civilizing step forward. Nothing of the sort can be found in the historic practice of mob lynching. As for capital punishment being the law, so at one time were slavery, the Black Codes, and more recently Jim Crow. All have been abolished for their manifest and extensive unfairness; it is not unreasonable to expect that the death penalty will join them.

Hypothesis 6: There is a direct link between mob lynching and the death penalty.

Comment: Stephen Bright, in his essay in the 1997 *International Sourcebook on Capital Punishment* (p. 8), and again in the 2002 book edited by David Dow and Mark Dow, The *Machinery of Death* (p. 45), asserts that "The death penalty is a direct descendant of lynching and other forms of racial violence . . . ." Timothy Kaufman-Osborne quotes Bright's remark favorably in his chapter, "Capital Punishment as Legal Lynching?," which appears in the 2006 volume edited by Charles Ogletree and Austin Sarat, *From Lynch Mobs to the Killing State* (p. 22). William McFeeley echoes this remark in his epilogue to Brundage's edited volume (p. 320), when he says that some scholars (whom he does not identify) "see a direct link between lynchings and the death penalty." What constitutes that "direct link," however, these writers never say in so many words. So what is the difference between direct and indirect linkage? Why do we have the one and not the other? Or do we have both? We are not told.

Hypothesis 7: Capital punishment serves the same functions as lynching.

Comment: This is an extremely important hypothesis. To decide whether it is true, we need a firm grip on what functions each practice performs. Well, what are those functions? Three of the most important are general deterrence, incapacitation, and retribution. Symbolic reaffirmation of the prevailing social order is a fourth and arguably the most important. Mob lynching served these ends at the cost of abandoning due process of law and having recourse to lawlessness, at least as seen by the opponents of mob lynching.

We owe to Kaufman-Osborne a more sophisticated account of the purpose of lynching when he writes, "The very purpose of a spectacle lynching was to produce and reproduce the conditions of racial domination within the context of a regime that openly affirmed white superiority" (pp. 45–46).

Hypothesis 8: Lynching involves mob action; capital punishment does not.

Comment: This is true in most cases; whether it is true by definition obviously depends on how lynching is defined. The classic legal definition of mob lynching in the United States requires that such acts involve a minimum of three participants—arguably not much of a "mob"—making common cause. In any case, the death penalty as practiced in our criminal courts does not involve mob action except in some cases where the crowd in the courtroom is hardly distinguishable from and merges into the mob outside the courtroom or jail clamoring to get in.

Hypothesis 9: Lynching and the death penalty have always been public events, spectator sports.

Comment: This is extensively confirmed by photographs since 1865 or so of public hangings whether by lawless mob action or as lawful executions. The evidence in lynching narratives from pre-colonial days as well as in death penalty literature shows in loving detail the way local white citizens—women as well as men, children as well as adults, public officials as well as ordinary citizens—turned a hanging into a festive event. So-called private executions, introduced in the 1830s were anything but. No wonder that Kaufman-Osborne calls these events "spectacle lynchings . . . highly ritualized expressive performances" (p. 29).

Hypothesis 10: The history of lynching is "deeply and hopelessly entangled" with the history of the death penalty.

Comment: This is the thesis advanced by Michael Pfeifer, in his 2004 book, *Rough Justice: Lynching and American Society 1874–1947* (p.152). Is it true? One would not know from our first history of the American death penalty, Stuart Banner's book, *The Death Penalty* (2002), as he cites only three references on the topic of lynching. And these references fail by a wide margin even to consider, much less support, Pfeifer's thesis. On the other hand, several recent books on lynching come much closer to making some use of the history of the death penalty by interspersing lynching narratives. But none of them really does justice to the topic, either. Much remains to be told by historians about the two practices.

Hypothesis 11: The demography of those killed by mob lynching is essentially the same—in sex, race, age, and so on—as those who are executed under law.

Comment: This is certainly true in many cases, and necessarily so, because the victims of mob lynching often were convicted offenders waiting further disposition in their cases, for example, appeal of a conviction or sentence to a higher court, or a clemency hearing.

Hypothesis 12: Women and children under 18 at the time of the crime are rarely lynched, and rarely executed by law.

Comment: This is true. The ratio, among those lawfully executed or lynched, of men to women and children is about 100 to 1.

Hypothesis 13: Capital punishment, like historic mob lynching, has been inflicted disproportionately on African Americans.

Comment: The evidence amply supports this claim (see Dow and Dow, 2002, p. 70, n. 5). Between 1882 and 1968, three-fourths (72.7 percent) of all those lynched were African Americans. More than nine out of ten (90 percent) of all lynchings during that period took place in the South. Whether lynching has everywhere been more racist than the death penalty, however, is not clear. In the South such a racial preponderance is evident from the Tuskegee records, but elsewhere in the nation it is probably otherwise. Although not all the American victims of mob lynching were African American males (perhaps 10% of the victims were either white or female), it was the lynching of black males by whites of every description that set the tone of this practice.

Hypothesis 14: The demography of those who carried out mob lynching is the same—in sex, race, age, and so on—as the demography of those who carry out capital punishment.

Comment: Traditionally, lynching was carried out by a mob, whereas a trial jury, prison employees, and others with official status in the criminal justice system administer the death penalty. Are the people involved in the one the same as those involved in the other? I know of no interviews with members of a lynch mob that might give us evidence one way or the other. It seems plausible in any case to doubt whether there are any great differences between the two classes of persons. Lynching records show that, whether the killing was legal or by a mob, there are many cases where the mayor, county sheriff, trial judge, or other stalwart local citizens are among those who carried out the lynching, with the result that the two groups do sometimes have some of the same members.

Hypothesis 15: The popular legitimacy of lynching shows up in the fact that lynchers were rarely arrested, tried, and convicted, just as the officials who have carried out legal executions have never been arrested, tried, and convicted.

Comment: True. The virtual immunity of members of lynching parties (including those who might in fact hold official government positions) from any interruption of their conduct carrying out extra-legal executions shows up in virtually every account of lynching. As Cutler noted, "popular justification was the sine qua non of lynching" (p. 276). More recently, Eliza Steelwater states in her book, *The Hangman's Knot* (2003), that "Extra-legal execution has scarcely been punished throughout our history" (p. 94). Philip Dray, in his book, *At the Hands of Persons Unknown* (2002), writes that ". . . capital punishment for rape, particularly if only black men were receiving [death] sentences, amounted to nothing less than an authorized lynching" (p. 394).

Hypothesis 16: The geography of mob lynching is the same as the geography of capital punishment.

Comment: This is one of the most important common traits of the two practices. Both are rooted in the dark past of slavery, and both flourished in its aftermath in the Deep South. Today, mob lynching in the old Confederacy has vanished, whereas the death penalty flourishes in the Bible Belt. And whereas one can envision a day when Illinois and Ohio have abandoned the death penalty, no one is predicting a future in which Texas or Virginia is likely to do the same.

Hypothesis 17: Most of those who supported mob lynching also supported capital punishment but not the converse.

Comment: I know of no evidence to support this pair of plausible claims. A careful and thorough review of the available lynching narratives and newspaper journalism ought to shed some light on this hypothesis.

Hypothesis 18: A majority of the public has always supported the death penalty; only a minority ever supported mob lynching.

Comment: This is true today, as it was throughout the past two centuries. It seems plausible to believe that all those who supported mob lynching would also support the death penalty, with one exception. The supporters of mob lynching were typically impatient with the slow workings of the criminal justice system and to that extent would oppose efforts to administer the death penalty under some semblance of due process of law. This impatience, amply evidenced in the narratives of mob lynching, tends to corrupt the criminal justice system. To speed up the process is to increase the likelihood of convicting the innocent.

Hypothesis 19: The crimes for which persons have been executed by capital punishment are the same as the crimes for which mobs lynched persons.

Comment: This is essentially true. Both lynching and the death penalty were most widely used against accused murderers and rapists. No third kind of crime, for example, arson, burglary, or kidnapping for ransom, comes even close to these two in providing victims for mob lynching and for the death penalty.

Hypothesis 20: Vigilantism, not racism, is the dominant cause among the several that explain the role of lynching in American culture.

Comment: This is the implicit thesis of Franklin Zimring's important 2003 book, *The Contradictions of American Capital Punishment.* What tends to obscure the dominance of vigilantism is that lynching historically has been concentrated in the South, and "The South is the region with the highest prevalence of provigilante values…" (p. 103; see also pp. 109–110 and 117–121). Zimring also notes what he calls "a striking parallel" between the death penalty and "lynching a century earlier" (p. 89). Not only that; he further asserts that "lynching history predicts modern executions" (p. 96). That thesis requires more interpretation and evidence than Zimring provides.

Hypothesis 21: The methods of execution used by lynch mobs were the same as those used to carry out the death penalty.

Comment: This is not true. During the past century five different methods of execution under law have been used: hanging, shooting, lethal gas, lethal injection, and the electric chair. No mob lynchings (to the best of my knowledge) have been carried out using lethal gas, lethal injection, or the electric chair. Instead, mob lynchings almost always involved death by hanging plus shooting and often involved in addition burning at the stake and mutilation, as well as shooting and dismembering.

Hypothesis 22: There was little or no discussion of capital punishment in the literature of a century ago on mob lynching.

Comment: If this is true, it suggests that the two practices were quite distinct in the minds of most people. Those engaged in mob lynching seem to have been so convinced that they were meting out appropriate "justice" that they saw no need to discuss the supposed superiority of their practices over the institution of capital punishment.

Hypothesis 23: Early scholarship (say, around 1900) on the connection between lynching and the death penalty resulted in very few empirical hypotheses worth testing.

Comment: This is essentially true. Our main sources are the books by Cutler and Bye. Cutler begins cautiously, allowing that there seems to be "a relationship between legal executions and lynching" (p. 163); he continues just as tentatively: "[T]he punishment of crimes by law may tend to make recourse to lynching less frequent" (p. 164). He seems to endorse this hypothesis (although he never formulated it in so many words). Finally, he suggests that the crime of rape may increase in frequency after a lynching for rape (pp. 224–225). Bye considered three main hypotheses. Did abolishing the death penalty give rise to an increase in lynching? He concluded that it did not (p. 67). Would increasing the use of the death penalty reduce the volume of lynching? Once again, he concluded that it would not (p. 70). Finally, was the death penalty administered in a racially biased manner especially where African American offenders and white victims were concerned? He concluded that it was, at least for the crime of rape by an African American male whose victim was a white woman (p. 63).

Hypothesis 24: During the heyday of mob lynching, killings by this method never exceeded the number of victims of the death penalty.

Comment: Not so. According to Stuart Banner, in his essay "Traces of Slavery," in the Ogletree and Sarat edited volume, "At its peak, lynching was much more common than official capital punishment" (p. 107). But Banner cites statistics from only one jurisdiction (Kentucky) to support this claim. Was Kentucky unique? Unusual? Typical? We are not told.

Hypothesis 25: As the use of capital punishment increases, mob lynching decreases.

Comment: One might think this is true, and Pfeifer comes close to asserting it on the strength of some evidence (pp. 7–8 and152–153). One might also think that opponents of mob lynching who were willing to embrace the death penalty as a substitute would hope this proposition is true, because if it were then society would have a ready-made practice to put in place of mob lynching but roughly equivalent in its effects. What the available evidence shows, however, is that a century ago the two practices existed side by side.

They differed in their use: mob lynching went into steady and apparently irreversible decline, whereas the death penalty has had peaks and valleys in its use since the Civil War. There is little or no evidence that the decline in mob lynching was caused by an increase in the use of lawful executions. On the other hand, James Marquart and his co-authors in their 1994 book, *The Rope, the Chair, and the Needle* (p.18), report that a Texas politician endeavored to enact a death penalty statute in 1922 in order to reduce the likelihood of further lynchings.

Hypothesis 26: Execution by law has in some cases probably prevented mob lynching.

Comment: This is an important claim and may well be true. If it were widely true and known to be true, it could have been an argument in favor of the death penalty. As things stand, however, no one—to my knowledge—has searched the lynching literature and produced evidence to confirm or disconfirm this claim.

Hypothesis 27: The reasons used to support mob lynching in its day are the same as the reasons used to support the death penalty in our day.

Comment: This is yet another example of a hypothesis that needs to be addressed by interested researchers.

Hypothesis 28: In mob lynching the victim's body is typically mutilated, not so with executions.

Comment: This is true and important, although one needs to consider whether the cases of "botched" executions ought to count as exceptions. Each of the five methods of lawful execution has resulted in one or more cases where the execution procedure malfunctioned. However, the cruelty and savagery of mutilation in lynching far exceeded that from such botched executions, both in frequency and intensity. Furthermore, the savagery typical of racist lynching was intentional, whereas botched executions are not. It is nevertheless sobering to realize that the century-long search for a foolproof humane method of lawful execution continues to elude the friends of the death penalty.

Hypothesis 29: The reasons that led to the decline and virtual disappearance of mob lynching are the same reasons that will lead to the end of the death penalty.

Comment: This interesting proposition may well be true. Indeed, there is some evidence already that the objections to lynching are resurfacing in the effort to abolish the death penalty. The very concept of capital punishment as legal lynching is an important step in this direction. The two practices share aspects of lawlessness, runaway populism, and the risk of killing wrongfully arrested and wrongfully convicted persons.

Hypothesis 30: It is unfair and unreasonable for opponents of the death penalty to insist on its affinity with historic mob lynching.

Comment: This is false. What would be unfair is to exaggerate the variety, scope, and significance of those linkages. Conversely, it would be unfair to deny or trivialize those linkages when they reveal important features shared by these two practices.

Hypothesis 31: There is no good explanation for the fact that there has been a rising interest in the past decade or so in searching for linkages between mob lynching and the death penalty.

Comment: Looking for and finding such linkages is one more tactic used by the opponents of the death penalty to discredit it by using a form of argument akin to guilt by association. Here is the argument: if the death penalty shares many important features with lynching, and decent people have always known that lynching is a terrible criminal act, then for that reason we ought to oppose and abolish the death penalty. Why this argument was not prominently employed by abolitionists in the 1950s or earlier, or more recently in the 1960s and 1970s, I do not know.

Conclusion

What, after all this, is the bottom line? We might borrow from the philosopher Ludwig Wittgenstein and suggest that our investigation so far shows that lynching and the death penalty have a "family resemblance." That is, the two practices have a number of features in common—some are in parallel and others are identical—but there are still other features they do not share; instead they go their separate and independent ways. Whether the shared features are more important than the others is difficult to say. In these remarks I have not tried to draw a conclusion either way.

Index

R

S